SHARING THE COSTS OF HIGHER EDUCATION

Sharing the Costs of Higher Education

Student Financial Assistance in the United Kingdom, the Federal Republic of Germany, France, Sweden, and the United States

D. BRUCE JOHNSTONE

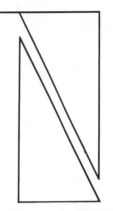

New York, College Entrance Examination Board, 1986

Authors are encouraged to express freely their professional judgment. Therefore, points of view or opinions stated in College Board books do not necessarily represent official College Board position or policy.

Editorial inquiries concerning this book should be addressed to: Editorial Office, The College Board, 45 Columbus Avenue, New York, New York 10023-6917.

Copies of this book may be ordered from College Board Publications, Box 886, New York, New York 10101. The price is $10.95.

Library of Congress Catalog Number: 86-072714
ISBN: 0-87447-278-4

Printed in the United States of America

9 8 7 6 5 4 3 2 1

CONTENTS

3 The Federal Republic of Germany

6 The United States   112

7 Summary Observations on Sharing and Shifting the Costs of Higher Education   143

Appendix A

Appendix B

TABLES AND FIGURES

Figures

FOREWORD

As the countries of the world become increasingly interdependent, there is growing awareness among policy analysts that governments face many common questions of social policy. The financing of higher education is no exception. Who should go to college? What proportion of the relevant age group? Who pays the cost? Who benefits? Who *should* pay? What is the appropriate mix of parental contribution, student self-support, and taxpayer subsidy? How can college opportunities be equalized for low-income and other disadvantaged, previously excluded groups in the society?

These are universal issues, and debate on them has intensified in many nations as fiscal resource constraints have tightened during the 1980s.

This book looks across national boundaries, lending comparative perspective and depth to an examination of a subject that, at least in the United States, typically bogs down in the operational technicalities of existing student loan, grant, and other assistance programs. Administrators, analysts of student aid, and international educators in this country have long been inquisitive about the experience of other countries in this field, but aside from a few useful investigations sponsored by the World Bank and the Organization for Economic Cooperation and Development, fairly little comparative research has been available.

Sharing the Costs of Higher Education examines and contrasts student financing arrangements in five Western countries—the United Kingdom, Sweden, West Germany, France, and the United States. Rarely are lessons, models, and mechanisms readily transferable from one country's educational system to another. History, political ideology, social customs, and economic conditions shape the policies and idiosyncratic patterns in each country. But cross-national comparisons can enlighten and influence policy analysis.

The book represents a prodigious endeavor. The author, D. Bruce Johnstone, not only surmounted daunting language and cultural barriers to understand and describe the several systems included in the study, but he reconciled and analyzed a huge amount of incongruent statistical data from the five countries. The author has cut through all these complexities to produce a distinctive work of comparative education scholarship.

The College Board provided partial support for the research and is pleased to publish this book. Sponsorship by the College Board springs from three sources of interest and commitment: the Washington Office, which conducts policy research on education financing and related issues; the Office of International Education, locus of the Board's overseas services and activities; and the College Scholarship Service, which has as its mission to foster equity and consistency in the administration of student assistance.

The idea for the book evolved from discussions by the staff and Advisory Panel to the Washington Office beginning several years ago. D. Bruce Johnstone is a former member of the panel, a veteran authority on student aid policies, and a frequent participant in College Board forums.

We hope this work will prove useful not only to state and national policy makers, administrators, and scholars in the United States, but to their counterparts in other countries of the world as well.

In his preface the author acknowledges the many people who contributed to the project along the way. I thank them as well. Janet S. Hansen, director for policy analysis in the Washington Office, played an especially important part in facilitating the project.

Finally, I thank the author himself for his intellectual provocations, good humor, persistence, and hard work in creating this volume. The Board has learned much in the process and is proud to be associated with its publication.

George H. Hanford
President
The College Board

PREFACE

The origins of this study go back to 1971, when I directed a Ford Foundation study of the income-contingent loan concept (under the acronym PAYE, for Pay-As-You-Earn) and first learned about the world of student financial assistance. That year, through a study tour of Scandinavia, I also had my first exposure to student finance in other countries and thus to the comparative study of higher education. Since that time, I have written and taught about the economics and finance of higher education, always with a special interest in student finance and student loans, combining (I hope with occasionally useful insights) perspectives from my earlier studies of economics with my later experiences as a college and university administrator.

As president of the State University of New York College at Buffalo since 1979, I have been fortunate to serve for most of those years on the Advisory Panel of the Washington, D.C., office of the College Board as well as on the National Student Aid Coalition. Through those continuing associations with both the Washington-based policy analysts and with some of the ablest practitioners in the student financial aid profession, I maintained my interest in the economics of student assistance and in the policy implications of parental contributions, student "self help" and debt loads, the equity implications of alternative price and aid systems, etc. I first used the construct of "sharing and shifting the costs of higher education" as a discussion leader in the College Scholarship Service's Thirtieth Anniversary Colloquium, "An Agenda for the Year 2000," held in Aspen, Colorado, in the fall of 1984, and in the spring of 1985 in an address to the Eastern Association of Student Financial Aid Administrators in Boston.

The cost-sharing model assumes the costs of higher education to be borne by parents, students, taxpayers, and institutions/philanthropists, with changes in the costs borne by any particular party usually having a zero sum impact on total costs and thus merely shifting the burden to other participants. This construct seemed not only useful in looking at U.S. financial aid policies and practices, but potentially universal in its applications, recalling my earlier investigations of student loans in Scandinavia and the adamant opposition to loans in the United Kingdom. Several colleagues with whom I have long toiled in the vineyards of financial aid and student loan policy analysis shared and encouraged my interest in an international comparative education perspective on student financial assistance policies.

Serious pursuit of the cost-sharing construct in a comparative study was made possible for me by the marvelously enlightened policy of the State University of New York in granting three-month study leaves to college presidents after five or six years of acceptable hard labor. The purpose of the presidential study leave is to recharge the scholarly batteries of the chief administrative officer and to give both the institution and the president a refreshing, if momentary, rest from each other. I now had the opportunity as well as the topic.

With intellectual encouragement and some financial support from the College Board, I laid plans and reviewed the minimal literature during the spring of 1985. June and July began my study leave and were spent gathering data and ideas in England, West Germany, France, and Sweden. I had originally wanted a Socialist Bloc nation as well, and I tried to gather enough data and insight about Romania, encouraged by an invitation to visit and work out of the UNESCO European Centre for Higher Education in Bucharest. Sufficient data proved very difficult to get in that nation, however. Thus, although I remain confident that the cost-sharing construct can be usefully applied to higher educational finance in a centrally planned economy, a case study demonstrating this will have to await either a more fruitful trip to Romania or a more accessible Eastern Bloc nation.

An important colleague throughout the study, who established many of my European contacts for me and whose deep knowledge of both East and West European higher education helped shape the initial proposal as well as the final product, is Jan Sadlak, currently on the staff of CRE, or the European Rectors Conference. Sadlak is a Polish economist who has worked in higher educational planning in Poland, Romania, Paris, and now Geneva, and who was a Ph.D. student at the University of Buffalo when our association began.

Key to both the initial planning and the subsequent writing were Larry Gladieux, executive director of the Washington, D.C., office of the College Board, and Janet Hansen, director for policy analysis of that office. Without them this project would not have taken place. Joseph Cronin, president of the Massachusetts Higher Education Assistance Corporation and a fellow traveler in the fields of student finance and loan policies, contributed encouragement, insights, and valuable editorial suggestions.

Many persons at Buffalo State College and the State University of New York made this study possible, either by contributing to it directly or by keeping the college on a steady course during my absence. I am grateful to State University of New York Chancellor Clifton R. Wharton, Jr., and to Buffalo State College Council Chairman

Ross Kenzie for their support of my study leave, which made this adventure back into scholarship and writing possible. My executive secretary, Anna Tiberia, managed the enormous complications of a two-month research trip abroad, kept track of voluminous notes and dictation, and generally made it possible for me to be away from the office, undistracted, for a total of four months. Richard Wiesen, academic vice president, filled in ably as acting president of Buffalo State College during my leave. My executive assistant, Marianne Vallet-Sandre, not only helped make possible my leave from the presidency, but provided French translations of many documents on my return. My director of financial aid, Daniel Hunter, provided valuable assistance in my chapter on financial aid in the United States. Finally, my two secretaries, Mary Lou Littlefield and Susan Kendt, typed many drafts of the manuscript, composed the tables, and maintained their supportive good humor even while keeping up with all of the other tasks in the office of a college president. I am indebted to all of them.

I had many wonderful hosts and colleagues during my visits to the United Kingdom, France, the Federal Republic of Germany, and Sweden. Maureen Woodhall deserves special mention not only for the hospitality she arranged at the University of London's Institute of Education, but for her encouragement and guidance during the entire study. No one knows as much or writes as well about comparative student finance as she, and I trust that this work will lead to our further collaboration. Others who helped me in London include Gareth Williams, also of the University of London Institute of Education; Richard Bird, Clive Booth, and David Lewis of the U.K. Department of Education and Science; Adam Gaines, Geoffrey Ferris, and Christopher Hall of the National Union of Students; John Davies of the Anglian Regional Management Centre; Rupert Bristow of the Polytechnic of the South Bank; and M.G. Bruce of Thames Polytechnic.

In Paris, I was given space and assistance at the European Institute of Education and Social Policy headed by Ladislaw Cerych, an extraordinary source of insights on European higher education policy. Also helpful to me during my stay in Paris were Brian Smith and Madeleine Bouillet of the European Institute of Education and Social Policy; Guy Allain and M. Chevasson of the National Ministry of Education and the Student Assistance Bureau (Bureau de Bourse); C. Moha of the Paris Student Services Agency (Centre Regional des Oeuvres Universitaires et Scolaires, or CROUS); Louis Levy-Garboua of the Centre de Recherche pour L'Etude et L'Observation des Conditions de Vie (CREDOC) and the University of Paris I; Dorothea Furth and C. Soumelis of the Organization for Economic Cooperation and Development; Bikas Snayal of UNESCO's International Institute for Educational Planning; and professors Alain Bienaymé and B. Giroud de l'Ain of the University of Paris IX.

For the Federal Republic of Germany, I was fortunate to be given the name of Karl Roeloffs, currently of the German Academic Exchange Service and formerly of the Students Grants Office of the Federal Ministry for Education and Science. Roeloffs wrote a long and marvelously comprehensive letter in reply to my first inquiry and then met me in Baltimore, making my later trip to Bonn much easier and more fruitful than it might otherwise have been. Others who supplied data and insights in Germany were Karsten Brenner and several colleagues from the Federal Ministry for Education and Science; Burkhard Hoffmeister of the German National Student Union; Dieter Iversen and Horst Bachman of the Bonn Student Service Agency (Studentenwerk Bonn); Gerald Koeniger of the Dortmund Fachhochschule; Klaus Schnitzer of the Higher Education Information System Agency (HIS) in Hanover; and Rolf Hoffman of the Alexander Von Humboldt Foundation.

My Swedish visit was made useful and pleasant by Gabriella Hansson, Deputy Head of Division at the Central Study Assistance Committee (CSN, or Centrala Studiestödsnämnden). Additional insights in Sweden were given by Stefan Bjorklund of the National Board of Universities and Colleges (UHA); Lief Lindfors of the Ministry of Education; and Thomas Persson of the National Union of Students.

As is the case in any such study, I must convey my deep gratitude to all who gave assistance while absolving them from responsibility for any errors that may have persisted in my interpretation of the data. Such responsibility is mine alone, but I trust that future research will not only update and correct my work, but go beyond and extend the comparative study of higher educational finance and student assistance to many more nations.

D. Bruce Johnstone
Buffalo, New York

COST SHARING IN HIGHER EDUCATION

This is a book about the costs of undergraduate higher education. But it is mainly a book about a particular portion of those costs: namely, the direct "out-of-pocket" expenses that initially face students and their parents as they attempt to meet the costs of student living (room, board, books, travel, and all other such expenses) plus whatever portion of the costs of instruction may be passed on to them through tuition or fees. More specifically still, it is about the way those costs are ultimately borne by the parents, the student himself or herself, the taxpayer (a word that will generally be employed in preference to the more euphemistic "government" or "public"), and institutions or philanthropists.

Further, this book is a comparative study, combining both theoretical constructs and empirical descriptive data about the way these particular costs of higher education are shared among parents, students, taxpayers, and philanthropists/donors in five countries: the United States, the United Kingdom, the Federal Republic of Germany, France, and Sweden. It was a major premise of this study, borne out by the research, that these and other countries must balance very similar public policy goals in apportioning these costs (e.g., equal higher educational opportunities, efficient use of public resources, and equitable distribution of costs and benefits) and that each country can benefit in the refinement of its objectives and in the choice of its instruments (e.g., parental-need analyses, means-tested grants, student loan programs) by understanding what countries with similar higher educational systems and public policy objectives are doing.

THE COSTS OF HIGHER EDUCATION

The "cost of higher education" concept admits to many different meanings, as shown graphically in Figure 1.1. The broadest and most theoretical, constituting the sum of all resources devoted to, or lost from alternative use because of, higher education as shown in Figure 1.1. under Definition "A" combines the direct costs of instruction plus the forgone earnings of students (i.e., as a monetary approximation of lost real production by virtue of the students' withdrawal from the labor force) plus the special educational costs usually borne by the student or his or her parents such as books and supplies, but excludes the basic costs of living, such as room, board, clothing, and entertainment, that would be expended whether or not the student were engaged in higher education. Forgone earnings are often ignored, particularly in the United States, where college-going is so highly valued and socially expected among such a wide socioeconomic range of the population that the decision to attend college and to forgo the alternative of a job immediately out of high school does not weigh heavily in most students' decision whether to attend a college or university. Furthermore, youth unemployment is high enough, particularly among those on the decision edge—that is, among those truly ambivalent about college or among those whose academic preparedness is most marginal—that the income in fact lost to the individual or his or her family (or indeed, the production lost to the nation's GNP) by virtue of the choice to go to college may be quite negligible. Thus, the costs of forgone earnings will not often be encountered in the volume. Nevertheless, forgone earnings and the lost real production they represent constitute a very real cost of college-going, particularly in societies, and to individuals in those societies, for which the decision to go to college is a real choice and in which a likely job with real earning potential is quite clearly given up by virtue of the decision to go on to higher education.

The total cash, or monetary, cost associated with higher education, represented by Definition "B" in Figure 1.1, omits forgone earnings but adds all the costs of student living as shown in Definition "F," whether or not these costs are peculiar to the college student, plus the direct costs of instruction, which are included within the budgets of the institutions and which are represented by Definition "D." The gross cash cost, then, is all the costs of instruction outlays by colleges and universities and all the costs of educational living outlays by students and/or parents. This sum minus those living costs such as room, board, and entertainment that would have to be met by students and nonstudents alike yields the total net cash, or monetary, cost of higher education, shown in Figure 1.1 by Definition "C."

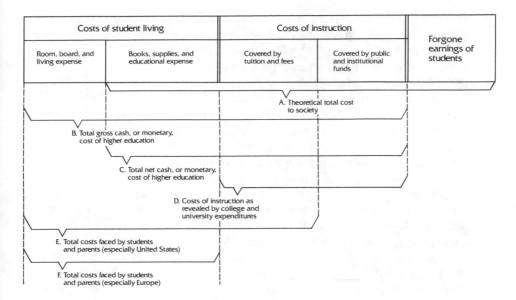

FIGURE 1.1 The costs of higher education: the range of concepts.

The costs of principal concern to this study are those that must be met by the student, most often with the help of his or her parents, including all the costs of student living in addition to whatever instructional costs are passed on to the student and family as tuitions or fees. Thus, the costs faced by students and parents in the United States are represented by Definition "E" in Figure 1.1, which includes tuition, while the costs faced by most students and parents in the European cases in this study include only those of student living represented in Figure 1.1 by Definition "F."

THE SOURCES OF REVENUE

Whatever the set of costs in question, and regardless of the system, society, or country, the costs must be shared by some combination of the following four sources of revenue: parents, students, taxpayers, and institutions (i.e., colleges or universities which derive extra revenues from philanthropists or donors to help students).

Parents are expected in most, although not all, countries to contribute at least to the costs of student living. In the United States, they are also expected to contribute a portion of the instructional costs through the payment of tuitions and fees: a large portion at private institutions, which receive relatively little (in some cases, no) direct governmental, or taxpayer-borne, aid; and a relatively small portion at public colleges and universities, where tuitions are lower. Parental contributions are limited by ability to pay—generally as measured by current income, sometimes also by wealth or assets, and usually modified by special considerations such as number of dependent children. Parental contributions may come from savings, from reduced current consumption, or from borrowing against future earnings. Parental contributions may be through cash or "in kind," particularly in the support of students living at home.

Students may pay a portion of the costs of student living and also, if tuition is charged, a portion of the instructional costs. Student-borne revenues may come from their own assets or savings, from term-time earnings, or from loans to be repaid from future earnings. Spouses, too, may be possible contributors to the costs of higher education and are treated for the purpose of this analysis as though their earnings were an extension of the students' own. Similarly, the unmarried partner or mate (in France, the *conjoint*) may be a significant, though unofficial, source of support. At the same time, public policy in Scandinavia holds the working spouse not responsible for contributions to living costs of his or her student spouse—a principle that releases the student from dependence on his or her working spouse, but that necessarily places a somewhat greater burden on the student and the taxpayer.

Taxpayers in most European countries pay all or nearly all of the direct instructional costs plus some portion of the costs of student living. In the United States, the taxpayer pays most of the instructional costs in the public sector and a portion of those in the private sector, either through direct institutional grants or through payment of a portion of the tuition costs. The costs of student living in the United States and in most European countries are supported by some combination of direct cash grants; loan-repayment subsidies (e.g., in the form of low interest rates or forgiveness of a portion of the principal amount borrowed); indirect subsidies of room, board, and other expenses (e.g., as in some European countries, through government-subsidized canteens, low-cost housing, or special travel fares); or by special tax advantages to the parents of students, which have the effect of shifting costs from taxpayers who happen to have children in college to taxpayers generally. Living costs are supported in most countries according to parental means, or "need": that is, are reduced as parents' incomes increase and as the need for the taxpayer subsidy declines.

Institutions/Philanthropists in some countries may contribute to

TABLE 1.1
Costs of Higher Education and Sources of Revenue

Sources of revenue	Costs of higher education	
	Costs of educational living	Costs of instruction
	● Room ● Board ● Books, travel, entertainment, and all other	● Faculty and staff salaries ● Operation and maintenance of plant ● Supplies and equipment ● Amortization and depreciation of plant
Parents	Any parental contribution toward children's educational living expenses	Tuitions and fees as paid by parents, net of any portion covered by grants, scholarships, or loan subsidies
Students	Any student contribution from savings or own assets . . . plus term-time work and summer savings . . . plus loans net of governmental subsidies	Tuitions and fees as paid by students, net of any portion covered by grants, scholarships, or loan subsidies
Taxpayers	Any student grants, need-based or otherwise, for costs of living . . . plus any direct governmental subsidies specifically for students' room and board . . . plus indirect subsidies via tax preferences to parents of students or loan repayment subsidies	Educational and general portions of public institution budgets, net of any revenues derived directly from students or parents via tuitions and fees . . . plus any portion of that tuition and fee revenue that is covered by governmental grants or loan subsidies . . . plus governmental grants to private institutions
Institutions/ Philanthropists	Scholarships or grants to defray living costs supported by endowment earnings or current gifts	Current gifts or endowment earnings for the support of basic instructional budgets plus any portion of philanthropically originated scholarships covering tuitions or fees
Business* (consumers, employees, or stockholders)	Scholarships or grants to defray living costs through gifts to institutions	Unrestricted gifts to institutions plus any portion of tuition or fees paid on behalf of employees or other grant recipients

* Business is presented here as a potential fifth source of revenue. The true incidence, or impact, of business contributions, however, is passed on to consumers, employees, stockholders, or even to the general taxpayer. For this reason, as explained in the text, and because its contributions are generally minor, "business" will not be covered in this text as an independent fifth "bearer of costs."

a portion of direct instructional costs through endowment income or current gifts applied to operations. They may also contribute to a portion of the costs of student living through grants or scholarships originating from endowments or current donations and most often given by the institution according to need. Institutional/philanthropic support is particularly prevalent in the United States, most likely because of the tradition of the autonomous private institution, which has always required alumni support in order to survive and which therefore assiduously cultivates the loyalty of alumni to their alma mater, and also because U.S. tax laws very substantially reward donations to tax-exempt, not-for-profit corporations, thus reducing the real cost of giving and, in effect, shifting some of the ultimate burden of such gifts onto the general taxpayers, who must make up the lost revenue.

The costs of higher education and the distribution of these costs among the four sources of revenue, or "bearers of the burden," are summarized in Table 1.1. It is a fundamental premise of this study that *all* costs, by whichever of Figure 1.1's definitions, are borne by some combination of these four sources—regardless of system or nation—and that any cost shifted *from* one source must perforce be shifted *to* another. This interlocking of revenue sources is portrayed in Figure 1.2. The costs of student living plus the costs of tuition and fees (if any) constitute the total costs faced by the student and his or her parents, which costs are in turn met by the parents' contribution, the student's contribution through work and loans, the taxpayers' contribution through grants and subsidies, and institutional grants originating in gifts from philanthropists or donors. Figure 1.2 also shows, in the bottom row, those shares of costs that are termed "financial assistance" in the United States.

CONTRIBUTIONS FROM BUSINESS

Business may also contribute to the costs of instruction, and occasionally to the costs of student living as well, through unrestricted gifts to colleges and universities or through tuitions paid on behalf of employees or other recipients of business scholarships. Business gifts to higher education are much more significant in the United States than elsewhere for the reasons cited above in connection with philanthropic giving in general. Furthermore, even in the United States, much business giving to higher education is restricted as to purpose and cannot be said to contribute significantly to covering the overall costs of undergraduate instruction.

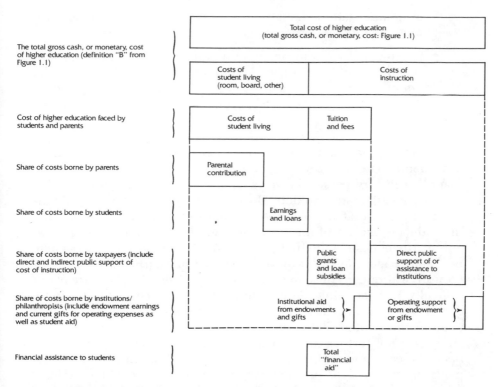

FIGURE 1.2 Apportioning the costs of higher education (size of shares roughly approximates U.S. public colleges).

But a much more serious qualification to the inclusion of business as a true partner in the bearing of college costs is the question of ultimate incidence. After all, only people or institutions on behalf of people—not businesses or corporations themselves—own assets and ultimately derive (or forgo) income. When a business is said to make a contribution to a college or to an employee scholarship fund, the burden of that contribution actually falls on some combination of the following:

- the consumers of the product or service produced by that business, as the cost of the contribution, like all production costs, is passed on to be reflected in the price; or

- the general taxpayer, who must make up the revenue lost from the tax deduction that lowers taxes and lessens the burden that would otherwise be felt in the business; or

- the employee, whose compensation package may include a tuition grant program, but only inasmuch as some other element of compensation, including a possibility of additional cash wage, is forgone; or

- the stockholder or owner, whose profits may decline as a result of contributions made to higher education, but only to the extent that the costs incurred are not absorbed or mitigated by the consumer, general taxpayer, or employee as suggested above.

Business, then, is not an ultimate bearer of costs in the manner of students, parents, taxpayers, and donors, but is rather an intermediary that in turn passes the costs on to consumers, employees, general taxpayers, or stockholders. Business remains a potentially significant player in that it can support higher education to an extent that the ultimate bearers of this burden—e.g., the consumers—might not voluntarily choose to do. In this sense, the business contribution may be likened most to the taxpayer contribution, particularly within a typically European consumption-based tax system. But because of the difficulty in specifying the true ultimate incidence of the business contribution, and because such contributions are still relatively small even in the United States and even less significant elsewhere, this study will not further consider business as a separate contributor, or bearer of cost, and will instead deal with the three principal participants of *parent, student,* and *taxpayer* and also consider, at least within the United States, the fourth participant of *institution/philanthropist.*

SPREADING THE BURDEN OVER TIME

A final perspective on higher education costs and the sources of revenue to cover them is summarized in Table 1.2, which shows the spreading of costs, or the bearing of the burden, over time. The parental contribution, for example, can come from the past, through a depletion of savings; from the present, through a reduction in family consumption; or from the future, if the parents wish to take out a loan or later to replenish their depleted savings and other assets.

Students, too, may pay their share of costs by drawing either on the past, through depleting their own savings or other assets; on the present, through current term-time work; or on the future, through loan repayments or other devices, such as a tax on future earnings, that shift the actual burden forward in time.

The taxpayer share is borne mainly in the present, through taxa-

TABLE 1.2
Sharing the Burden over Time: Spreading the Contributions from Parents,
Students, Taxpayers, and Institutions/Philanthropists over the Past, Present,
and Future

Contributions from	Past	Present	Future
Parents	Depletion of savings or other assets	Contributions from current income . . . reduction of current consumption and/or savings	Repayment of loans or replenishment of depleted savings
Students	Depletion of savings or other assets	Contributions from current earnings	Repayment of student loans, net of public subsidies
Taxpayers	Publicly endowed scholarships or grants (rare)	Instructional budgets of public institutions, instructional grants to private institutions, and student grants, all as covered by taxes, plus governmentally capitalized loans less present value of repayments	Public subsidies of repayments of privately capitalized loans, plus higher education's share of public deficit
Institutions/ Philanthropists	Income from endowments	Contributions from current giving to operating budgets or student assistance	Indirect capitalization of future gifts through inadequate depreciation of private-sector plant or depletion of real value of endowment

tion. To some degree, the taxpayer-borne burden may be shifted to the past If the current taxpayer contribution is kept below what it might be through deferring maintenance or otherwise depleting public capital. Also, the taxpayer contribution can be shifted to the future through deficit financing, by which the actual burden—that is, the loss of current consumption and private savings possibilities—is borne by future rather than present taxpayers.

Finally, philanthropy, too, can represent a burden borne in the past, as endowments continue to provide current revenues from gifts long since made; in the present, as current gifts come in; or even in the future, as colleges and universities "bank on" future donations, particularly via notoriously underfunded depreciation or replacement costs.

PUBLIC POLICY IN APPORTIONING THE COSTS

The foregoing analysis has presented the universe of potential contributors to the costs of higher education. The proper apportioning of costs, however, is a matter of intense public policy debate in the United States and at least Western Europe. Specifically, what is the relative share of costs to be borne by parents, students, and the general taxpayer?

About the only point of total agreement both within and among nations is that the costs faced by the student and his or her family should not be so daunting as to exclude children from low-income families from the opportunity to go to a college or university. Thus, the principles of social welfare and the nearly universal goal of equalizing access to higher education, at least for the academically able, have led to very substantial taxpayer subsidization both of the costs of instruction itself, making college or university attendance free or low-cost for all who qualify, and of the costs of student living, at least for those whose families could not afford to pay and who would otherwise be discouraged from higher education even with little or no tuition cost.

Beyond this point, which itself admits to varying degrees of tax-payer-borne subsidy, there is little agreement either within or among nations. Not surprisingly, most students want a smaller burden on themselves in the form of less debt and part-time work and also want smaller burdens on their parents in order to lessen their dependence on them and to minimize the personal and financial discomfort of parental undersupport. Everything else being equal, parents, too, generally prefer a lighter burden. Most students and parents would probably support a larger share borne by the taxpayer, either in the form of more generous taxpayer-supported aid to students or more aid directly to institutions to hold down, or prevent the imposition of, tuition charges. Parents are also taxpayers, however, and some may feel more financially threatened by taxes than by the expenses of college, some of which, after all, can be borne by their children. Also, the average taxpayer without a child currently in college would almost certainly prefer to have at least some of his or her tax burden lifted and picked up by someone else—especially if the "someone else" is the parent of a college student and thus likely to be more affluent than the average taxpayer. Finally, in the United States, which has the complication of the dual public–private sector, advocates of the private or independent sector generally want more of these costs picked up by the taxpayer; but they may also want students in the public institutions and their parents to have to pay more, thus perhaps relieving the taxpayer somewhat, but more importantly reducing the price differential between the highly subsidized public sector and the much less subsidized private, or independent, sector.

Any particular pattern of apportioning the costs of higher educa-tion and any proposal to shift these portions, especially among general taxpayers, students, and parents of students, has ramifications with regard to at least five major kinds of public policy issues. Central to this study, of course, is the proposition that these five policy issues are comprehendable in, and important to, all countries—a proposition that is amenable to a test in the five countries covered in this volume, the United States, the United Kingdom, the Federal Republic of Germany, France, and Sweden. The five issues are:

1. *The level of enrollments in, or the proportion of the relevant age cohort going on to or continuing in, higher education.* Other things being equal, the lower the proportion of costs that must be borne by the student, or by the student plus the family, even to the point of "negative costs" as suggested by the concept of the "study wage," the more some students will prefer higher educational studies as opposed to direct partici-pation in the labor force or some other alternative. On the other hand, higher costs borne by students may force out of college and back into the work force some of those students whose abilities or interests are most marginal. Part of a national policy toward cost sharing, then, depends on the priority placed on inducing more persons into higher education at the expense of the general taxpayer or consumer.

2. *The participation in higher education by those from poor, minority, geographically isolated, or otherwise disadvantaged families or from older persons who were once excluded or discouraged from higher education.* It stands to reason that any significant costs passed on to students or parents and not compensated for by financial aid will discourage higher edu-cational participation most among those (the poor, minority, geographically isolated, or otherwise traditionally bypassed)

whom most societies most want to encourage toward higher education. Cost sharing that discriminates in favor of under-represented sectors of the population may be an important ingredient in national policies to equalize opportunities—or even to equalize attainments.

3. *The relationship between the distribution of the benefits of higher education, both public and private, and the costs, as ultimately borne by students, parents, taxpayers, and perhaps the general consumer.* The benefits of higher education in virtually all countries, at least as reflected in participation rates and private returns, are disproportionately partaken of by the sons and daughters of the middle and upper classes; while the costs, at least that proportion borne by the general taxpayer or general consumer, are carried more-or-less by all or, to the degree that public finance is regressive, are carried disproportionately by the lower-middle and lower classes. This issue raises questions of distributional justice and may yield quite different policy recommendations than Issue 2, above.

4. *The responsiveness of higher educational institutions to consumer (student) pressures for quality, kind, and cost of education.* While the apportioning of costs is not the only factor bearing upon the efficiency or responsiveness of universities, it can be argued that the greater the share of costs borne by the student and his or her parents, particularly in the presence of competitive providers, the more the universities will seek to keep overall costs down, to seek certain economies, and to provide the kind and quality of higher education sought by the student. (In fairness, it is at least possible to argue against such commercial virtues as economy and consumer sovereignty in higher education and thus to employ the same premise to argue against costs being borne by students or parents.) This issue raises the proposition that the burden of the costs—which must mainly be borne, in any event, by some combination of students, parents, taxpayers, or consumers—might be seen as a positive good when borne in some measure by students, so long as national policies of equal opportunity, etc., were still achieved.

5. *The viability of institutions or sectors of higher education that are either not, or are only partially, subsidized by the taxpayer.* The strong private and proprietary sectors in the United States depend not only on their often special missions or ambiance, but upon the existence of governmental subsidies

in the form of need-based aid to their students, plus the fact of substantial tuitions and other costs borne by students and parents at public colleges. Both policies together serve to narrow the price disparity between the public and the private and proprietary sectors and to better preserve the private and proprietary institutions. A tradition of a considerable portion of the costs being met by the students and/or their families, then, helps keep alive alternatives to institutions of higher education that are mainly taxpayer-financed—and that may also be substantially governmentally controlled.

A COMPARATIVE PERSPECTIVE ON COST SHARING

A comparative perspective is especially valuable in the examination of policy issues stemming from a universal situation or proposition such as sharing the cost of higher education. For example, parents are one of the three principal sources of support for higher educational costs: They form the backbone of the U.S. system of cost sharing, and they are expected to contribute to some measured limit of their ability in most European countries. Yet, parents in the United States are not expected to contribute anything until their annual adjusted gross income is about $15,000 or higher. The comparable income in France, above which parental contributions are expected, is about $6,000. Such differences lend a special flavor to otherwise universal questions: How much can, should, and will parents contribute toward the higher education of their children? How much sacrifice, particularly at low incomes, should parents be expected to make? How steeply should this contribution rise with income—that is, at what rate should marginal income effectively be taxed for support of the costs of college? At what age of the student or by whatever other criteria should the responsibility of the parents cease? And what of Sweden, where parents aren't officially expected to contribute at all? Is not the Swedish policy an advantage only to the well-to-do, since it is primarily they who send their sons and daughters to college and who in most other countries would be expected to contribute most to the costs of student living? And how does this observation square with the dominant social democratic egalitarianism for which Sweden is so justly well known?

Or, consider the student's share. In the United States, students regularly work part time and incur debts of $2,000–$2,500 and more a year to handle their share of costs, especially at high-priced private colleges. Students play an even more important role across the board in meeting college costs in Sweden. Students in the United Kingdom bear almost no share of costs, neither borrowing nor working. Yet relatively few U.K. students are eligible for the grants generously supported by the British taxpayer, and the nontraditional or marginally prepared (even if well-motivated) student has few options to help himself or herself. What are the factors or beliefs upon which a nation's policy with respect to the appropriate student share is based, and what are the trends that may foretell future policy?

Student loans, in fact, are a controversial element of student finance virtually everywhere. Does the mere existence of a generally available student loan program tempt policymakers over time to shift more of the financial burden of college from taxpayers and parents to students? U.K. students assert this to be so, and both the American and the Swedish experiences suggest some credence to the fear.

Where student loans have become an integral feature of student finance, as in the United States, all of Scandinavia, and more recently in the Federal Republic of Germany, how much debt can, will, and should students be expected or allowed to bear? If loan subsidies effectively apportion the real costs of the loan between the student and the taxpayer, what is the proper amount of subsidy? Should loans be mainly like grants, as in Germany, with its 5-year grace period, 20-year repayment period, and zero interest? Or should they be more like "real loans," as in the United States, with its 6-month grace period, 10-year repayment period, and interest rates that fluctuate in the range of 7 to 9 percent? Should subsidies be upon all loans, or should they flow somewhat more generously to students whose parents happen to have been poor at the time the debt was incurred, as in America's National Direct Student Loan Program? Or should subsidies flow more to students whose own incomes are low at the time of repayment, as is the case on a limited basis in Sweden and as often proposed in the United States?

The evidence is overwhelming, in centrally planned as well as in market-oriented countries, that free tuition and generous maintenance grants are insufficient in themselves to achieve socioeconomic, ethnic, or regional distributions within the student population that mirror those distributions in the general population. Conceivably, even higher grants (like "study wages") to underrepresented students, coupled with reduced subsidies to overrepresented students, could achieve a more nearly equal distribution of student places. To what degree can and should policies manipulating the sharing of costs be used in this way to affect the socioeconomic, ethnic, or regional distribution of higher educational opportunities? Also, if the socio-economic inequalities in higher education enrollment originate at the level of secondary education, such as in countries with substantial dropout rates among low-socioeconomic youth, should available financial support, even to the point of study wages and augmented family support, be targeted more at this level than at the collegiate or tertiary level?

These and similar policy questions do not admit to easy answers. What is significant to this study is that they are being asked in many countries—and being answered often in very different ways. While knowledge of one system generally does not lead to an otherwise unanticipated answer to an issue or dilemma posed in another system, comparative knowledge nevertheless lends perspective and depth to policy analysis.

The comparative literature on cost sharing, student support, or financial assistance is extremely thin, not highly analytical, and too often out of date by the time of publication. The most extensive is Maureen Woodhall's 1978 review of student support schemes in the Organization for Economic Cooperation and Development (OECD) nations of Australia, Canada, France, Germany, Japan, the Netherlands, Norway, Sweden, the United Kingdom, and the United States.[1] Woodhall has an excellent grasp of the issues and is particularly insightful on student loans, about which she has become the foremost comparative authority.[2] Her 1978 OECD work, however, relies perforce on country data mainly from 1974–75—virtually obsolete by 1985 given the rapid development of student support policies.

Michael Vorbeck, from the Council of Europe's Section for Educational Research and Documentation, is similarly well situated to review financial support practices in many countries, and his 1983 review is based on more recent data (1980–81), but the only available published report is too cryptic for analysis and does not provide an analysis of issues nor any real comparative policy perspective.[3]

Furthermore, neither Woodhall nor Vorbeck looks at student support from the perspective of burden sharing. Woodhall's data is most often aggregate, relating to such issues as total national student support budgets, percent of all students receiving grants, or percent of total support estimated to come from parents. Such data do not get at the issue so critical, at least to Americans (and perhaps becoming more so to other countries), of the amount of contribution that parents at a particular level of income and assets and with specified other parental obligation are willing and able to devote to the higher education of their son or daughter, or the amount of contribution that students, either from own assets, spouse's earnings, own current earnings, or loans, are willing and able to contribute.

COST SHARING IN THE UNITED KINGDOM, THE FEDERAL REPUBLIC OF GERMANY, FRANCE, SWEDEN, AND THE UNITED STATES

Four countries in addition to the United States were chosen to begin building a base of data and policy description for a comparative analysis of cost sharing:

- the United Kingdom (actually, England and Wales), because of the extensive literature available and the extremely generous grants combined with a virtual zero "self-help" (i.e., student-borne) expectation;

- the Federal Republic of Germany, because of its highly developed needs-analysis system and its recent changeover from a mostly grant to an all-loan (albeit very highly subsidized) system;

- France, because of a national needs-analysis system quite different from that employed in the United States, a very strong tradition of parental support, and a substantial literature on the economics of higher education; and

- Sweden, because it has been a leader in the world in the use of student loans and has also moved completely away from any expected parental contributions.

Contacts were made and literature gathered during the spring of 1985. The four European nations were visited during the summer of 1985. From this information, profiles were developed on higher education generally, and cost sharing specifically, for each of the four European countries and the United States. Special attention was paid to securing comparable data on:

- the total out-of-pocket costs of higher education as faced by students and their parents;

- the expected parental contribution, if any, and how it is derived from income and other factors;

- the expected student contribution, from savings, term-time work, and/or loans;

- the taxpayer-borne contribution, whether from need-based grants, loan subsidies, or indirect support of student living expenses;

- the institutional/philanthropic contribution (in the United States);

- trends and issues regarding the sharing of higher education costs within each country; and

- problems or issues common to all five countries.

Chapters 2 through 6 present the five country profiles. Chapter 7 draws the data together and makes some comparative observations. Appendix A describes the concept of "purchasing power parity," by which all units of national currencies are also given in U.S. dollars derived not from the current and highly volatile market exchange rates, but from ratios that reflect relative purchasing power in the two countries. Appendix B presents the concepts and calculations for separating subsidized loans into a "true loan" and an "effective grant."

2

THE
UNITED KINGDOM

HIGHER EDUCATION IN
THE UNITED KINGDOM

Structure and Governance[1]

Higher education in the United Kingdom is structured according to the so-called binary principle, by which the mission, governance, and finance of the university and nonuniversity sectors are sharply distinct. In the nonuniversity, or "public," sector, the structure and governance of the institutions, as well as the student support systems, vary further between England and Wales, Scotland, and Northern Ireland (in which, however, the nonuniversity sector is very small).

The United Kingdom's 46 publicly funded universities are autonomous entities, each with its own charter and with degree-granting authority.[2] They included such venerable institutions as Oxford, Cambridge, and Edinburgh as well as the new universities created in the 1960s from former colleges of advanced technology. Ministerial oversight, such as there is, of the universities is provided in Great Britain by the Secretary of State for Education and Science and in Northern Ireland by the Department of Education. The mission of the universities is that of the classical Western university: scholarship and advanced training in the disciplines and in certain professions, such as medicine and law. Admittance is highly competitive. Financing is principally from the central government, but—and this is a key feature, highly prized by the universities—is disbursed by the University Grants Committee (UGC), a quasi-autonomous body established by the Treasury in 1919 when it became obvious that Britain's universities would need sustained public subsidies, but with the recognition even then of the advantage to the universities as well as to the government of a buffer between the source of funds and the all-important decisions about their disbursement.

The nonuniversity, or public, sector comprises the 30 polytechnics in England and Wales, the 14 Scottish Central Institutions, the 54 voluntary colleges in England, and more than 300 other institutions, described collectively as "colleges and institutes of higher and further education," between 50 and 60 of which are engaged predominantly in *advanced* further education and correspond to what in the United States would be termed "higher education." The Scottish institutions are quite distinct from the others, as is their system of student support, and so will not be considered further in this report. The "voluntary colleges," mainly the legacy of a once-church-supported sector and providing primarily teacher education, are funded directly by the Department of Education and Science without local intervention, and the Department of Education and Science also funds a small number of "direct-grant" institutions, mostly specialized colleges, such as the Royal College of Art and Cranfield Institute of Technology. The rest of the public sector—principally, for the interest of this report, the polytechnics—is controlled and financed jointly by the local education authorities (LEAs) and the central government, with ministerial oversight by the Secretary of State for Education and Science in England and the territorial secretaries of state for Scotland, Wales, and Northern Ireland.

The mission of the polytechnics, founded since the late 1960s, is education and training, largely of an applied orientation, with scholarship being a secondary and almost unofficial expectation of the faculty, even though there is a tendency of polytechnic faculty (as of comprehensive college faculty in the United States or *Fachhochschule* faculty in Germany) to drift toward the norms of the university.[3] Degrees given by polytechnics and other further education institutions (i.e., by all but the universities, which are authorized to grant their own degrees) must be validated by the Council for National Academic Awards (CNAA). Higher certificates and diplomas must be validated by the Business and Technician Education Council. Funding for the polytechnics is from the central government and the local education authorities, coordinated since 1982 by the National Advisory Body for Public Sector Higher Education (NAB) in England and a counterpart body for Wales (WAB), with similar advisory structures for Scotland and Northern Ireland.

Recent Developments

Higher education in the United Kingdom has been powerfully shaped by the 1963 Report of the Robbins Committee, which set forth the still-accepted rationale for general public support of higher education. The Robbins Report led to the great expansion of both university and nonuniversity institutions and enrollments in the 1960s and 1970s, and it formed the economic and social policy rationale for the then-emerging system of student support. The core principle of the report was that programs of higher education should be available for all those who are qualified by ability and attainment and who wish to pursue them to do so.[4]

What emerged in the decades after Robbins was a dominant university sector, characterized by (a) a young, very selective, and almost totally full-time student body; (b) high per-student costs (although costs per graduate were lower than in other countries because of the high retention rate compared to other university systems); and (c) substantial autonomy from governmental or other external intrusions, particularly when compared with continental European universities. The polytechnics, formed during the 1960s mainly from other institutions, have had a much more volatile existence but have carried much of the burden of expanding higher education's clientele and relating more closely to local communities. Finally, there arose during this same period a system of student support grants, described more fully in the following section, that were, and remain, among the most generous in the world for those who receive them but that also elude many students and potential students because of strict eligibility requirements and reductions based on expected parental contributions.

The proportion of the traditional age cohort going on to higher education (that is, to either the universities or to a program elsewhere of advanced further education) has hovered around 13–15 percent. Those entering the university sector remain overwhelmingly from high-socioeconomic-status families. The Conservative Government, in power since 1979, has cut operating support very substantially, to which the universities, with the Government's blessing, responded by cutting enrollments in order to maintain their per-student support.

The Government's 1985 "Green Paper" calls for (a) greater linkages with the private sector and with the needs of the economy in general, especially on the part of the universities; (b) expanded nontraditional forms of delivery, especially within the public (nonuniversity) sector; (c) greater efficiency, accountability, and attention to academic standards; (d) only the most minimal expansion of enrollments; and (e) more nontaxpayer sources of revenue.[5] The last refers to research grants, private donations, and "full cost fees," paid by overseas students and by students or business sponsors of special nondegree "short courses." The press for nontaxpayer revenue also included, albeit with great ambivalence, the Government's strong desire to shift some additional financial burden both to students, in the form of a loan program, and to parents, in the form of increased family contribution expectations—neither of which options, however, proved politically feasible in 1985 and both of which appear to have been abandoned, at least temporarily, by mid-1986.

SHARING THE COSTS AMONG PARENTS, TAXPAYERS, AND STUDENTS

Costs to the Student and Family

Tuition and Fees. Although there are tuition and fee charges at U.K. institutions, these have been paid automatically by the Government directly to the institution since 1977 for all students within the mandatory grant network, which comprises nearly all "home" (i.e., British resident) students in full-time study at the higher education level (see the next section for a more complete description of the students eligible for mandatory awards).[6] Thus, for most students, the level of tuition or fees is immaterial. The institutions receive for each mandatory award-holder up to £520 [$877]* in 1985–86—up from £480 [$809] in 1982–83, which was, in turn, over one-half of the £900 [$1,518] in 1981–82.

The reason for tuition and fees at all, when they are paid by the taxpayer anyway and are further assumed to be offset against the direct recurrent grant that is also borne by the taxpayer, is not completely clear, particularly when one attempts to understand the very great recent yearly fluctuations as well. It is apparently thought by some that the tuition and fee income is sufficiently distinct on paper that it constitutes an alternative source of income to the direct recurrent grant and is thus of some value to the institutions. Perhaps more important, if not entirely consistent, is the supposed symbolic function of tuition: a reminder to the students that the education received has real value—even if neither they nor their parents are paying for it directly, and even if the nominal tuition amount clearly bears no meaningful relationship to the real cost of university operations. To the institutions, the tuition payment might be viewed as an incentive

* All pound units in this chapter are followed by a U.S. dollar equivalent according to a 1985 purchasing power ratio of $1 = £0.593. See Appendix A.

to increase enrollments, although the reduction in tuitions by nearly half in 1982–83, to an amount clearly below the real marginal per-student cost of instruction, was explained by the government at the time as an attempt to discourage the expansion of enrollments in the polytechnics at a time when university enrollments were being trimmed. It is assumed anyway that whatever additional tuition revenue might be generated, whether by raising tuitions or by increasing enrollments, might (and quite clearly could) simply be removed by a corresponding reduction of the direct recurrent grant.[7] Finally, the tuition does generate some revenue, from those British resident students who are outside the mandatory grant network and whose tuition is not covered by a discretionary grant, and certainly from the overseas students, who since 1980–81 have been paying full-cost tuitions.[8] For the purpose of this study, however, because the vast majority of full-time undergraduate students do not face any real tuition charge, we will assume there to be no tuitions or fees within the costs faced by the student/family unit.

Costs of Living. Because the maintenance grants, along with any officially expected contributions from parents', spouse's, or student's own sources, are ostensibly designed to cover the full costs of living for a normal nine-month academic year, the maximum grant—before any deductions for expected contributions—might be taken as the *de facto* governmental estimate of a student's minimal living expenses. The maximum grants in 1984–85 were £2,100 [$3,541] for students living in London, £1,775 [$2,993] for students living elsewhere, and £1,435 [$2,420] for students living at home and commuting—these amounts increasing in 1985–86 to £2,165 [$3,651] in London, £1,830 [$3,086] elsewhere, and £1,480 [$2,496] for commuters.

The adequacy of student grants is difficult to measure in any country. Governments tend to associate "adequacy" with "minimal," and they tend to view as corroborating evidence for the adequacy of the status quo the fact that students live on whatever they have to in order to remain as students. That the governmental grants may be supplemented by sources not officially assumed necessary by the government, or that students may have to live at standards far below their nonstudent age peers, may not bother (indeed, may be welcomed by) government officials. Students, on the other hand, especially in the United Kingdom and Northern Europe, define adequacy more along the lines of a minimally adequate living standard for their age peers in the "outside" working world. While U.S. students view higher education as a very expensive, yet very valuable and pleasurable, experience for which they and their parents should expect to pay, British students view the universities (somewhat less the polytechnics) more as their proper workplace, not unlike the factory for their less fortunate age peers, and thus view study as a service they are performing for society which incurs an expense (the costs of living, as well as any tuition or fees) for which they should be paid rather than one that should be paid by them or their parents. In addition, politically astute students realize that grant levels are set through a kind of indirect bargaining process, wherein the government (particularly a fiscally conservative one) can be expected to maintain a constant downward pressure on grants, as indeed on nearly all governmental expenditures, while students, like any other interest group, are expected to maintain a constant upward pressure. In this light, for students to proclaim that current grant levels were fully adequate, or even as high as could reasonably be expected, could be seen as an admission that the grants were actually higher than necessary and as an invitation to reductions.

Hence it is not surprising that the National Union of Students should proclaim the current mandatory grant levels as inadequate, although their major argument with current policy remains their adamant opposition to the very principle of the expected parental contribution. It is true that award levels have failed to keep pace with living costs and that the current (1985–86) Conservative Government has an undisguised agenda of (a) reducing or at least restraining governmental expenditures generally; (b) eliminating or at least reducing student eligibility for public assistance outside the student grant system, such as housing, unemployment, and supplemental benefits; (c) reducing or at least restraining enrollments; (d) forcing additional resources from parents, at least from more affluent families; and finally (e) generating some student contribution to these living costs, specifically through the student loan program that has long been sought by some Conservatives.[9]

At the same time, the British student grant system—disregarding for the moment the related but distinct issue of the expected parental contribution offset—is widely assumed to be one of the most generous in the Western world. Also, several hundred thousand students are evidently "making it" somehow with the available grants, many or most of them probably without substantial additional resources from parents, because the current expected contribution is already high, and probably without substantial additional resources from themselves, because British students are actively discouraged from taking part-time work except during summer vacations and because student loans are virtually unavailable. Thus, the maximum grants, with the various official supplements that are available for special demonstrated needs, seem to be at the very least a reasonable estimate of the minimum living costs facing U.K. students.

An extensive survey of actual student expenditures undertaken during the 1982–83 academic year by the National Union of Students

TABLE 2.1
Costs Facing Undergraduate Students and Families, England and Wales,
1985–86, by DES and NUS Estimates

	DES estimated costs, elsewhere than London[a]		Estimated from NUS Survey data, all U.K.[b]		DES estimated costs, London[c]	
	£	$	£	$	£	$
Tuition and fees[c]	0	0	0	0	0	0
Room and board	1,100	1,855	1,180	1,990	1,300	2,192
All other costs	730	1,231	765	1,290	865	1,459
Total	£1,830	$3,086	£1,945	$3,280	£2,165	$3,651

[a] Department of Education and Science estimated costs are the mandatory grant totals divided 3/5 room and board and 2/5 all other according to NUS survey findings.

[b] National Union of Students estimated costs are taken from data reported in John Saxby, *Undergraduate Income and Expenditure: Survey 1982/83* (London: NUS, 1984) for 1982–83, extrapolated by 12 percent to approximate 1985–86 costs.

[c] Tuition and fees assumed to be covered and thus not a real cost, per discussion in the text.

(NUS) supports the conclusion that the maximum mandatory grant—assuming full expected parental contribution—underestimates only slightly what students actually spend.[10] Student expenditure diaries revealed average weekly room-and-board expenditures in 1982–83 of about £34 and all other expenses of about £22, for a total expenditure in a 31-week academic year of £1,736 [$2,927], compared to the 1982–83 mandatory grants of £1,900 [$3,204] for London and £1,595 [$2,690] for elsewhere. The NUS study found that the mandatory grant provides sufficient money (again, assuming that the parents pay their share) to cover room, board, travel, and course-related expenses, but that additional sources (e.g., student earnings or additional parental assistance) may be needed for noneducationally related essentials. But the study concludes that: "Those who are underfinanced are invariably those students whose parents for one reason or another do not make their contribution in full or at all. . . ." In short, the maximum mandatory grants, if understood to assume relatively austere budgets, are not unreasonable estimates of the cost in England and Wales to the student and family.[11] These estimates, with a somewhat higher extrapolation from the NUS survey data, are summarized in Table 2.1.

Student Grants

Nearly all full-time home (i.e., non-overseas) students in England and Wales are eligible for grants that pay tuition and fee charges

TABLE 2.2
Maximum Undergraduate Cost-of-Living (Mandatory) Student Grants for
England and Wales, 1984–85 and 1985–86

	1984–85		1985–86	
	£	$	£	$
Elsewhere than London	1,775	2,993	1,830	3,086
London	2,100	3,541	2,165	3,651
Living at home	1,435	2,420	1,480	2,496
Receiving free room and board	755	1,273	780	1,315
Mature student 26 yrs.	165	278	170	287
supplement 27 yrs.	330	556	340	573
28 yrs.	505	852	520	877
29 yrs. and up	665	1,121	685	1,155

Sources: Department of Education and Science, *Grants to Students: A Brief Guide
1984,* and "Student Grants for 1985–86," 31 May 1985, DES news release.

For the mature student supplement, students must be age 26 before the start of the
program of studies.

Additional supplements are available for academically mandated travel and additional
weeks' study, special equipment needs, etc.

directly to the institutions, as described in the preceding section,
regardless of the incomes of their parents. Eligible students who are
enrolled in designated courses ("programs" in U.S. nomenclature)
also receive means-tested grants that, together with any expected
contribution from parents', spouses', or students' own assets, are designed to cover the student's minimal academic-year living expenses.
The basic awards for 1984–85 and 1985–86 are shown in Table 2.2,
with supplements for mature students. Other supplements are paid
to cover required study abroad, study during vacation periods, special
equipment needs, and the like.

The current student-grant system has existed since 1962, when
the system of *mandatory* and *discretionary* grants was set forth in
law, based on the recommendations of the Anderson Committee.[12]
The mandatory grants are administered through the local education
authorities (LEAs) but must be paid to all eligible students enrolled
in designated programs. Eligible students, with certain technical exceptions, are those residents of the United Kingdom who have not
previously been enrolled in a designated course of higher or advanced
further education. Designated courses are generally full-time or
"sandwich" (i.e., alternating full-time study and prescribed full-time
work) programs of study leading to a first degree (equivalent to a U.S.
bachelors and to some advanced professional degrees) or to a diploma
or certificate program of at least three years' duration and comparable
to a first-degree program, given by a university, a polytechnic, or

another college of advanced further education. In 1982–83, some 370,500 mandatory awards were given in England and Wales—72 percent of all student awards given.

Generally excluded from the mandatory grant system are post-graduate students who are eligible instead for competitive grants from one of the five national research councils; students in nondegree fields such as occupational therapy and dental hygiene, who are eligible for competitive grants from the Department of Health and Social Security; students pursuing nonadvanced certificate programs or still working at the advanced secondary level, even if studying at a college; most part-time students; and most students who have already at some time begun another designated program with support of a mandatory grant.

Any student not falling within the mandatory-grant network may still apply for, and possibly receive, a discretionary grant of either full value (i.e., equal to what a mandatory grant would have been) or lesser value from his or her local education authority. Discretionary grants, however, vary by year and by LEA and may be smaller than, or less available than, the mandatory awards, in part because the local discretionary awards have had to bear a share of fiscal austerity that the LEAs have been unable, by law, to pass on to those students within the mandatory grant program. In England and Wales in 1982–83, 45,400 full-value and 85,900 lesser-value discretionary awards were given—9 percent and 17 percent respectively of all awards given that year.[13]

Woodhall wrote in 1983:

> It is widely recognized that the system of discretionary awards discriminates against part-time students and those taking non-advanced courses. The rules governing the mature student allowance make it difficult for married women to qualify, since a "mature student" must have been in full-time employment for three out of the six years immediately before the start of a course, and no exceptions are made for looking after children or unemployment. The level of the mature student allowance and the dependents' allowance means that it is particularly difficult for adult students with financial responsibilities to finance higher education. The rules about grants for those who change their minds about . . . [programs of study] or careers are not designed to encourage flexibility, and reflect the fact that the system of higher education grants was designed before the idea of continuing education had any real influence on policy.[14]

Parental Contributions

All students receiving mandatory or full-value discretionary grants (the overwhelming majority of full-time undergraduates) have their tuitions paid in full. The maintenance grants, however—except for a minimum award that was £410 ($691) in 1983–84 and £205 ($346) in 1984–85 but was eliminated altogether in 1985–86—are subject to means-tested reductions according to parents', spouses', and students' own abilities to contribute toward these costs. The expected parental contribution is based on "residual income," which is the combined gross taxable income of both parents in the year preceding that for which the grant is to be awarded, less such deductions as a flat £980 [$1,653] for each nonspouse adult dependent, tax-deductible mortgage interest, and certain other expenses such as pension contributions, but not including the large and ubiquitous expenses of income taxes and National Insurance (similar to U.S. Social Security). The Department of Education and Science estimates that gross income is, on average, about 10 percent higher than residual income.[15]

Expected parental contributions—i.e., the amounts by which grants are reduced—are shown in Table 2.3 for 1984–85 and 1985–86. The resulting expected contributions were reduced for each dependent child (other than the award holder) who is not also an award holder by £80 [$135] in 1984–85 and raised to £85 [$143] in 1985–86; for each additional dependent child who is also an award holder it was reduced by £225 [$379] in 1984–85 and raised to £240 [$405] in 1985–86.

Example:

What would be the expected parental contribution and the mandatory grant in 1985–86 for a student resident in London from a family with one other nonstudent dependent child, a gross prior-year combined family income of £18,000, deductible mortgage payments of £1,200, and deductible pension and life insurance payments of £700?

Calculation (refer to Tables 2.2 and 2.3):

Prior-year gross family income £18,000
less deductible mortgage payments 1,200
less deductible "other" payments 700
equals prior-year residual income £16,100

Expected parental contributions,
by Table 2.3, of £1,274 plus one-quarter
of residual income over £15,000 1,549
less deduction for dependent child 85
equals expected parental contribution 1,464
Maximum Award, London, by Table 2.1 2,165
Actual Award (Maximum less Expected
Contribution) £701

In the example above, an £18,000 [$30,354] prior-year gross family income converts to a £16,100 [$26,981] residual income, which

TABLE 2.3
Expected Parental Contributions for England and Wales, 1984–85 and
1985–86

Prior-Year Residual Income		1984–85[a]		1985–86[b]	
£	$	£	$	£	$
7,600	12,816	20	34	0	0
8,100	13,659	71	120	20	34
9,000	15,177	220	371	148	250
12,000	20,236	703	1,185	674	1,137
15,000	25,295	1,203	2,028	1,274	2,148
18,000	30,354	1,703	2,872	2,024	3,413
21,000	35,413	2,203	3,715	2,774	4,678
24,000	40,472	2,703	4,558	3,524	5,943

Sources: Department of Education and Science, "Student Grants for 1985–86," 31 May 1985 News Release, and DES, *Grants to Students: A Brief Guide 1984*. The 1986–87 schedule is from *The Times Higher Education Supplement*, 20 Dec. 1985.

[a] The 1984–85 scale begins with an expected contribution of £20 and increases at a ratio of £1 expected contribution for each £7 from the starting income of £7,600, changing to a ratio of £1 in £6 for incomes above £9,700. The minimum grant in 1984–85 was £205.

[b] The 1985–86 scale begins with an expected contribution of £20 and increases at a ratio of £1 expected contribution for each £7 of income from the starting income of £8,100, changing to a ratio of £1 in £5 at £10,300, then at a ratio of £1 in £4 at £15,000 until the maximum contribution (for all children in higher education) of £4,000 is reached at a residual income of £25,294. There is no minimum grant beginning in 1985–86.

The 1986–87 scale, not shown above, begins with an expected contribution of £20 at a residual income of £8,700 and moves all of the thresholds up by 8.7 percent. Contribution rates change at £11,100 and £15,000, and the maximum contribution for all children in a single family is £4,300, reached at a residual income of £28,000.

yields an expected family contribution (less the £85 [$143] dependent-child deduction) of £1,464 [$2,469], which is in turn subtracted from the maximum 1985–86 basic London resident award of £2,165 [$3,651] for a net mandatory award of £701 [$1,182].

Figure 2.1 shows the family net residual income at which point there begins to be an expected contribution and thus an award reduction, and also the upper range of income, at which point the expected contribution equals the full maximum award, beyond which there is thus no award. For 1985–86 for a family with one student in London and one additional nonstudent child, there are no expected parental contributions, and thus a maximum mandatory grant of £2,165 [$3,650] would be awarded, up to and including a prior-year residual income of £8,520 [$14,368]. After that point, expected parental contributions begin, which increase at a fairly steep rate, although with two slightly progressive kinks in the curve, to a prior-year resid-

Assume: • student resident in London, and
⠀⠀⠀⠀⠀⠀• one additional dependent nonstudent child in family

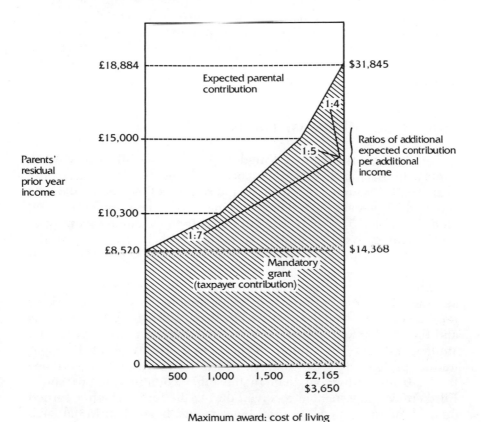

Parents'
residual
prior year
income

Maximum award: cost of living
for academic year as estimated
by Department of Education and Science

FIGURE 2.1 The division of estimated maintenance costs between the expected parental contribution and the mandatory award as a function of parents' prior-year residual income, 1985–86, England and Wales.

ual income of £18,884 [$31,845]. At this point, the full £2,165 [$3,651] is expected to come from the parents and the grant is phased out altogether. The Department of Education and Science estimated that 70 percent of all dependent students eligible for a full-value award (either mandatory or discretionary) in 1982–83 had their awards reduced by an expected parental contribution.

⠀⠀⠀Many parents—just over one-half, according to the 1982–83 NUS survey reported earlier—make their contributions by deed of covenant to the student. Payment by covenant is treated as taxable income to the student, but the majority of students pay no income tax, as their total income falls below the tax threshold. But the amount so paid is no longer taxable to the parents, and the covenant account is entitled to a rebate on the taxes that have already been withheld from that portion of the parents' income. The net effect, therefore, is to reduce the after-tax burden of the parental contribution by as much as 30 percent.[16]

Student Contributions: The Issue of Loans

Students in the United Kingdom are not officially expected to contribute even to their maintenance expenses during the academic year. The NUS survey of expenses and sources of income in 1982–83 reported 55 percent of students working during the summer, earning an average of £251 [$423]. It would be safe to conclude that most of these earnings went to support the students themselves during the summertime, with some earnings doubtless saved to supplement parental contributions during the academic year.

British university tradition, though, discourages term-time work, and the NUS survey showed only 12 percent of the students working term-time, earning on the average less than £100 [$169]. The students and the government both view term-time work as a distraction from studies and as a contributor to the twin maladies of attrition and unduly prolonged study—both of which are much less in evidence in the United Kingdom than in the other countries of this study. Furthermore, any income received during the term, whether earned on a job or "unearned," as from investments, beyond an initial £425 [$717] in 1985–86, reduces the mandatory grant "pound for pound," clearly discouraging any but the most occasional term-time job.

Finally and most important, there is no generally available student loan program in the United Kingdom, and without loans there can be little systematic student participation in sharing the costs of higher education. Opposition to student loans in any form and at any level has been one of the principal planks in the platform of the National Union of Students since large-scale student loan programs emerged in Europe and North America in the 1960s. On its face, the controversy over student loans seems to pit students and their political allies, mainly on the left, who could be expected to favor grants over loans and therefore resist the introduction of loans where none now exist, against some conservative party leaders and market-oriented economists, who could be expected to favor loans as a way to reduce the burden on the taxpayer and to introduce some elements of the market into the financing of higher education. In fact, the loan controversy in the United Kingdom has a number of arguments on either side, many of which are subtle and hard to verify, and some of which seem to draw opposite conclusions from the same observation. Some of the arguments are based on observations of North American and Scandinavian experiences with student loans.

The Case for Loans. For example, the proponents of a student loan program in the United Kingdom may cite any one or more of the following alleged benefits:[17]

1. *Lower governmental expenditures,* on the intuitively plausible assumption that a given level of student assistance can be made available at less cost to the taxpayer with governmentally guaranteed or even governmentally capitalized loans, even with subsidies, than with direct, nonrepayable governmental grants.

2. *A more equitable distribution of governmental costs and benefits,* on the assumption that taxpayer-supported higher education is paid for by all, including the poor, but is partaken of disproportionately by the sons and daughters of the wealthy, who will, in turn, do well financially because of this higher education; and on the assumption, therefore, that passing more of the costs on to the students themselves would more fairly align the burden of the costs with the recipients of the benefits.

3. *A greater sensitivity on the part of institutions to the needs of students,* on the assumption that students who must pay for some of their higher education will be more astute consumers and the universities and polytechnics, presumably, more responsive suppliers.

4. *A more efficient use of the resources of the universities as well as the time of the students,* on the assumption that students who must pay for a portion of their higher education will neither linger unduly at their studies nor flit wastefully from program to program.

5. *An opportunity for people in their early 20s facing several years of study, followed by good job and earning prospects, to shift some consumption and investment opportunities from the future to the present,* i.e., the same reason anyone borrows money, as long as he or she can find a willing lender who will sell some of his or her present opportunities in return for future opportunities plus interest.

6. *An opportunity for those excluded from the mandatory grant network, or whose parents refuse to help, to pursue some*

program of study in a university or polytechnic, on the assumption that it may be appropriate for the government (i.e., the taxpayer) *not* to assist with mandatory grants those whose parents are dilatory or those who want a second program of study or to study only part time or to pursue a "nondesignated" course of study, but on the further assumption that it would be most appropriate (and socially egalitarian) to help such persons pursue their own higher educational goals at their own expense, with just a bit of governmental assistance through a guaranteed or directly capitalized loan program.

Points 1, 3, and 4 are standard articles of conservative economic faith. Point 1—the allegedly lesser burden on the taxpayer of loans as opposed to grants—is undoubtedly true in theory. However, opponents of loans point to the high costs of subsidies (depending, of course, on the rate of interest charged), to the high costs of administration and collection, and to the high level of defaults (especially in the United States) and dispute the claim of substantial economy in a loan program. In reference to point 4, opponents of loans in the United Kingdom also cite the almost unparalleled efficiency of the current U.K. system and claim that reliance on loans could scarcely improve upon the United Kingdom's low attrition and short time-to-completion, and that it could just as well worsen both measures of efficiency.[18]

Pro-loan argument 2—on behalf of greater distributive justice—is a good example of the intersection of the intellectual left and the political right: in this case, the neo-liberal assertion that certain kinds of governmental expenditures (e.g., higher education) may, by virtue of benefits that are skewed to the middle and upper classes and burdens that are borne substantially by the working class, actually increase rather than decrease income disparities and help perpetuate the intergenerational transmission of wealth and status. Such an argument is enormously threatening to those who either work for, or otherwise benefit from, those parts of the public sector, such as universities, that are consistently targeted by this neo-liberal critique. As such, and because the argument is a bit sophisticated and generally counterintuitive (i.e., most people consider free goods and public grants to be beneficial to the poor), point 2 is made more often by the academic or intellectual left, who on this issue may find themselves uncomfortable bedfellows with the political right and at odds with their generally more ideologically compatible colleagues on the mainstream political left.

The most broadly appealing argument on behalf of *some kind* of loan program in the United Kingdom, probably as purely supplemental to the existing programs of mandatory and discretionary grants, is summarized in point 6. The United Kingdom has one of the lowest higher educational participation rates of any western country, particularly among working-class and low-income youth as well as among adults and others who would be termed "nontraditional" in the United States. Because the mandatory grant system excludes most older, part-time, and marginally prepared students, it is not a useful instrument to pull the educationally bypassed back into the higher-educational mainstream. While the relatively narrow and decidedly traditional concept of "student" in the mandatory grant system may be a reasonable public policy construct, the absence of any supplemental system to self-finance—i.e., the absence of even a "back-up" student loan program—means that students excluded from the mandatory and discretionary grant systems have almost no way to help themselves.

Similarly, students whose parents refuse, or otherwise claim to be unable, to meet the expected parental contribution also have no recourse. Again, it is not unreasonable for public policy to decline to reward such a refusal on the part of the parents with a grant to the student, even if the student may thus become an innocent victim of parental behavior that runs counter to prevailing norms. However, it may be unduly harsh to deny such a student even the option of a loan through which he or she might prevail in spite of the nonsupport of his or her parents. In the words of Maureen Woodhall, probably the foremost advocate in the United Kingdom for some kind of student loan program:

> . . . a combination of loans and grants would enable more students to receive support than under the present system of mandatory grants for the fortunate who qualify, and a steadily diminishing chance of a discretionary grant or nothing at all for large numbers of potential students who wish to study part-time, change courses, or fail to meet residence requirements. . . . Those who do not now qualify for a grant have no recourse to any alternative, and this discriminates against certain categories of student far more effectively than a loan system.[19]

The Case against Loans. The opposition to loans in the United Kingdom, led by the NUS, is adamant and powerful.[20] The principal NUS position paper on student financial assistance, issued in February 1985, states flatly that "the concept of any form of 'loans' system is wholly unacceptable."[21] A 1985 NUS study of student loan programs in the United States, Canada, Denmark, and Sweden found nothing to commend the student loan concept to the United Kingdom, and concluded that ". . . the [student loan systems] studied do not meet the criteria of maintaining an efficient education system of high quality combined with equality of access and freedom of choice of study and efficient [degree-program] length."[22] NUS president Phil Wollas in his foreword to that study stated that "The proponents of student loans . . . have not, in principle or practice, been able to show that such a system of student financial support would benefit students, education, government, or the country."[23]

Some principal arguments marshalled by the NUS against student loans include the following:

1. *The distortion of students' choices of courses of study, advanced degrees, careers, and even plans for marriage and family*, on the plausible assumption, albeit with very little supporting evidence, that students will be fearful of their high debt loads and may either avoid debts or else move into programs and careers with high earning expectations simply in order to manage them.

2. *The prolongation of study*, from observing the greater time to completion of study in countries with student loans (the United States, Sweden, Denmark, Canada) and inferring that students may be taking time off from study in order to work and thus to minimize debts.

3. *A possible adverse impact on low-socioeconomic-class student enrollments*, based on the conventional view that working-class and low-income rural families have an aversion to debt and on the inference that potential students from such backgrounds may avoid higher education altogether in lieu of taking on loans.

4. *The high costs of administration and collection, of interest subsidies, and of defaults*, all of which must continue to be borne in large measure by taxpayers and which together diminish the presumed savings of loans over grants.

Point 4—the high cost (to the taxpayer) of student loan programs— is demonstrable and is dealt with in the chapters that follow on Germany, Sweden, and the United States. The extent of complexity and administrative costs, as well as the division of burden between the taxpayer and the borrower, are amenable to policy decisions; a combination of Swedish default rates and American interest rates, for example, would yield a student loan program capable of delivering financial assistance at far less cost to the taxpayer than an equivalent program of grants. In all student loan programs, however, there are very substantial costs still to be borne by the taxpayer, and the simplistic view of loans as a clear alternative to grants, borne by students instead of taxpayers, is fallacious.

Points 1, 2, and 3, however, are more in the order of "plausible conjecture." There is no concrete evidence from the countries with substantial student loan experience that borrowing significantly distorts career choice, length of time to the degree, or participation rates by socioeconomic class. But what makes even the "plausible conjectures" difficult to demonstrate or refute is the failure to control for a given level of taxpayer-borne expenditure, whether on grants, loans (i.e., subsidies, guarantees, and administration expenses), or a combination of the two. Opponents to loans in the United Kingdom like to contrast a given amount of loan with the same amount in the form of a grant. Disincentives to further degree work or to taking on low-paying jobs in the face of the debt, as opposed to the loan, are most plausible under such scenarios.

Most proponents of student loans in the United Kingdom, however, do not propose to abandon all grants in favor of a system of pure loans at no cost to the taxpayer, but, rather, to shift *some* of the taxpayer-borne support (whatever the total amount is to be) from grants to the support of a back-up, or supplemental, loan system. To the proponents of a supplemental student loan system, the total amount of governmental, or taxpayer-borne, support is a given, arrived at through some public process that is itself independent of how the funds will be spent; they would merely divert a portion of the public grant funds to the support of a considerably greater amount of student loan funds—perhaps for those older, part-time, or "second-chance" students that are currently excluded altogether from the mandatory grants and who are insufficiently helped, if at all, by their LEAs discretionary grants.

Student leaders privately acknowledge that a generally available, subsidized loan program would be useful to many current and potential students, especially to those whose parents were failing to meet the full expected parental contribution, as well as to those nontraditional, part-time, or second-chance students who do not get grants and who have neither parents, spouses, nor part-time jobs to cover the living costs of higher education. For such students, in fact, a loan program might be the only way to meet the costs of higher education and go on to realize their academic and career goals.

However—and this is the real heart of the opposition to any form of student loans, however limited—the NUS believes that the total amount of governmental assistance is not determined independently from the available forms of assistance, but would, in fact, be significantly lowered if only the government could shift some costs to students in the form of loans. Of equal concern is the specter of having the expected parental contribution finally abolished, which has been the principal goal of the NUS for many years, and having that contribution shifted not, as planned, to the taxpayer via the abolition of means-tested reductions in the mandatory grants, but to students via a standard self-help expectation of loans and/or jobs.

In short, the students fear even the mere introduction of a purely supplemental, or back-up, loan program as "the camel's nose into the tent"—that is, as the opening wedge in what would likely be a steady erosion of taxpayer contributions on the grounds that the student, once a generally available loan program is in place, can easily bear a bit more of the costs himself or herself. In this fear, the leadership of the National Union of Students finds corroboration in the experiences of the United States and Sweden, which have seen just such a steady increase in loan burdens on students and a commensurate easing of the burdens borne by both the taxpayer and the parent. Without any loan program at all, there is virtually no way for students to bear a portion of their living costs except for the modest amounts possible through term-time and vacation work—and students in the United Kingdom seem determined to keep things that way.

Trends, Issues, and Summary Observations

The United Kingdom's (England's and Wales's) scheme of financing higher education is characterized by:

- generous grants (although diminished in real terms in recent years) for traditional, full-time students within the mandatory grant system, particularly for low- and middle-income students whose grants are not substantially reduced by the parental contribution;

- minimal assistance for other-than-traditional students, e.g., part-time students, students attempting to change programs, or those wanting a course of study that is not deemed "advanced";

- an expected parental contribution that, while not onerous by German, French, or U.S. standards, seems to be deeply resented by students and often ignored by parents; and

- a very low share of costs borne by students themselves, either through work or loans.

The Conservative Government attempted in November of 1984 to shift some of the costs from the taxpayer to wealthier parents by abolishing the minimum grant and by returning to a means testing of the tuition grant as well. More affluent parents (one estimate was approximately 140,000 in all of England and Wales) would have had their expected contributions increased by as much as £750 [$1,265]. The outcry from students, parents, and members of all parties was thunderous, and the Government backed down completely from the proposal to pass the £520 [$877] tuition on to the wealthiest parents, but it did retain the abolition of the minimum grant.[24]

At the same time, the Government promised a review, followed by a "green paper" on student finance by the summer of 1985, a paper that was expected by most observers to introduce finally into the United Kingdom, in the face of certain tremendous opposition from the students and the opposition parties, a proposal for some kind of student loan program—perhaps merely a supplement to other sources of income (i.e., not to become part of an actual expected student contribution to be deducted from the grant) and perhaps available only to postgraduate students.

Instead, the Government announced in July of 1985 that the introduction of student loans had been "ruled out for the time being." By the summer of 1986, neither the review nor the green paper has emerged. So strong is the political opposition in the United Kingdom to student loans—and so little else remains to be said or proposed worthy of a governmental "green paper" without the proposed start of some kind of loan program—that the secretary of state, Sir Keith Joseph, finally declared, in a written statement in Parliament in November: "I have been considering the publication of a consultative document in which student loans would not feature as an option, but have concluded that no useful purpose would be served by the publication of such a paper."[25]

The agenda of the Labour and Liberal parties—to eliminate the expected parental contribution and to widen the range of grant recipients to nontraditional student clienteles—carries a heavy price tag, estimated in 1983–84 as high as £180 million [$304 million][26] for eliminating the parental contribution alone. Given financial conditions in the United Kingdom, such massive new expenditures would seem unlikely even with a change in government—particularly when the abolition of the parental contribution, for all the problems it would solve, would clearly bring substantial and immediate financial gains to the wealthiest and almost nothing to the poorest, while the nontraditional student currently outside the mandatory grant network would continue to be helped only minimally. At the same time, any substantial further shift of costs to parents also seems unlikely, given the Conservative Government's inability to pass even a relatively modest cost increase on to those most able to pay.

The immediate future, then, seems to hold little prospect for any significant shift in the proportion of costs currently borne by students, parents, and taxpayers. The longer-term prospects are, of course, riskier to project but may well hold some diversion of taxpayer-borne expenses to an expansion of the mandatory grant network, met eventually by some slight increase in student-borne costs, through less disincentive to work and/or a student loan program to at least make up for shortfalls in parental contributions and perhaps to take care of more of the "extra needs" that are currently handled by the grant program.

3

THE FEDERAL REPUBLIC OF GERMANY

HIGHER EDUCATION IN THE FEDERAL REPUBLIC OF GERMANY

Structure and Governance[1]

Higher education in the post–World War II Federal Republic of Germany is primarily the responsibility of the 11 states, or Länder, with coordination provided mainly by the standing Council of the State Ministers of Education and Culture, the Council of University Rectors (with representatives, as well, from the nonuniversity sectors of higher education), and the Federal Ministry for Education and Science. Higher education in the Federal Republic includes: (a) the universities, which in turn include the old classical universities, the newer universities established since the War, and the technical universities that more recently have been accorded university status; (b) teachers colleges, the former teacher-training institutes that are now free standing (others having been absorbed into various universities); (c) the remaining independent theological seminaries, which, like the teachers colleges, have university status; (d) the independent colleges of art and music; (e) the *Fachhochschulen*, which are nonuniversity, vocationally oriented institutions of higher education similar to the British polytechnics; and (f) comprehensive institutions, or *Gesamthochschulen*, which combine university- and *Fachhochschule*-type programs within a single institution

39

with common internal governance, some interchangeability of faculty, and enhanced student mobility between levels.

The universities are entered from the academic secondary school, or *Gymnasium*, which extends through grade 13 and from which one graduates with the *Abitur*, or academic secondary school leaving certificate. In 1984, some 22 percent of 18-year-olds were receiving the *Abitur* (a low proportion by U.S. standards, but up from 17 percent of the 18–20-year-old population in 1980); 10.8 percent in 1970; and 5.5 percent in 1960. Some 14 percent of the age group in 1980 were entering a university or a university-level institution (e.g., a teachers college or theological college) either immediately or after military service, compared with 11.3 percent in 1970 and 6.5 percent in 1960.[2] Preliminary data from the mid-1980s suggests an increasing proportion going on to the university after several years of work, sometimes earning the *Abitur* through evening classes or other alternatives to the traditional *Gymnasium*.

The universities dominate in both numbers and status despite efforts to diminish the special status of the universities vis-à-vis other sectors and, indeed, to establish by the Higher Education Frame Act of 1976 the comprehensive model as the principal model for Germany's future higher educational development. The comprehensive model, developed in the late 1960s and early 1970s, has emerged in only eleven institutions, six of which are in North Rhine-Westphalia, with eight of the eleven Länder having formed no institutions on this model and with no additional ones likely anywhere as of mid-1985.[3] Altogether, those institutions with university status and university degree-granting authority enrolled in 1984 some 1,022,000 students (German and foreign), or some 78 percent of the total 1,314,000 students enrolled in higher education in West Germany.[4]

Most of the rest of the students—about 276,000, or just over one-fifth—were enrolled in 1983 in the country's nearly 100 *Fachhochschulen*, created in the late 1960s and early 1970s from technical and other advanced vocational schools and specializing today primarily in engineering, business, social work, design, and public administration. Students may enter the *Fachhochschulen* from the *Gymnasium*, with or without the *Abitur*, but the secondary track specially designed for *Fachhochschule* entry are the advanced secondary level vocational schools, or *Fachoberschulen*, entered after the tenth grade, often with some apprenticeship or work experience. Studies at the *Fachhochschulen* are supposed to be of shorter duration than at the universities (e.g., three or three and one-half years as opposed to four, five, six, or more) and more practically and professionally oriented. Faculty teach heavier loads than their counterparts at the universities and are not required to engage in research. As with the British polytechnics and

American comprehensive colleges, however, the overlap with university curricula and with university-type systems of faculty expectations and rewards has been considerable.[5]

Persons possessing the appropriate qualifications for entry into a particular sector of higher education have a constitutional right to that education and thus to entry into that sector. The *Abitur* is evidence of qualification to do university-level work, and no further evidence need be provided—indeed, no further entrance requirements are allowed to be imposed by any of the universities. Only when there is severe overcrowding in all the universities, and when the long-range limitation of additional job opportunities makes an expansion of university places socially and economically unwise (such as in medicine, for example), can there be a general limitation of numbers, called *numerus clausus*. (A similar, short-term limitation, in rare cases, can be extended to a particular department or departments in particular universities that are intolerably overcrowded.) The application of entry limitations, or *numerus clausus*, must be agreed upon by the education ministers of all of the Länder and is a matter of enormous political volatility. When *numerus clausus* or departmental restrictions have been agreed upon, a central office handles all applicants and assignments. Formulae combining academic high school performance, "social hardships," and number of years on the waiting list assure that no one with the basic qualification is excluded from consideration altogether, but some students of course abandon the waiting and go on to other studies and other fields.

Student Services

The universities, *Fachhochschulen*, and other institutions of higher education in West Germany, like those elsewhere on the European continent and unlike the Anglo-Saxon institutions in the United Kingdom, the United States, and the Commonwealth countries, provide virtually no services directly to students. Low-cost health insurance, subsidized transportation, and subsidized tickets to cultural events are provided to students through the Länder. Whatever housing, canteens, and nonacademic services (e.g., student activities, cultural events, or personal or career counseling) are made available to students come through the *Studentenwerke*, which are loosely translated as "social welfare organizations at the universities."[6] *Studentenwerke* originated in voluntary associations of students, faculty, and citizens formed prior to World War I to provide university students with affordable meals and lodging. These associations became increasingly dependent upon governmental assistance and after World War II were brought under Länder control, although they were retained as nongovernmental institutions. Länder regulations provide for student, faculty, employee, and citizen representation on the boards of directors, with administrative liaisons to the institutions whose students are being served.

Forty-nine local *Studentenwerke* serve the institutions and students within their respective geographic areas. Although there are differences among the Länder, the *Studentenwerke* all provide low-cost subsidized meals (limited to the cost of food used in preparation of the meals) and housing (limited to operating costs), and most provide some additional services such as day care, counseling, and cultural events and activities. Approximately 40 percent of students take meals in the *Studentenwerke* restaurants, and about 10 percent reside in the residence halls. The residence halls have no programmatic activities and are not necessarily proximate to the associated institutions, so their only function is to reduce the cost of housing to some students.

In addition to serving as indirect sources of taxpayer-borne subsidies via the low-cost meals and lodging, the *Studentenwerke* administer the principal student grant/loan program, the BAföG, to be described in the next section. Thus these associations, and their national umbrella organization, the *Deutsches Studentenwerk*, serve as a major focus of assistance and advocacy for students generally and especially for the approximately 30 percent of students who in 1984–85 received financial assistance in the form of student grants/loans.

Recent Events and Trends

The two decades from the mid-1960s to the mid-1980s have been a period of great expansion and political turbulence for higher education in the Federal Republic of Germany. The post-war baby boom, the extraordinary affluence of the 1960s and 1970s, and the flowering spirit of egalitarianism in this era all combined to fuel in Germany, as in most of the industrialized West, an enormous increase in student enrollments (from 291,000 and 4.3 percent of 19–21-year olds in 1960 to 1,273,200 and nearly 22 percent of the traditional age cohort in 1983). The mission of higher education was extended to include responsibility for national economic growth and social mobility as well as the traditional missions of scholarship and advanced learning for the very able. The number and types of institutions maintained at public expense expanded to serve these new institutional missions and new student numbers.

At the same time, the universities and other higher-educational institutions in the Federal Republic of Germany were caught up in the so-called reform movement of the late 1960s and early 1970s. The movement, under the main banner of "equality of chances" (*Chancengleichheit*), and drawing on the U.S. university model for such concepts as departmental governance and curricular organization, also sought to diminish the power of the senior professoriate within the university as well as the authority and status of the universities within the expanding sector of higher education.[7] Finally, and with parallels in other Western nations, especially the United States and the United Kingdom, West German higher education in the 1980s entered a period of mild "counterreformation," mirroring the political ascendancy of the conservative Christian Democrats. The movement rightward also reflected the fiscal austerity of the 1980s, as well as a dissatisfaction with some of the earlier experiments (e.g., the comprehensive university) that seemed to have failed to take hold.

From the vantage point of mid-1985, the following trends and countertrends seem evident in the Federal Republic of Germany:

- Enrollments may have peaked, at least through the mid-1990s: The fall of 1985, in fact, saw the first decline in new enrollments in decades. The size of the total university-age cohort will decline sharply due to the low birth rates of the mid-1960s. While the proportion of that cohort going to the *Gymnasium* and completing the *Abitur* continues to rise, this factor is more than overcome by the increasing proportion of *Abitur* holders who are choosing not to go to the universities or *Fachhochschulen* because of the dearth of job prospects, especially in the humanities, social sciences, and the law. The public sector, which used to absorb about 60 percent of university graduates, can now absorb only about 20 percent, and there is no prospect of the private sector quickly taking up this slack.[8] If the proportion of youth going on to higher education stays at its current approximately 22 percent, enrollments will decline significantly.

- Resources allocated to higher education have already peaked, and the institutions are becoming increasingly overcrowded. As early as the mid-1970s, the Länder governments decided to cap the facilities and faculty at a level best able to support about 850,000 students. Authorities knew even then that enrollments in the subsequent decade would swell far in excess of that figure, but apparently concluded that financial austerity was a proper reflection of the available public resources as well as of the longer-range demographic projections and needs, and that an expansion of the proportion of the 18–20-year age cohort entering higher education was no longer in the public interest because of the shortage of new job openings requiring university degrees. Some attempt is being made to reduce overcrowding and to increase efficiency by encouraging more rapid completion of studies (traditionally, the Germany student essentially determines when his or her studies are completed).[9]

- The student grant program, created in the early 1970s to remove financial barriers to higher education and to increase the proportion of students from working-class families, has been converted from what was initially an all-grant program to a grant program with a small loan component, and finally in 1984 to an all-loan program. The proportion of students qualifying for this assistance has declined from more than 40 percent in the mid-1970s to 35 percent in 1981 and to only about 30 percent in 1984–85.[10] Although loans are less expensive to the taxpayer than grants, the enormous subsidy built into the German student loan program diminishes the public savings argument in favor of the conversion. More important seem to be the symbolic and ideological arguments advanced by conservatives in favor of loans over grants, such as the allegedly greater appreciation on the part of the recipient for the true cost of public benefits received, or perhaps the greater likeness of loan financing to a market transaction.

- Some of the 1970s reforms in university structure and governance have been quietly abandoned, or at least partially reversed. The movement toward the comprehensive university as the favored ultimate model for West German higher education, for example, has been abandoned. The current Conservative government, under the banner of differentiation and competition (*Differenzierung und Wettbeberb*), has stated its determination to restore the traditional power of the senior professors (at the expense of assistants, students, and nonacademic staff) and to reassert the need for institutional autonomy, academic quality, and research alliances with private industry. The public policies of the 1970s that sought to "level downward" and to diminish the authority and status of the elite universities (and the elite senior professoriate within them) seem to have been abandoned in the apparent expectation that status differentiation and a corps of prestige institutions will re-emerge.[11]

- The 1970s goal of expanding the proportions of working-class youth, women, and older students within higher education (and especially within the universities) has diminished, and advances seem to have slowed. The full-time German student is on the average older than his or her American counterpart because of a longer secondary level preparation for the university, a longer average period of study, extensive work and apprenticeship experience for the *Fachhochschule* student, and compulsory military service for many between school and the university. The number of truly nontraditional adult students—those over the age of 30, say, or those who never aspired to higher education as secondary school students—increased by the mid 1980s, particularly with alternatives to the *Gymnasium* for earning the *Abitur*, often in conjunction with employment. Compared to the United States, however, the nontraditional student population remains low.[12] The proportion of female students was far higher in 1980 than in the 1960s, but it was still considerably lower than the female proportion either of the population as a whole or of those qualified for university entry, and the aggressive extension of opportunities to women does not appear to be continuing into the 1980s. Finally, the proportion of working-class youth in higher education, and especially in the universities as opposed to the *Fachhochschulen*, remains low and, in the mid-1980s, seemingly fairly static.[13]

SHARING THE COSTS AMONG PARENTS, TAXPAYERS, AND STUDENTS

Costs to the Student and Family

There is no tuition in the state-supported universities and colleges in the Federal Republic of Germany, and as of 1985 there were only two private institutions, so tuition as it is known in the United States is not a factor in the costs faced by students and their families. There were proposals from the government in 1984 for imposing tuition on students who took too long at their studies—apparently a common, and costly, phenomenon—but this was abandoned in favor of other incentives to induce timely completion. Students do face small fees of about DM60 [$28]* for the costs of student government and certain student-run services.

The relevant costs, then, are for maintenance and educational

---

* Amounts in Deutschmarks in this chapter are followed by a U.S. dollar equivalent according to a 1985 purchasing power ratio of DM2.16 = $1.00. See Appendix A.

expenses for either 10 or 12 months. A minimum, "austere budget" estimate of these costs can be inferred from the subsidized loan entitlements, which, together with the official means-tested expected parental contributions, and assuming some use of the subsidized meals and/or housing through the *Studentenwerke*, are supposed to cover fully the student's living costs and educational expenses without the need for part-time work, additional parental contributions, or other sources of income.

The basic loan award in 1985–86 is DM690 [$319] a month for students living apart from their parents. Students living at home are entitled to a basic loan of DM560 [$259] per month for a calendar year. These amounts can be supplemented for certain documented additional expenses up to DM98 [$45] a month. Official estimates of costs, then, can be inferred to be in the range of DM560 [$259] to DM750 [$347] or more per month, depending mainly on commuter or resident status. The lowest estimate—that is, a mirror of the available loan amount—is more reasonable if the student is also assumed to be taking advantage of the subsidized meals available through the *Studentenwerke* restaurants, which provide meals for DM1.8–DM2.5 [$.83–$1.16], and the subsidized housing, which is in short supply but which can provide a room for less than DM200 [$93] a month or DM2,000 [$926] for a 10-month school year.[14]

However, students claim that these expense estimates are unrealistically low, and many observers, even within the Ministry, seem to agree. A "correct" student expense budget, of course, inevitably flounders on the conceptual difficulty of agreeing on the proper living standard for students, with the claims ranging between subsistence poverty, on the one hand, to a study wage comparable to what non-student age peers are earning, on the other. A student-union spokesman estimated in the summer of 1985 that most students who take part-time jobs and whose parents provide at least close to the full expected contribution live on DM1,100–DM1,200 [$509–$556] a month, but that the absolutely necessary expenses were between DM800–DM900 [$370–$417].[15] The low end of this "minimal range" actually corresponds to 1985 "more realistic" cost estimates given directly to the author by Ministry officials—DM9,700 [$4,491] for 12 months or DM808 [$374] monthly[16]—and is not that far from the maximum amount of student aid (interest free loans), which with supplements can extend to DM788 [$365] monthly, DM7,880 [$3,650] for 10 months, or DM9,456 [$4,378] for 12 months.

The 1985 survey of student expenses and revenues commissioned by the *Deutsches Studentenwerk* has not, as of this writing, been analyzed; the last survey, conducted in 1982, revealed a considerable range of expenditures, with a median of about DM840 [$389]

TABLE 3.1
Costs Facing Undergraduate Students and Families for 10 Months, Federal
Republic of Germany, 1985–86

	Commuter student ministry estimate[a] 10 months		Resident student ministry estimate[b] 10 months		Resident student more adequate budget[c] 10 months	
	DM	$	DM	$	DM	$
Fees	60	28	60	28	60	28
Room and board	2,540	1,176	4,380	2,028	4,950	2,292
All other	3,000	1,389	3,060	1,417	4,490	2,079
Total	5,600	2,593	7,500	3,472	9,500	4,398

[a] The commuting-student budget, "Ministry estimate," is based on the BAföG for
students living at home: DM560 a month.

[b] The resident-student budget, "Ministry estimate," is based on the BAföG for students
living away from home of DM690 a month, plus housing and insurance supplements
estimated here at DM60 a month.

[c] The "more adequate" budget is the author's estimate based on discussions with
current and past Ministry officials and student leaders.

monthly.[17] Not surprisingly, such a survey shows that students will
get by on what they can obtain from all sources: that it is possible to
live frugally (even within the DM690 [$319] monthly government
loan amount), but also that many students, at least by 1985, manage
to put together parental support, term-time and holiday earnings, and
loans to support themselves at a higher level than this minimum.

Table 3.1 summarizes a range of 10-month expenditures, from a
low 10-month commuter budget of DM5,600 [$2,593], to an "official
estimate" 10-month resident budget of DM7,500 [$3,472], to a more
realistic 10-month budget of DM9,500 [$4,398], which corresponds
to what student leaders and Ministry officials alike believe to be more
representative of actual student living styles. A 12-month student
budget, of course, would be proportionately higher, and the truly
independent student easily needs DM11,400–DM13,200 [$5,278–
$6,111] for the full 12-month year.

Subsidized Loans to Students: BAföG

The Grant Program Prior to 1984. Governmental support to students at both the upper secondary and higher education levels was
strengthened in Germany with the enactment in 1971 of the Federal
Law for the Promotion of Education, *Bundesausbildungsförde-
rungsgesetz,* or colloquially, "BAföG." At its origin, BAföG was a
means-tested program of grants designed to meet necessary minimal

costs of student living less an expected parental contribution. (There were, and still are, expected student and spouse contributions as well, but they are of limited significance). The basic amounts, before and after 1984, differed for commuter and resident students and also allowed for coverage of certain receipted special expenses such as health insurance and unusually high housing expenses. The cost of the BAföG was, and is, shared between the Länder and the central government; the award is a statutory entitlement and the government must provide funds for all who meet the award criteria. Administration has been handled by the appropriate *Studentenwerk*. From the advent of the program until its radical change to an all-loan scheme in 1984, between 40 and 50 percent of eligible students received BAföGs.

Prior to 1984, the principal controversies surrounding the program related to the size of the maximum award and the severity of the rate of increase of expected parental contributions. Both criticisms continue to be made today by the national student unions and others, although they may be overshadowed by the controversy over the change from grants to loans. The size of the maximum award has always been thought by many to be unrealistically low, particularly given the ostensible official principle that the BAföG was to support students without the need for part-time or summer work, loans (beyond the very small portion of the BAföG grant that was always in the form of a loan), or additional support from parents (beyond the expected contribution that was already subtracted from the BAföG award). The maximum regular award in 1974–75, for example, was DM500 [$231] a month or DM6,000 [$2,778] for a 12-month year for resident students, and DM410 [$190] a month or DM4,920 [$2,278] for a 12-month year for students living with parents. By 1985, these awards had increased to DM690 [$319] a month for students living away from home and DM560 [$259] a month for students living with parents, with supplements for higher housing and insurance costs as shown in Table 3.2. The charge of inadequacy is based on the fact that these grants (now loans) have not risen as fast as the incomes and living standards generally of the West German people, and also on the fact revealed in the periodic surveys commissioned by the *Deutsches Studentenwerk* that many students are "forced" to work part time (which is not supposed to be necessary) either because of the inadequacy of the maximum grant or the failure of their parents to provide the expected supplement or both. The Ministry, on the other hand, has generally responded by citing the incontrovertible fact that a great many students were evidently managing to remain at their studies with the available BAföGs—which, by at least some principle, was the only rationale for taxpayer-borne grants to stu-

TABLE 3.2
BAföG Entitlement (Loans), University and *Fachhochschulen* Students,
1985

	Living with parents				Living away from home			
	Minimum		Maximum		Minimum		Maximum	
	DM	$	DM	$	DM	$	DM	$
Base (month)	500	231	500	231	500	231	500	231
Housing (month)[a]	60	28	60	28	190	88	250	116
Insurance (month)[b]	0	0	38	18	0	0	38	18
Total (month)	560	259	598	277	690	319	788	365
Total (10-month)	5,600	2,593	5,980	2,769	6,900	3,194	7,880	3,648
Total (12-month)	6,720	3,111	7,176	3,322	8,280	3,833	9,456	4,378

[a] Housing expenses in excess of DM190 [$88] a month are 75 percent covered up to a maximum of DM60 additional.
[b] Insurance of up to DM38 [$18] a month is provided if student is not covered by family insurance.

dents—and that the allegation of inadequacy confused "needs" and "wants."

The other criticism antedating the conversion to a loan program—that the expected parental contribution is too severe—is just as hard to establish or refute conclusively. The annual income at which parents are expected to contribute to the costs of their child's higher education—about DM23,820 [$11,028]—is lower than the income at which the U.S. and U.K. parent is officially expected to begin contributions. Also, the expected contribution rises with increasing incomes at a very steep rate—by 1984, in fact, taking from the family with one student and one nonstudent dependent child the equivalent of 55 pfennigs of every marginal Deutschmark. At this steep rate, the expected contribution in 1984 reached the full prevailing BAföG at an annual net taxable income of only DM38,220 [$17,694], phasing out the award completely. The relationship of annual income and expected contribution is shown graphically in Figure 3.1. Clearly, parents at incomes just above the cutoff point, or even in the range in which additional income is being "taxed" for the costs of their children's higher education at a marginal rate of 55 percent, can be said to be bearing a heavy load, at least in comparison to those with incomes either just below DM23,820 [$11,028], who need contribute nothing, or those with incomes high enough that the full expected DM8,000-[$3,704]-or-so contribution to their children's living expenses is no longer a burden.

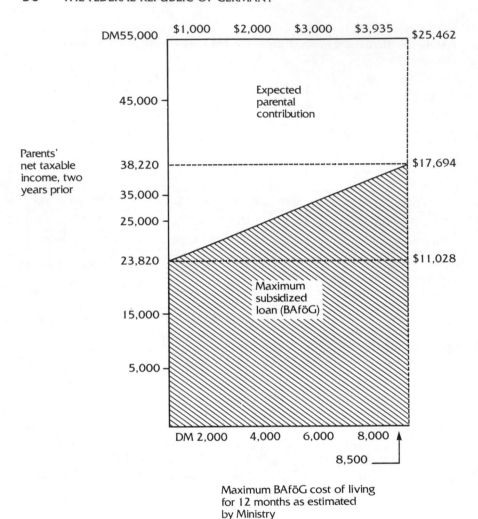

FIGURE 3.1 The division of estimated maintenance costs between the expected parental contribution and the maximum BAföG as a function of parents' net taxable income two years prior, 1985–86.

Conversion of BAföG to an All-Loan Program.[18] Early in the BAföG program, the first DM150 [$69] monthly payment was made as a loan, apparently in the hope that those who were entitled to only a very small award would find a loan—albeit long term and interest free—sufficiently inconvenient that they might not claim it at all and thus save the government both the cost of the loan and the attendant bookwork. The loan portion, then, was 15–20 percent of the total at minimum. Students who received small maximum awards anyway would end their studies with a higher proportion of their accumulated BAföG as a loan, but still with a very small and very manageable debt. Students who changed programs of study or added a second course to one for which BAföG support had already been granted, and who were thus ineligible for a BAföG grant, might be given all of their award in the form of a loan. But this loan was clearly a convenience to students who would otherwise have few resources at their disposal to cover their living costs while at the college or university.

In 1984, in a highly controversial measure with deep symbolic, but less clear financial and social, ramifications, the Conservative Government converted the BAföG system to one of all loans. The amounts remain the same (with periodic increases as under the former grant program), as does the means-tested reduction through the expected parental contributions. But BAföG awards accumulated from 1984 on are considered all loans, repayable beginning five years after the normal completion of the particular program of study at no interest. Other repayment provisions include:

- up to 20 years to repay, with minimum monthly repayments of DM120 [$56]—which thus requires an initial accumulated debt of DM28,800 [$13,333] to extend the repayment period to the full 20 years.

- deferment of repayments if the borrower's monthly income falls below DM1,030 [$477] a month; cancellation of the remaining debt after 20 years (a particularly significant feature to a non-working spouse with a large initial debt).

- automatic forgiveness of DM5,000 [$2,315] of debt for any student who finishes his or her program at least four months ahead of the normal schedule.

- forgiveness of 25 percent of all principal amount due for the 30 percent of BAföG recipients who finish their studies with the best academic records. (It is not known at the time of this writing exactly how the top 30 percent is to be determined, particularly in comparing students from different programs and kinds of institutions.)

True Loan and Subsidy: Sharing the Cost of the All-Loan BAföG. Although the only generally available student support program in the Federal Republic of Germany is an all-loan program, the loans also carry enormous subsidies for all borrowers, who have the use of money for up to 20 or more years at zero interest, and even greater subsidies for those who finish early or in the top 30 percent of their

TABLE 3.3
Student Loan Terms and Present Value of Repayment, Federal Republic of Germany

	Top 30% academically[a]	All others
Initial loan	DM 1,000	DM 1,000
In-school period[b]	1.5 yrs	1.5 yrs
Grace period[c]	5.0 yrs	5.0 yrs
Interest charged during in-school and grace periods[d]	0%	0%
Debt at beginning of repayment	DM 750	DM 1,000
Interest charged during repayment	0%	0%
Repayment period	20 yrs	20 yrs
Repayment mode	equal monthly	equal monthly
Present value of repayments[e] { Discount rate 8%	DM 223	DM 297
Discount rate 10%	170	227
Discount rate 12%	131	175

[a] The academically top 30 percent of borrowers have debts reduced by 25 percent. Further decreases of principal owed, not shown here, are possible by completing schooling ahead of normal schedule.

[b] Period between origination of loan and end of schooling, assumed here to be 1.5 years for the purpose of simplification and comparison.

[c] Period between end of schooling and first repayment period.

[d] Student loans in FRG acquire no interest during in-school and grace periods and are repaid thereafter at no interest.

[e] See Appendix B for full explanation of principle and method for present value calculations.

class or both. The level of loan subsidy—in effect, a stream of small grants back to the borrowers that lessens what the repayment burden would otherwise have been—as opposed to level of "true loan" can be measured by the present value of the repayment stream, as explained in Appendix B. Essentially, the true loan is the amount of principal that the actual repayments would amortize at some reasonable, market-related rate of interest; the present value of the subsidies can be derived either by discounting the stream of effective subsidies for each payment or, more simply, by subtracting the calculated true loan from the total actual principal received.

Table 3.3 shows the present value of repayment, and thus the division of the repayable BAföG between true loan, borne by the student, and "effective subsidy," borne by the taxpayer, under discount rate assumptions of 8, 10, and 12 percent. Assuming an average of 1.5 years between the BAföG awards and the completion of studies, a full 20-year repayment period, a top-30-percent academic rank, and a discount rate of 10 percent, the present value of the repayment stream for an accumulated BAföG loan of DM1,000 would be only

DM170—that is, would amortize a true loan bearing a 10 percent interest rate of only DM170, or just 17 cents on the dollar. This is the amount, if the discount rate assumption is appropriate, that can be said to be fully borne by the student lender. The other DM830—more than 80 cents on the dollar—can be said to be the taxpayer-borne share of the DM1,000 BAföG. Clearly, within any conceivable range of discount rates, the post-1984 BAföG, while certainly shifting some burden from taxpayer to student, in fact shifted very little and has kept most of BAföG's costs, even as a loan program, a responsibility, in the end, of the West German taxpayer.

The Parental Contribution

Unlike the United States or United Kingdom, where parental support toward the costs of college is expected but not legally required, the expected parental contribution in West Germany is a legal obligation of the parents, who must by law support their children through whatever level of education equips them for their first entry into a profession or vocation. Their obligation is limited, of course, by (a) the financial ability of the family to provide such support and (b) the ability and inclination of the child to learn or to be trained at a particular level. Within those constraints, the parents' obligation, limited to the prevailing BAföG maximum, is enforceable by the courts through action brought either by the child or by the government, which can bring suit to recover funds that it may have provided the student in the event of the parents' nonsupport.

With no tuition and no fees to speak of, the maximum parental share is limited to the student's living expenses, minus any amount of those that can be taken up by either a BAföG loan or by the student's term-time or holiday earnings. There is an official expected parental contribution which, as in the United Kingdom, is subtracted from the maximum BAföG award. The expected contribution is based on the net taxable income two years prior to the year for which the grant is being sought—unless the current actual income is less than the income two years prior, in which case current income may be used as a better indication of ability to pay.

For a BAföG being sought for 1985–86, the first DM1,540 [$713] of monthly income in 1983–84 is "free," as is an additional DM85 [$39] for the student, another DM360 [$167] for each child under the age of 15, and DM470 [$218] for each dependent child over age 15. Of the total net income (after any additional possible deductions) in excess of the free income, 25 percent is "protected" for the parents themselves and an additional 10 percent is protected for each dependent, including the student. All remaining income is considered available to meet the child's higher education maintenance expenses—up to the amount of BAföG that would otherwise have been awarded. By another perspective, all income in excess of the free amount is effectively taxed at a marginal rate of 100 percent minus 35 percent for parents and student, minus an additional 10 percent for each additional dependent child.

Example:

Consider a family with one child at the university otherwise entitled to a DM690 [$319] monthly BAföG, one additional child under age 15, and a net taxable income in 1983–84 (i.e., two years prior) of DM 28,000 [$12,963] for the year.

Free income:

DM1,540 [$713] plus DM85 [$39] for the student, plus another DM360 [$167] for the additional child under 15, for a monthly total of DM1,985 [$919] and a 12-month free income of DM23,820 [$11,028].

Remaining income:

DM28,000 − 23,820 = DM4,180 [$12,963 − $11,028 = $1,935]

Contribution rate:

1.00 − [.25 + .10 + .10] = .55

Expected 12-month parental contribution:

.55 (DM4,180) = DM2,299 [$1,064]

Maximum 12-month BAföG loan:

DM690 × 12 = DM8,280 − DM2,299 = DM5,981 [$2,769]

Expected contributions according to the 1985–86 schedule are shown in Table 3.4 for 12 months and for 10 months. Table 3.5 shows the range of parental incomes over which the expected contribution increases with increasing family income. The bottom of the range may be viewed as the maximum low income before any contribution is expected—or as the minimum income that still calls for a parental contribution. As shown in Table 3.5, contributions begin (and the maximum allowable BAföG begins to be reduced) at an annual net taxable income of DM23,820 [$11,028], which corresponds to an annual gross income in 1983–84 of about DM25,020 [$11,583], conservatively assuming additional deductions of DM1,200. Income in excess

TABLE 3.4
Expected Parental Contributions and BAföG Entitlements for 10 and 12
Months, Federal Republic of Germany, 1985–86

Assume: • monthly BAföG entitlement DM690, and
         • one additional child in family under age 15

Net Taxable income two years prior (1983–84)		12 Months				10 Months			
		Expected parental contribution		BAföG entitlement		Expected parental contribution		BAföG entitlement	
DM	$	DM	$	DM	$	DM	$	DM	$
20,000	9,259	0	0	8,280	3,833	0	0	6,900	3,194
24,000	11,111	99	46	8,181	3,788	83	38	6,817	3,156
28,000	12,963	2,299	1,064	5,981	2,769	1,916	887	4,984	2,307
32,000	14,815	4,499	2,083	3,781	1,750	3,749	1,736	3,151	1,459
36,000	16,667	6,699	3,101	1,581	732	5,583	2,585	1,317	610
40,000	18,519	8,280	3,833	0	0	6,900	3,194	0	0

See text example for explanation of how a DM28,000 net taxable income in 1983–84
yields a 1985–86 expected parental contribution (offset to the BAföG) of DM1,916
monthly.

At a net taxable income of DM38,220, the normal parental contribution would be
DM7,920 for 12 months, leaving a BAföG of DM360. Because that is the minimum
BAföG (DM30 a month), the entitlement is phased out completely for incomes above
DM38,220 [$17,694] a year.

of this amount (for the family with one child at the university or
Fachhochschule and another under the age of 15) is "taxed" at a rate
of 55 percent, as explained above, which reduces the maximum allowable BAföG to DM30 [$14] a month—the minimum BAföG
award—at an annual net taxable income of DM38,220 [$17,694], com-
parable to an estimated gross annual income of about DM42,557
[$19,702], after which no BAföG can be obtained as long as the
student remains a dependent.

Parental Contribution Offsets

Against this official parental contribution may be considered several offsets, principally in the form of tax deductions and child allowances, that accrue to the parents as long as the child is enrolled full
time at an institution of higher education and that are lost if and when
the child ceases to be a student.[19] The child allowance pays DM50
[$23] monthly for the first child and DM100 [$46], DM220 [$102],
and DM240 [$111] for the second, third, and fourth (and any subse-
quent) children, respectively. Prior to 1984, the child allowances were

TABLE 3.5

Maximum Annual Net Taxable and Estimated Annual Gross Parental Incomes for Maximum BAföG and for Phase-Out of BAföG Entitlement, 1985–86

Assume one additional dependent child under age of 15 in the family.	Point just before start of parental contribution and reduction of BAföG; award still at the maximum allowable		Point of maximum parental contribution and phase-out of allowable BAföG; lowest income that is still too high for award	
	DM	$	DM	$
Net taxable family income in 1983–84 (two years prior)	23,820[a]	11,028	38,220[b]	17,694
Estimated gross family income in 1983–84 (two years prior)	25,020[c]	11,583	42,557[d]	19,702

[a] The statutory "free income" in 1985–86 is DM1,540 monthly plus DM85 for the student and DM360 monthly for the single additional child under the age of 15, or DM1,985 total monthly or DM23,820 [$11,028] per annum—before any parental contribution is expected.

[b] Parental income above DM23,820 is "taxed" at a rate of 100% minus 25% for the parents, minus another 10% for the student and another 10% for the additional child, or $100 - (25 + 10 + 10) = 55\%$. Because entitlement actually ends when the allowable BAföG falls to DM30 a month, the annual income at which BAföG ceases is:

$$DM23,820 + 12 \left(\frac{690 - 30}{0.55} \right) = DM38,220 \ [\$17,694].$$

[c] Calculated as in "a," but assuming additional deductions of DM1,200 as free income, this amount is based on conversations with current and former Ministry officials.

[d] Calculated as in "b," but assuming 15% additional deductions as free income and further assuming a maximum BAföG loan of DM725 a month. Thus the annual income cut-off is at $12 \ (1,540 + 85 + 360) + .15(12) \ (1,540 + 85 + 360) + 12 \ (725 - 30/.55) = DM42,557 \ [\$19,702].$

paid regardless of family income: The wealthy family with five children received a monthly allowance of DM50 + DM100 + DM220 + DM240 + DM240, or a total of DM850 [$394], or an annual allowance of DM10,200 [$4,722]. Since 1984, the monthly allowances for higher-income families have been reduced to DM50, DM70, and DM140 [$23, $32, and $65] for the first, second, and third (and subsequent) children, respectively.

What is significant to the matter of the parental share of the cost of higher education is that these allowances are paid to parents of children beyond the age of 16 only if the child remains in higher education (or national service) up to the age of 27 and in some cases even beyond. The two-child family with an annual income of DM40,000 [$18,519], which as shown in Table 3.4 is not entitled to BAföG and which must therefore come up with all or most of the necessary DM8,000–DM9,000 [$3,704–$4,167] to keep the child in the university, has this burden mitigated somewhat by the continuation of a child allowance for the student of DM70 [$32] monthly or DM840 [$389] a year.

There are also tax deductions for families with children in higher education who have incomes above the range of eligibility for BAföG. In 1985, these deductions were up to DM1,200 [$556] annually to families whose student children were at home and up to DM2,100 [$972] for those whose children were out of the home. With a top income tax bracket of 55 percent, this amounts to a further effective reduction, for the family whose child is out of the home, of .55 (DM2,100) or DM1,155 [$535].

Finally, it was widely reported that parents very often do not provide the full expected contribution, at least in part out of a belief that their child ought to work part time or during some of his or her holidays to earn some income.[20] Anecdotal evidence suggests that this supplement—or offset—to the parental contribution may be a significant part of the total picture of West German student finance.

Taking these three parental contribution offsets and inserting conservative estimates into each, it would appear that what might well look like an annual DM8,500 [$3,935] expected parental contribution for an upper-middle-income West German family can easily be reduced, or offset, by a continuation of the child allowance of DM840 [$389], a tax deduction of DM1,155 [$535], and an earnings expectation passed on to the child of DM1,000 [$463], resulting in an effective net parental contribution of only about DM5,505 [$2,549].

Student Contributions

Student contributions toward meeting their costs of living occur in four ways, the first two listed below being relatively insignificant.

1. A student's own assets and/or income great enough to offset the BAföG entitlement, treated conceptually similarly to the expected parental contribution (rare).

2. Student loans other than BAföG, available to certain students through foundations or associations within trade unions, polit-

ical parties, or churches; to medical and some other advanced professional students on a strictly commercial basis; and to some students through their *Studentenwerk* on a short-term, emergency basis. These loans are still not generally available and thus are not a significant source of income for students.

3. The BAföG loan, which for the average student (i.e., one not eligible for either the "early completion" or the "top-30-percent" principal reductions), and assuming a very low discount rate of 8 percent, has a "true loan" component of just under 30 percent (Table 3.3).

4. Part-time or temporary work, which according to the 1982 *Deutsches Studentenwerk* survey is engaged in by 39 percent (term-time) and 46 percent (summertime or holiday) of university students and by 36 percent (term-time) and 42 percent (summertime or holiday) of *Fachhochschule* students.[21] The declining proportion of students with BAföG loans and the reported failure of either BAföG or the parental contribution to keep pace with inflation and student needs suggest that the proportion of students who work in order to bear a portion of their living costs (excluding those students in academic programs that combine work and study) could well be 50 percent by the 1985–86 academic year.

Given the great range of student academic programs, life-styles, and ways of meeting the cost of student living, there would seem to be little merit in attempting to calculate the proportion of expenses borne by the "average" student in the Federal Republic of Germany. Examples can nevertheless be both illustrative and representative.

Example of Student A. Student A is from a low-income family and so is entitled to, and takes out, the full BAföG loan of DM690 [$319] plus DM30 [$14] supplement each month for four years, for a total BAföG debt accumulation upon graduation of DM34,560 [$16,000]. He does not finish early and is not in the top 30 percent academically, so he repays the loan in equal monthly installments spread over 20 years beginning five years after leaving school. Student A supplements his BAföG with part-time work averaging DM75 [$35] a month for total earnings over four years of DM3,600 [$1,667]. He does not take appreciable advantage of either meal or housing subsidies available through his *Studentenwerk*.

- *Total four-year expenses (resources available)*: DM38,160 [$27,667].

- *Total expenses borne by student* A: total earnings + present value of loan repayments discounted at 8 percent[22] = DM3,600 + .223 (34,560) = DM11,307 [$5,235].

- *Proportion of expenses borne by student* A: DM11,307 ÷ DM38,160 = 30 percent.

Example of Student B. Student B is from an upper-middle-income family whose expected parental contribution exceeds the maximum BAföG. Her parents provide DM650 [$301] a month. She lives for two of her three years at the *Fachhochschule* in *Studentenwerk* housing and takes many of her meals there, enjoying subsidies conservatively estimated at DM100 [$46] a month. Student B also works part time and holidays, averaging DM150 [$69] a month.

- *Total three-year expenses (resources available)*: DM23,400 [$10,833] from parents + DM5,400 [$2,500] from earnings + DM3,600 [$1,667] in *Studentenwerke* subsidies = DM32,400 [$15,000].

- *Total expenses borne by student* B: total earnings of DM5,400 [$2,500].

- *Proportion of expenses borne by student* B: DM5,400 ÷ DM32,400 = 17 percent.

Trends, Issues, and Summary Observations

As it pertains to students and parents, higher educational finance in the Federal Republic of Germany is characterized by:

- taxpayer support of all institutional costs: no tuitions.

- a legally enforceable obligation of parents to support their children (i.e., cover the costs of living) to the best of their ability through the level of education—including, if appropriate, the university or *Fachhochschulen*—necessary for entry into a profession or vocation. The expected parental contribution rises quite steeply with parental incomes, but the burden on parents is substantially lessened by child allowances and tax deductions that are not available to those parents whose children elect not to go on to higher education.

- governmentally sponsored assistance to students limited for the most part to means-tested loans, available only as supplements to the parental contribution and thus used primarily by the one-third or so of students from the lowest-income families. No loans are generally available to middle- or upper-middle-income students. There are no generally available grants.

- enormous implicit subsidies built into the loans through very long terms, generous forgiveness provisions, and no interest, so that only between 15–30 percent or less qualifies as a true loan.

- indirect support to 25–30 percent of the student population who take advantage of subsidized meals and housing from the local *Studentenwerke*.

The Federal Republic of Germany has for some years been experiencing a sluggish economy and high unemployment—a special trauma to a nation that enjoyed such extraordinary growth and prosperity throughout the 1960s and much of the 1970s. The government has been determined to cut public expenditures generally and to introduce measures of efficiency and discipline into higher education. The conversion of the BAföG program from grants to loans was a highly controversial and deeply symbolic act. The change, of course, fell only on those who were BAföG awardees, that is, those mainly from the one-third or so lowest-income families. The conversion was in particularly stark contrast to the spirit and policies of the previous decade, in which expansion of enrollments and of higher educational opportunities were paramount.

At the same time, the loan program is, as loan programs go, extraordinarily generous to the student borrower—and perforce expensive to the taxpayer. While distinctions between true loans and effective subsidies may be small consolation to needy students whose counterparts received four years' worth of grants in the early 1980s, but who themselves will now get only four years of loans, the fact remains that the loan burden is not great. Nevertheless, the claim is made that German families, particularly low- and middle-income workers or farmers, simply do not believe in debt and may discourage their children from aspiring to higher education because of the specter of a high BAföG debt upon conclusion of studies. The declining proportion of BAföG recipients among the total West German student body lends some credence to this fear.

At the same time, the limitation of the only generally available student loan program to BAföG recipients means that students from middle- and upper-income families have no recourse to any generally available student loans, whether to supplement the family contribution, to become financially independent of parents, to increase the standard of student living, or to add additional fields of study or return to college as a mature student. It is not clear that this lack of student borrowing opportunities for middle- and upper-middle-income students is a major problem.

Nevertheless, one obvious alternative open to the West German Government is to lessen substantially the amount of subsidy within the current loan program, open the less-subsidized loans up to students from a wider range of financial backgrounds, and shift the savings into at least some restoration of grants or partial grants for students from low-income families—at no actual increase in taxpayer-borne costs.

FRANCE

HIGHER EDUCATION IN FRANCE

Structure and Governance[1]

Higher education in France can be viewed as a binary system, although with little resemblance to the binary system of the United Kingdom described in Chapter 2. By far the larger of the two sectors, and by most measures the most important although the lesser in status and prestige, is the university sector with its affiliated institutions. Smaller, but greater in status and quite different in governance and finance, is the sector of the *Grandes Ecoles*.

The universities in France (with a few exceptions, such as the medical faculties) accept all holders of the French academic secondary school "leaving certificate," or baccalaureate. Prior to the 1968 structural reforms, the French universities were large (even by U.S. standards—the University of Paris in 1968 had nearly 230,000 students), relatively monolithic institutions organized according to the five traditional faculties of law and political science, medicine and dentistry, pharmacy, humanities and social science, and science. The first three prepared those entering their respective professions; the latter two prepared mainly secondary school teachers. (The French universities have never been strong in engineering, applied science, or the management sciences, these being left to the other side of the binary line, the *Grandes Ecoles*, discussed below.)

By the 1968 Orientation Law, sometimes known as "the Faure

Law" for the then Minister of Education, the dominant University of Paris was broken up into more manageable units. Several of the other large provincial universities were similarly broken into smaller units. The university faculties were then reorganized into "units of teaching and research" (*Unités d'Enseignement et de Recherche*, or UERs), corresponding closely to American university departments or groups of cognate disciplines. Finally, the universities were given what was supposed to have been a substantial measure of institutional autonomy, although all university faculty were still governmental employees and all universities remained under the authority of the Minister of Universities. (The universities had a separate cabinet minister in the 1970s as well as a separate minister for research and technology. The return of the Parliament to the Conservatives in 1986 has brought a reconsolidation of the education and research ministries.)

In 1965, the Government created two-year institutions of technology (*Instituts Universitaires de Technologie*, or IUTs) and attached them loosely to the universities. They were to combine a practical, vocational orientation with enhanced transferability into the university—a bit like the U.S. community college in curricular mission, although closer to the British polytechnic in selectivity and the academic preparedness of their students. However, the IUTs remain much less popular than originally envisioned, and they never acquired the status that the Government attempted to bestow upon them by decree.[2]

The universities are large, politically volatile, and quite underfunded, whether measured by student/faculty ratios, percentage of G.N.P., or per-faculty research support, at least compared to Northern European, British, or North American universities. They have borne nearly the entire brunt of the enormous expansion of enrollments over the past 20 to 30 years. While very high dropout and "no-show" numbers make French university enrollments hard to stipulate with real meaning, the enrollments can be estimated at between 900,000–950,000 in 1984–85, with 50,000–60,000 of these in the IUTs.[3] The stated aim of the recent Socialist Government was to increase these enrollments by the end of the 1980s by some 350,000 students, with the overwhelming majority assumed to be absorbed by the approximately 75 universities[4]—a daunting prospect for institutions that are already, by most Western university standards, vastly overcrowded and without prospect for significant augmentation of faculty or facilities.

Quite distinct from the universities are the *Grandes Ecoles*, which are entered upon passage of a highly competitive examination, *le concours d'entrée*, taken after two or even sometimes three full years of post-*lycée* study in special *classes préparatoires*. The *Grandes*

Ecoles are of two types: *Les Ecoles d'Ingénieurs*, or schools of engineering, and *Les Ecoles Normales Supérieures*, or advanced colleges for the preparation of secondary-school (*lycée*) teachers. Most of the *Grandes Ecoles* are very prestigious; collectively, they form the gateways into the highest-status positions in engineering, science, management, and public administration. They are small, individually and collectively, numbering approximately 150 and enrolling fewer than 70,000 students.[5] They are very well funded, especially on a per-student basis as compared with the universities. Some are privately affiliated with professional associations, chambers of commerce, and the like. Many of these charge tuition. Of those that are fully public, many are funded and thus controlled by Ministries other than the Ministries of Education or of Universities. Together, the *Grandes Ecoles* constitute a small, disparate, quasi-independent, well-supported, and very prestigious sector of higher education, which over the past two decades has also suffered far less political damage than has the university sector, either from internal strife or external interference.

Scholarly research in France is conducted partly in the universities but more so in independent, publicly supported research institutes, the largest of which, the *Centre National de la Recherche Scientifique*, or CNRS, has the largest share of public research funds and throughout most of the 1980s has been essentially independent from both the Ministry of Education and the Ministry of Universities. (The new Conservative Government, formed after the 1986 Parliamentary elections, immediately abolished the separate Ministry for Science and Research, combining this portfolio with the Ministry for National Education. The Government's announced aim, as of the summer of 1986, is to place curbs on the size and autonomy of the CNRS.[6])

Services to Students

Nonacademic services to students, including personal and career counseling, activities (including athletic programs), and cultural events, in addition to the provision of subsidized meals and lodging to students who qualify on the basis of need, are provided through the local *Centre Régional des Oeuvres Universitaires et Scolaires*, or CROUS.[7] Like its German counterpart, the *Studentenwerk*, the French CROUS is quasi-independent, governed by a board consisting of students, university administrative or faculty representatives, and citizens within a framework established by law and with public (i.e., taxpayer-borne) support. Full membership, and thus entitlement to the subsidized meals and rents, is limited to higher-education students in good standing under the age of 26 (at the beginning of their studies) whose own resources do not exceed a certain low-level civil service pay grade.

Formerly, the Ministry reimbursed the CROUS for each subsidized meal served to its membership—allowing, in the Paris CROUS in 1984–85, for example, meals to be served for 8F [$1.08], or 15.8F [$2.12]* for those not entitled to the subsidy. Recently, however, the government changed to a total subvention for the entire center (based, of course, on some projection of students and meals served), and the CROUS must now manage with whatever pricing and selling policies the board wishes to put into effect—provided that the operation at least breaks even on its subvention plus its earned revenue. In this process, the state share has declined from about 50 percent to under 40 percent. A basic meal can still be served to the membership, however, for about 8.5F [$1.14].

The CROUS residences, at least in Paris, are very inadequate to meet the demand, having only 1,368 places which are disbursed on the basis of need and student seniority. In 1984–85, a single room in a Paris CROUS dormitory was 488F [$66] a month, probably one-half the cost of a comparable room in private quarters in Paris.

The Paris CROUS also provides lists of temporary and permanent jobs, general information for students, travel services, and listings of student clubs and associations. It maintains two art galleries for student work and athletic facilities for basketball and other sports. Students can obtain very short-term emergency grants and loans. In summary, the CROUS, perhaps even more comprehensively than the German *Studentenwerk*, provides a full range of free and subsidized services to students.

Recent Events and Trends

During the 1960s and 1970s the French universities, like their German counterparts (and for similar reasons), experienced a combination of enormous growth and turbulent change, fueled first by rising expectations and general economic prosperity, followed by the clash of opposing agendas (e.g., of the students, the junior faculty, the senior faculty, the political right, and the political left), growing disenchantment, and finally the recent financial austerity. The 1968 Faure Law was an attempt both to modernize the university (espe-

* All franc units in this chapter are followed by a U.S. dollar equivalent according to a 1985 purchasing power ratio of 7.44F = $1.00. See Appendix A.

cially its governance and authority, and desirably its curriculum) and to respond to the demands of the student movement and its allies, most frequently the junior faculty and the political left, who saw the universities as engines of social justice—but only as long as access and job security were guaranteed. The government (then Conservative) and the business community also had a stake in changing and expanding the universities for the sake of economic growth and world technological parity. The breakup of the University of Paris and the other very large universities, together with new measures of institutional autonomy and decentralized decision-making, were supposed to crack the allegedly stultifying combination of ministerial bureaucratic rigidity and university academic conservatism and to turn loose the fresh winds of diversification, innovation, and entrepreneurship.[8]

By most accounts, none of these agendas was fully realized. The experience of the 1970s made it clear that higher education is not very good at reducing income disparities, eradicating disadvantage, or breaking the transmission of wealth and status from parents to children—not just in France, but anywhere. The universities did not seem to be preparing young people particularly well for the world of work, nor (in the United States, the United Kingdom, Germany, or France) was higher education seeming to assure the technological advancement that was increasingly presumed to be key to the economic future of the advanced industrialized West.[9] It has also been observed that "autonomy was only given lip-service by the government," and that most universities kept with traditional degrees and research programs rather than take advantage of the freedom that the 1968 law had supposedly given them.[10]

The 1976 reform was aimed much more specifically at the alleged lack of ties between the traditional university curricula and the world of work. The law imposed on the universities a new vocationally oriented degree at the *Maîtrise* level (given at the end of the second stage of university work, after three or four years of study), which at first promulgation would also have required substantial changes in curriculum requirements, departmental budgets, and academic job opportunities. The result was enormous opposition from faculty and students. Again, however, the agendas were mixed: some faculty feared the loss of jobs or promotional opportunities; some objected on academic grounds to the narrowing vocationalism of the proposed curriculum; and many were angered by the government's "top-down" heavy hand. Morale, particularly among the senior faculty, is reported by Bienaymé to have been shattered.[11] The government backed at least partway down, but by the early 1980s the new *Maîtrises*, according to Bienaymé, were "playing a growing role and attracting an increasing proportion of students."[12]

The next governmental intrusion was the 1983 Savary Law (after the first Education Minister of the Socialist Government), the first significant piece of higher education legislation enacted after the electoral victory of the Socialists in 1981. It reduced further the power of the senior faculty, made more difficult the screening out of non-productive faculty, created new teaching positions without scholarly expectations, and proposed new vocational/professional degrees and the strengthening of old ones. The 1984 legislation, passed the following year, virtually eliminated the selection (or the weeding out) of students, even at the second level of the university studies, and called for an increase in enrollments by fully one-third by the end of the 1980s—with minimal additional resources.

The Conservative Parliamentary victory in early 1986 provided yet another perturbation to French higher educational politics. One of the new Government's priorities was to be the repeal of the Savary Law and the restoration of what the Conservatives claimed to be lost university autonomy, selectivity, and competitive spirit.[13]

The future trajectory of French higher education is not easily discerned. As background to the sections to follow on student finance, however, the following observations appear to be supportable and relevant to the theme of this report:

- French higher education—at least the universities—has become highly politicized, buffeted both by French party politics and the changing agendas of changing governments as well as by internal politics, often also along party lines and pitting junior faculty and their union allies, frequently with the support of students, against the senior professoriate.

- The universities in France, overwhelmingly dominant in their share of enrollments, continue to be pulled in many different directions, not all of them compatible. In most fields, they have been and remain the pre-eminent institutions of education and scholarship, as "universities" are elsewhere. However, they are overshadowed in status, financial support, and quality of students in the key modern fields of engineering, applied science, management, and public administration by the *Grandes Ecoles*. The universities have lost much of their research funds to the stand-alone research institutes. Most recently, they are being expected to absorb enormous increases in enrollments without commensurate increases in resources and without the ability (in any but a few fields) to select students, even at the second level, who come with the baccalaureate from a *lycée*. The French universities experience very high dropout and no-show rates—not unusual for many U.S. universities, but much higher than would be found in, say, U.K., German, or Swedish universities.

- For all the sound and fury of the past nearly two decades, from the 1968 Orientation (Faure) Law through the Socialist Government's 1983 and 1984 legislation, the basic contours of French higher education seem, however, to have remained very much the same. The universities dominate by their size, broad mission, and largely open enrollments to holders of the academic secondary school degree. They apparently teach much the same curriculum in much the same way as in the 1960s. The IUTs and the even newer, more practically oriented university degrees are now established, but their enrollments are not large. The *Grandes Ecoles* have been practically untouched by any of the above.

- The *Grandes Ecoles* provide many options for the very able, and especially for the very able who can afford tuitions. In France, there does not seem to be the very high level of concern found in some other countries for the creation of higher educational opportunities for the older, nontraditional student, the less able student, or the disadvantaged young adult, other than the insistence upon open university enrollments to baccalaureate holders from the academic secondary schools, or *lycées*.

- Student finances—that is, those programs and policies of grants, loans, and expected parental contributions that constitute the real orientation of this report—seem to have been less of a burning issue than they have been in the United States, the United Kingdom, Germany, or Sweden. The grant program in France is very small, and there is no generally available, long-term student loan program. The key ingredient in France seems to be the generally accepted principle of family assistance, including widespread acceptance of young adult students living with their parents, buttressed by government policies of indirect support to students through subsidized meals and housing and to families through tax advantages available only to parents of students.

SHARING THE COSTS AMONG PARENTS, TAXPAYERS, AND STUDENTS

Costs to the Student and Family

The cost of higher education to the student and family is more difficult to specify in France than in many other countries for several reasons. First, perhaps even more than in the United States, is the enormous range of financial situations—from living at home while commuting to a nearly tuition-free university and taking highly subsidized meals at the CROUS to attending a semiprivate *Grande Ecole*, paying a substantial tuition, and living in a Paris flat while working part time. The French student is likely to be a bit older (in median or modal, if not in mean or average, age), to be either married or living-as-married, and to be from a somewhat higher relative socioeconomic class than his or her counterpart U.S. undergraduate, all of which characteristics extend the range of available resources as well as of budgetary requirements.

Second, the generally available, need-based financial aid system does not, at least ostensibly, begin with a budget or set of budgets and then subtract an expected parental and student/spouse contribution, as do other systems. Rather, it reaches a certain level of assistance through a combination of factors, obviously with a "cash need" somewhere in the mind of whomever devises the formula but not as a visible part of the award process. The national need-based aid system also reaches a very small proportion of students with relatively small grants, so that the assumptions of costs or need underlying the grant system do not form such clear benchmarks as in, e.g., the United Kingdom with its mandatory grants, the Federal Republic of Germany with its BAföG, or the United States with its Pell Grants.

Finally, French students tend to rely very heavily on their parents for both cash and in-kind assistance, and they also draw heavily on taxpayer-subsidized housing and restaurants. For example, the cost of a full meal listed in the 1984–85 Paris CROUS Handbook (1983 prices) is 8F [$1.08] for members and 15.8 [$2.12] for guests (presumably, nonsubsidized). Similarly, the cost of lodging in a CROUS dormitory is listed as 488F [$66] monthly for a single and 400F [$54] for a double room—as compared with private rooms on the CROUS lists that range from 700F–1,000F [$94–$134] for a single person.[14] These subsidies, together with the extensive family-provided meals and lodging, impose on the analyst the burden of imputing some estimates of real costs to lodging, meals, and other important goods and services that are consumed by students but that carry minimal cash price tags.

For example, a student living at home could probably live on as little as 500F [$67] a month for food, eating at home and at the CROUS, and another 500F for all other expenses, for an austere, ten-month cash budget of just over 10,000F [$1,344]. A low budget that included some of the family- and taxpayer-borne in-kind costs, especially of room and board, would add another 4,000F–5,000F [$538–$672]. A moderate university budget for ten months for a student living in a private room might be 13,000F [$1,747] for room and board, 6,000F [$806] for other expenses, and 300F [$40] for registration fees—for a total budget of about 19,300F [$2,594]. At the high end, a

TABLE 4.1
Range of Estimated Costs to Student and Family, France, 1985–86

| | Lowest budget: cash only | | Low: cash plus in-kind | | Moderate: university | | Higher: Grande Ecole | |
| | • commuter • CROUS member • no attributed in-kind costs | | • commuter • CROUS eligible • add family and public in-kind costs | | • private room • add family and public in-kind | | • private room • not CROUS eligible • tuition charged | |
	F	$	F	$	F	$	F	$
Fees	300	40	300	40	300	40	20,000	2,688
Room and board	5,000	672	9,000	1,210	13,000	1,747	17,000	2,285
All other	5,000	672	5,500	739	6,000	806	8,000	1,075
Total	10,300	1,384	14,800	1,989	19,300	2,593	45,000	6,048

Sources: *Infos Etudiants 1984* (Paris: Centre Regional des Oeuvres Universitaires et Scolaires, 1984); Nabil Abboud and Philippe Cazenave, "Budgets des Etudiants," *Education et Formations*, No. 2, 1983, p. 69; and Benoit Millot and François Orivel *L'Economie de L'Enseignement Supérior* (Paris: Cujas, 1980), p. 261.

ten-month *Grandes Ecoles* budget could easily be as much as 43,000F [$5,780], figuring in tuition and fees of 20,000F [$2,688], room and board of 17,000F [$2,285], and all other costs of 8,000F [$1,075]. These costs are summarized in Table 4.1. Although the great range of circumstances and the complexity of in-kind assistance diminishes the usefulness of averages, it would appear that a French student in 1985–86 needed about 16,000F–19,000F [$2,151–$2,554] to attend the university for ten months and to live away from home, with commuting budgets in the range of 10,000F–12,000F [$1,344–$1,613].[15]

These costs are met through the three principal sources: parents, students, and taxpayers. A fourth source, future employers, was once a significant contributor through pre-employment contracts, or *contrats de préembauche*, but is no longer so. Taxpayer support comes in three general forms: (1) grants, or *bourses*, to students, mainly need-based at the lower-division level and merit-based at the advanced (university third) level; (2) subsidized meals and lodging through the local CROUS; and (3) tax relief to parents whose children are in higher education through the special tax advantage of the *exonération fiscale*. The parental support comes through (1) the provision of cash to the student; (2) cash purchases made on behalf of the student (e.g., food for meals); and (3) in-kind services provided (e.g., housing, laundry)—all of these outlays offset somewhat by the tax relief previously mentioned. Student support comes through (1) part-time and vacation work; (2) short-term loans (rare); and (3) the earnings of the spouse or *conjoint*, as the French call the more-or-less permanent, but unmarried, mate of the opposite sex.

Need-Based Grants: The Bourse[16]

The French Ministry of Education administers three grant programs, or *bourses*. The *bourse d'enseignement supérieur sur critères sociaux*, or undergraduate need-based grants, are given to students in the first and second cycles of higher education (undergraduate years, to the approximate level of the U.S. master's degree) on the basis of criteria weighted predominantly by family income. The *bourse de licence* and *bourse à caractère spécial* are third-cycle scholarships given to students at the graduate level and do not vary according to family income, although, when the numbers are limited and the applicants are many, income might have some effect on the decision to whom to award them. They are limited within disciplines and are given for the first year or two of the third cycle rather than the final years, which are expected to be covered by grants from the research budgets of the appropriate ministries.

The *bourse* "social criteria," or undergraduate need-based grant, is awarded on nine levels, or *échelons*, ranging in 1985–86 from a low of 3,690F [$496] to a high of 12,744F [$1,713], with an additional 954F [$128] supplement possible for certain reasons, making the maximum ordinary *bourse* 13,698F [$1,841]. There is an across-the-board supplement for those students who have done National Service (principally military service), for whom the range extends from 4,878F [$656] to 13,698F [$1,841] plus any other supplement.

The *bourse* is given not only for the universities and *Grandes Ecoles*, but also for the *classes préparatoires*, which are those classes given within certain *lycées* generally for two years in order to prepare for the *Grandes Ecoles* entrance examinations. (If a student prepares for, say, two years but fails to pass the *Grandes Ecoles* entrance examination, those two years can generally be applied to university studies and the student can enter directly into the second cycle, or third year, of university study.) The *bourse* is good through the age of 25 or beyond as long as the first entry begins before the age of 26. A *bourse* is not normally given to a student beginning studies at age 26 or later. Such a mature candidate must get help, if available, through other ministries. A recent change in the *bourse* program, to help students from lower socioeconomic classes, is the assurance of a three-year award so that students do not lose the *bourse* and drop out for financial reasons if their first-year progress is not up to what may have been expected from students from the best academic *lycées*.

The kind of grant to which the student-family unit is entitled depends upon family income two years prior (or upon more recent income if circumstances have changed for the worse) plus a set of "situational" criteria such as other dependent children, the need to reside away from home, handicapping or disabling conditions for either student or parent, and so forth. The situational factors are summarized by a point system, which is then combined with income from two years past to determine the appropriate level of grant, as shown in Table 4.2. The student and the family begin with an automatic nine points. Additional points are added for other dependent children not in higher education (1 point each), other dependent children also in a university or school (2 points each), attending a school more than 30 kilometers from home, and so forth, most of which variables are summarized in Table 4.2. Given the appropriate number of points, the family income from two years prior as adjusted for tax purposes determines the grant to which the student is entitled, if any. The grant is increased by one step, also shown in Table 4.2, if the student has completed National (primarily military) Service.

As an example, consider a student who has not completed military or other National Service, who attends a university 80 kilometers

TABLE 4.2
Need-Based Grants (*Bourses*) for Undergraduates, France, 1985–86

Level of grant	Amount of grant — Regular		Amount of grant — Military or other National Service		Maximum family income to qualify for level of grant based on situation as measured by points (9–25)* — 9 points		10		11		12		13		17		25	
	F	$	F	$	F	$	F	$	F	$	F	$	F	$	F	$	F	$
1	3,690	496	4,878	656	55,800	7,500	61,900	8,320	68,300	9,180	74,400	10,000	80,700	10,847	105,700	14,207	155,500	20,901
2	4,878	656	6,084	818	53,100	7,137	59,100	7,944	65,000	8,737	71,000	9,543	77,000	10,349	100,700	13,535	148,100	19,906
3	6,084	818	7,308	982	50,900	6,841	56,700	7,621	62,400	8,387	68,200	9,167	73,700	9,906	96,800	13,011	142,200	19,113
4	7,308	982	8,352	1,123	48,500	6,519	53,900	7,245	59,100	7,944	64,500	8,670	70,000	9,409	91,500	12,298	134,700	18,105
5	8,352	1,123	9,378	1,260	46,200	6,210	51,400	6,909	56,600	7,608	61,700	8,293	66,800	8,978	87,400	11,747	128,900	17,325
6	9,378	1,260	10,440	1,403	42,600	5,726	47,500	6,384	52,100	7,003	58,300	7,903	61,700	8,293	80,600	10,833	118,800	15,968
7	10,440	1,403	11,466	1,541	40,200	5,403	44,800	6,022	49,300	6,626	53,300	7,204	58,300	7,836	76,200	10,242	112,300	15,094
8	11,466	1,541	12,744	1,713	35,600	4,785	39,400	5,296	43,400	5,833	47,500	6,384	51,300	6,895	67,200	9,032	98,800	13,280
9	12,744	1,713	13,698	1,841	33,100	4,449	36,700	4,933	40,400	5,430	44,100	5,927	47,400	6,371	62,500	8,401	92,000	12,336

Source: "Bourses d'enseignement supérieur sur critères sociaux. Modalités d'attribution pour l'année universitaire 1985–86" in *Enseignement Supérieur*, published by the French Ministry of Education, April 9, 1985.

*Family-Student Situations Qualifying for Points

	Points
• Family-student automatic entitlement.	9
• University city more than 30 kilometers away from home	2
• Each additional dependent child not a university student	1 each
• Each additional dependent also a university student	2 each
• Mother and father both working	1
• Others (e.g., student or parents handicapped, dependents of student)	1 each

Example: Parents both work, one additional child not in university, student must commute more than 30 kilometers: situation merits 9 + 1 + 1 + 2 = 13 points. Student not a veteran, thus entitled only to "regular" grant. A family income of 57,000F [$7,661] would yield a grant at Level 3, or 10,440F [$1,403]; an income of 72,500F [$9,745] would yield Level 3, or 6,084F [$818].

from home, who has one sibling not of college age, and whose parents, both of whom work, earned 57,000F [$7,661] net taxable income two years ago. The situational points would be as follows:

	points
• student and family automatic entitlement	9
• dependent sibling not in college	1
• more than 30 kilometers from university	2
• both parents working	1
Total	13

Table 4.2 shows that a 57,000F [$7,661] family income with 13 points entitles a student who has not completed national service to a grant of 10,440F [$1,403].

The normal range of points extends from a minimum of 9 to 16 or 17 points; totals can extend as high as 26, but only with many dependents in higher education and with multiple handicaps or other very special situations. Table 4.3 shows the normal range of low-grant and high-grant situations side-by-side. The low-grant situation (11 points) provides grants to families with incomes up to 68,300F [$9,180]; the high-grant situation provides them to an income of 105,700F [$14,207]. Clearly, the *bourse* imposes an extremely severe income test for relatively modest awards, at least by U.S., U.K., German, or Swedish standards. The fact that the awards are grants and not loans, unlike the German and a major portion of the Swedish and American awards, may make the *bourse* a little less ungenerous by comparison. Nevertheless, the awards are quite small, are available only to the very needy, and assist only about 10–12 percent of new students.[17] Furthermore, there is no generally available loan program to students in France. A small program, sponsored by the Ministry, provides loans for very special circumstances (e.g., the refusal of a parent to help a child), but only 3,465 loans were given out in 1984–85 at an average size of 8,000F [$1,075], so the program is not a significant supplement to the *bourse*.[18]

Such a low level of direct student assistance is a reflection of the severe needs-testing for the *bourse*—that is, the phasing out of any award for the average (13-point) family at an income of only 80,700F [$10,847]—plus the relatively low proportion of young people from very low-income families who make it through the rigorous academic secondary-level *lycée* and choose to go on to the university or to a *classe préparatoire* for candidacy to a *Grande Ecole*. At the same time, the small number of grants and the small average grant size[19] are also reflections of—or perhaps it should be said that they are only possible because of—the very substantial assistance available from

TABLE 4.3
Need-Based Grants (Bourses) and Family Income Ranges for Two Student-Family Situations, 1985–86

Student-Family Situation "A"

	Points
• No military or National Service	9
• One additional child (non-student) in family	1
• 6 km commute to university	0
• Parents both work	1
Total points	11

Student-Family Situation "B"

	Points
• Veteran	9
• One other nonstudent and two other student children in family	5
• 85-km commute to university	2
• Parents both work	1
Total points	17

Income Ranges and Grant Entitlements

Family income range Situation "A"		Grant Entitlement		Family income range Situation "B"	
F	$	F	$	F	$
more than 68,300	more than $9,180	0	0	more than 105,700	more than $14,207
65,001 – 68,300	8,738 – 9,180	3,690	496	100,701 – 105,700	13,536 – 14,207
62,401 – 65,000	8,388 – 8,737	4,878	656	96,801 – 100,700	13,012 – 13,535
59,101 – 62,400	7,945 – 8,387	6,084	818	91,501 – 96,800	12,299 – 13,011
56,601 – 59,100	7,609 – 7,944	7,308	982	87,401 – 91,500	11,748 – 12,298
52,101 – 56,600	7,004 – 7,608	8,352	1,123	80,601 – 87,400	10,834 – 11,747
49,301 – 52,100	6,627 – 7,003	9,378	1,260	76,201 – 80,600	10,243 – 10,833
43,401 – 49,300	5,834 – 6,626	10,440	1,403	67,201 – 76,200	9,033 – 10,242
		11,466	1,541		
40,401 – 43,400	5,431 – 5,833	12,744	1,713	62,501 – 67,200	8,401 – 9,032
less than 40,000	less than 5,430	13,698	1,877	less than 62,500	less than 8,400

Students without military or National Service are limited to a maximum grant of 13,698F; with an 11-point situation, as shown here, this would be available to students whose family incomes were below 40,400F.

Students with military service, as in the 17-point "Situation B" shown here, are entitled to a maximum grant of 13,698F, and their minimum grant is ≤ 8,878F.

TABLE 4.4
Additions to Undergraduate Need-Based Grants as a Consequence of
Attending a University Far from, Rather Than Near, Home, by Family
Income and Family Situation

Assume: • no National Service;
        • one additional nonstudent dependent child; and
        • both parents working.
Total points: 9 + 1 + 1 = 11

Maximum family income		Grant if university less than 30 km from home		Grant if university more than 30 km from home		Difference attributable to long commute or need to reside	
F	$	F	$	F	$	F	$
85,000	11,425	0	0	0	0	0	0
80,000	10,753	0	0	3,690	496	3,690	496
75,000	10,081	0	0	4,878	656	4,878	656
70,000	9,409	0	0	7,308	982	7,308	982
65,000	8,737	4,878	656	8,352	1,123	3,474	467
60,000	8,065	6,084	818	9,378	1,260	3,294	442
55,000	7,392	8,352	1,123	10,440	1,403	2,088	280
50,000	6,720	9,378	1,260	11,466	1,541	2,088	280
45,000	6,048	10,440	1,403	12,744	1,713	2,334	314
40,000	5,376	12,744	1,713	12,744	1,713	0	0

Note: The grants for "less than 30 km" are based on 11 points; the grants for "more than 30 km" add 2 points.

the government (taxpayer) indirectly via subsidized meals, lodging, and tax offsets and via even low-income parents through the continued provision of lodging, meals, and other support, both in-cash and in-kind. The *bourse,* in fact, virtually requires a recipient to live at home and take advantage of the family and taxpayer-borne in-kind assistance of low-cost meals and lodging. Table 4.4 shows the increase in the *bourse* to which an eligible student is entitled by virtue of attending a university more than 30 kilometers from his or her home. The maximum effect (and that only through the peculiarities of the cutoff points in the table) is 7,308F [$982]. The more usual effect of a resident as opposed to a commuting situation is that only 400F–500F [$54–$67] is added to the high-income end of *bourse* eligibility and only 200F–300F [$27–$40] to the *bourses* of the very poor. The commuting supplement, through the additional points allowed in a commuting situation, is thus regressive as well as inadequate and has the effect of making it very difficult for students from low-income families to attend a university in an other-than-commuting situation.

The Parental Contribution

French parents have a major role in meeting the expenses of higher education for their children. This role is met both by cash contributions and by the indirect contribution of lodging and other forms of assistance (e.g., laundry) made possible when students live at home with their parents. Data cited by Jarousse showed the direct parental contribution to be quite constant from 1963 to 1983, dropping from 55.7 percent to only 53.1 percent of student revenues.[20] This is very unlike the Swedish system, which encourages student independence and does not officially expect any monetary contribution from parents to students; the British system, which has an expected parental contribution that is deeply resented by the students and apparently not all that highly regarded by parents; or the German system, which depends heavily on parental support, but which also encourages independent living. Indeed, the French take it almost for granted that young people will have to live at home for at least much of their university studies unless the student is lucky and aggressive enough to find a well-paying, part-time job, or unless the parents are sufficiently well off and so inclined to support the expenses of full independent sudent living.

Public policy for the support of students, particularly for enhanced access for children from low-income families, is built on this tradition. Woodhall, probably the foremost comparative observer of student-support policies, wrote that ". . . public policy [in France] regards the student and the family as one entity for the purposes of financial aid."[21] This tradition embraces:

- a substantial expectation of cash contributions even at very low incomes, as reflected in an expected parental contribution offset to the *bourse* starting with incomes as low as 33,500F [$4,503], that is, the level of family income in a "9-point situation" that first causes a reduction in the *bourse*—in this case, from level 9, or 12,744F, to level 8, or 11,466F, for a loss of 1,278F [$172], which is presumably made up by an increased parental contribution;

- an acceptance of commuting as a way of student life, as well as of other forms of noncash parental support of students; and

- indirect, taxpayer-borne offsets to the parental contributions through the special tax advantage of having a nonminor dependent child enrolled in higher education.

This section will examine these three dimensions of parental support of students in higher education in France.

The Expected (Cash) Contribution: Offset to the Bourse. A "need-based grant" is understood to be one that makes up the difference between some target amount—usually the amount of money required by the student, less any amount the student is expected to earn or to borrow—and an expected contribution from the parents, which is usually nothing at all, at least in cash terms, at very low levels of income and then starts with a small contribution and increases as incomes rise until the expected parental contribution equals the target amount, or maximum grant, at which point (and at all higher-income levels) the grant has been phased out altogether. Presumably, the "expected parental contribution" is an amount that can reasonably, albeit with some hardship, be diverted from other family needs to cover the higher education costs of the child. Presumably as well, the increase in expected parental contributions (or the decrease in the grant) per unit of increased income—in effect, a "marginal tax rate"—is an amount of increased income that can reasonably be expected to be devoted to the cost of higher education rather than to the many other yet-unmet needs of the low-income family.

The French do not have a generally available loan plan to help the student bear a share of costs, and part-time work, while very common among French students, is resoundingly discouraged for *bourse* recipients by the official policy of reducing the grant franc-for-franc by student earnings. For low-income student-family units, then, it may be assumed that the combination of the *bourse* and an expected parental cash contribution will be sufficient to meet the very minimum needs, estimated above as 10,000F–12,000F [$1,344–$1,613] plus the costs of food consumed at home. The maximum grant of 12,744F [$1,713] for 1985–86 generally confirms this target cash budget. This means, then, that families with somewhat higher incomes will probably have to come up with cash to continue meeting this target as the *bourse* declines with rising incomes. Table 4.5 shows the expected parental contribution, by annual income, for 11-, 13-, and 17-point families. All contributions less than 13,000F [$1,747] assume a *bourse* to make up the difference, as per Table 4.2. Thus, the 11-point family (i.e., two wage-earners, one additional nonstudent child, and within commuting range of the university) must begin contributing 2,560F [$344] at an income level of 45,000F [$6,048] and must thereafter devote a little more than 1 franc for every 3 francs additional income to their child's university costs up to an annual

TABLE 4.5
Expected Parental Contributions by Parental Income and Family Situation,
France, 1985–86

Assume 13,000F [$1,747] minimal need

Family income		Expected parental contribution, by family situation					
		11 points[a]		13 points[b]		17 points[c]	
F	$	F	$	F	$	F	$
105,000	14,113	13,000	1,747	13,000	1,747	9,310	1,251
100,000	13,441	13,000	1,747	13,000	1,747	8,122	1,092
95,000	12,769	13,000	1,747	13,000	1,747	6,916	930
90,000	12,097	13,000	1,747	13,000	1,747	5,692	765
85,000	11,425	13,000	1,747	13,000	1,747	4,648	625
80,000	10,753	13,000	1,747	9,310	1,251	3,622	487
75,000	10,081	13,000	1,747	8,122	1,092	2,560	344
70,000	9,409	13,000	1,747	5,692	765	2,560	344
65,000	8,737	8,122	1,092	4,648	625	1,534	206
60,000	8,065	6,916	930	3,622	487	256	34
55,000	7,392	4,648	625	2,560	344	256	34
50,000	6,720	3,622	487	1,534	206	256	34
45,000	6,048	2,560	344	256	34	256	34
40,000	5,376	256	34	256	34	256	34
35,000	4,704	256	34	256	34	256	34

Each student-family unit begins with an automatic 9 points:
[a] 11-point situation: e.g., one additional dependent child in a university (2)
[b] 13-point situation: e.g., two additional dependent children, one in a university (2),
one not in a university (1), and both parents working (1)
[c] 17-point situation: e.g., one nonstudent and two student additional dependent children (5), both parents working (1), university more than 30 km away (2)

income of 70,000F [$9,409]. At this point the expected contribution
has displaced the entire *bourse* and the parents are expected, apparently, to come up with the full 13,000F [$1,747] or so. For a 13-point
family, shown graphically in Figure 4.1, the expected contributions
do not begin until an income of about 50,000F [$6,720], at which
point a parental contribution of 1,534F [$206] can be combined with
a *bourse* of 11,466F [$1,541] to yield the target sum of 13,000F
[$1,747]. Contributions rise with increasing incomes until an income
of just under 85,000F [$11,425], when the *bourse* disappears and the
whole need is up to the parents—or, at that point, the parents with
the help of the students' part-time earnings. (Part-time earnings are
discouraged only for low-income students, who stand to lose the
bourse.) Finally, for the 17-point family (generally one with many
dependents and other special needs), the contributions begin at an
annual income of about 65,000F [$8,737] and rise with increasing

• Assume 13-Point Situation

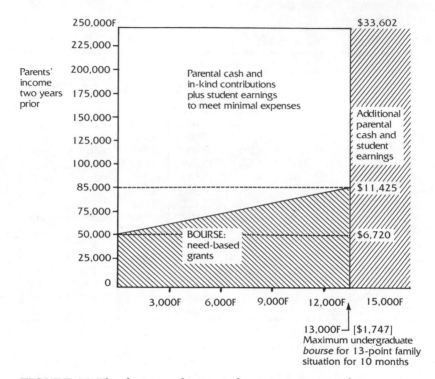

FIGURE 4.1 The division of estimated maintenance costs between expected parental contribution and maximum *bourse* as a function of two years' prior parental income, 1985-86.

incomes until an annual income of more than 105,000F [$14,113], at which point the *bourse* phases out. Although the students can begin to earn money themselves and simply forgo the small *bourses*, it is evident from the above data that the expected parental contribution is very rigorous and steeply sloped (i.e., taking a large share of marginal income), especially for the family with few or no dependent children.

The expected-family-contribution schedule is not at all progressive; even when the contribution is presumably increasing with income, it does so according to a roughly linear function, as opposed to a "kinked" or progressive function that would require larger additional contributions from additional units of income as incomes rise. Furthermore, the expected parental contribution peaks at a rather low income (depending, of course, on the family-situation points) and remains flat after that point, thus taking smaller and smaller proportions of income as incomes rise, in what the parlance of taxation would call a "regressive" function. Finally, it is especially important for the low-income family to come up with the full expected parental contribution because, at least by the regulations, the *bourse* cannot be supplemented by student earnings. Once the family income is beyond the level qualifying for a *bourse*, however, students may work part time and actually lower the amount of cash contribution that has to come from the parents. From the perspective of the expected parental contribution, then, the French *bourse*, at least as compared to U.S., U.K., German, and Swedish student support plans, provides a relatively small award to the student and reduces even this modest grant with an especially severe and nonprogressive expected parental contribution.

Parental Contributions Beyond the Range of the Bourse. Particularly for the 85 percent or so of parents who have incomes beyond the range of *bourse* eligibility, the contribution to their children's higher education is certain to include cash assistance and may continue to include meals and lodging, either for the academic year or vacation period or both, in addition to cash expenses borne by the parent on behalf of the student, as for clothing, insurance, medical care, and the like. Table 4.6 summarizes the gross and net parental contributions for a range of illustrative (a) total costs to be met and (b) family income levels. The total costs to be met are assumed to be either 15,000F [$2,016] or 20,000F [$2,688]. The "low," "moderate," and "high" family incomes are 50,000F [$6,720], 125,000F [$16,801], and 250,000F [$33,602]. Only the low-income family is entitled to a *bourse*. Student earnings for the other examples vary from 0 to 6,000F [$806]. The resulting gross parental contributions are reduced by an assumed taxpayer-borne offset of 3,000F [$403]—2,000F [$269] for the low-income example—as suggested by 1978–79 survey data.[22] The resulting net parental contributions for these examples are 2,560F [$344] for the low-income family and from 8,000F [$1,075] to a high of 17,000F [$2,285] for the other family income and total cost combinations.

The Student Contribution

Students contribute to the costs of their higher education mainly either by term-time and vacation work or by loans. The 1978–79

TABLE 4.6
Estimated Gross and Net Parental Contributions, Cash and In-kind, France, 1985–86

| | Low expense: living with parents Total cost 15,000F [$2,016][a] | | | | | | Moderate expense: living away from home Total cost 20,000F [$2,688][a] | | | |
| | Low family income 50,000F [$6,720] | | Moderate family income 125,000F [$16,801] | | High family income 250,000F [$33,602] | | Moderate family income 125,000F [$16,801] | | High family income 250,000F [$33,602] | |
	F	$	F	$	F	$	F	$	F	$
Total costs to be met, student and parents	15,000	2,016	15,000	2,016	15,000	2,016	20,000	2,688	20,000	2,688
less bourse[b] and	10,440	1,403	0	0	0	0	0	0	0	0
less earnings[c] equals	0	0	4,000	538	0	0	6,000	806	0	0
need from parents, in the form of	4,560	613	11,000	1,478	15,000	2,016	14,000	1,882	20,000	2,688
cash[d] and	2,735	370	6,600	887	9,000	1,210	8,400	1,129	12,000	1,613
in-kind,[d] which equals	1,825	245	4,400	591	6,000	806	5,600	753	8,000	1,075
gross parental contribution	4,560	613	11,000	1,478	15,000	2,016	14,000	1,882	20,000	2,688
less tax relief,[e] equals	2,000	269	3,000	403	3,000	403	3,000	403	3,000	403
net parental contribution.	2,560	344	8,000	1,075	12,000	1,613	11,000	1,478	17,000	2,285

This table is not presented as data-based averages, but as plausible and illustrative examples.

[a] Total costs are rounded estimates taken from Table 4.1 and surrounding text.

[b] Bourse taken from Table 4.2: 50,000F [$6,720] income and 12 points yields 10,440F [$1,403]; no other incomes qualify.

[c] No earnings for bourse recipient; earnings of 4,000F [$538] and 6,000F [$806] are consistent with averages reported in survey data and thus seem plausible for illustrations.

[d] The "cash" and "in-kind" contributions are divided 60:40, consistent with Abboud and Cazenave survey findings.

[e] The tax relief available to parents of university students is divided 60:40, consistent with Abboud and Cazenave 1978–79 data, which in turn doubled survey-reported data due to known under-estimation. See Abboud and Cazenave, "Budgets," p. 68, Fn. 2.

survey reported by Abboud and Cazenave reported extensive earnings. Those students who worked on a regular basis during the term were called *"salariés."* Such students constituted 21.7 percent of their survey population, although the proportion of *étudiants salariés* was highly correlated with age and stage of education—e.g., less than 20 percent of those under the age of 20, but more than half of those over the age of 21. The average earnings in 1978–79 were 15,399F [\$2,070]. A full 33 percent of first-stage arts students in the 1978–79 survey declared some kind of "remunerative" activity during the year; students at other stages and in other faculties varied considerably, but most worked less.[23]

Data on students and work for the mid-1980s was not available. Jobs may have become more scarce during the recent period of economic slowdown and higher unemployment. Nevertheless, it seems safe to assume that student earnings continue to play a significant role in meeting college costs for perhaps between one-fifth and one-quarter of all French students for whom these earnings meet most, and frequently all, of the cash needs (less the in-kind assistance for housing and meals provided by the family or the CROUS) of the academic year.

Student borrowing in France is much less prevalent. The 1984–85 Paris Region CROUS Handbook reported 10,000,000F [\$134,408] in loan funds available for only 500 students throughout the region.[24] The director of the national scholarship office reported only 3,465 government-sponsored loans in 1984–85 for the entire country, with an average loan of about 8,000F [\$1,075]. These loans are apparently available only on an emergency basis and do not form a regular part of the financing of French higher education.[25]

Most student loans in Franch are private banking transactions, and as such are generally short-term and require collateral or co-signers. The French journal *Le Monde de L'Education* reported in March of 1984 that loans were generally available only to students from wealthy families, or from the *Grandes Ecoles* or the university medical or dental schools. Loans were available to the other university students only upon presentation of two co-signers who could produce evidence of current employment, and even then often at a higher rate. Short-term (maximum 24 months) loans were available in 1983–84 at 0 percent with collateral or 9.5–10 percent without collateral, but only after qualifying with a savings balance. Longer-term loans, with up to four years to repay beginning after entry into the first job, were available only to the best credit risks (e.g., *Grandes Ecoles* or medical students), to a maximum of 12,000F [\$1,613] at up to 15 percent interest.[26] Clearly, then, student loans are not yet part of any general public policy designed to help students meet their share of the costs of attending a university.

Trends, Issues, and Summary Observations

The sharing of higher education costs in France is both varied and complex: varied because of the wide range of costs and family situations, and complex because of the public and private in-kind and transfer payments.

The reliance on parental support and the seeming acceptance of this support by parents and students alike is striking in France, particularly in contrast to Scandinavia, where parents' financial responsibility for their children's university living costs has been virtually abolished, but also in some contrast to West Germany, where the parental role seems to be begrudgingly accepted, and to the United Kingdom, where it seems greatly resented, at least by students and the Labour Party. Although the parents' contribution did not seem to be a major issue in France as of mid-1985, it is reasonable to expect growing pressures from several sources to reduce their burden.

One pressure, of course, is likely to be from those parents who now feel burdened or about to be burdened by a large expense and who believe that they will benefit by having some of what would be their share taken over by, perhaps, an expanded *bourse* or a much less rigorous means-tested reduction of the current grant program. This would be especially popular to those lower-middle-class families (with incomes from 85,000F–125,000F [$11,425–$16,810]) who currently just miss out on the *bourse* altogether. Another possible source of increasing pressure is from students who, while they are obviously far more comfortable with a continuing reliance on their families than are their British or Scandinavian counterparts, are likely in the future to prefer less financial dependence upon their parents—particularly as long as the burden can be passed on to the general taxpayers rather than to themselves. Finally, and to some degree overlapping with considerations just mentioned, there is a probable continuing pressure for something to be done to open the universities, and especially the *Grandes Ecoles*, to more students from the working and non-working poor. Surely, some will perceive a connection between, on the one hand, the paucity of low-income students in the universities, and even more so in the *Grandes Ecoles*, and on the other hand, the very great dependence on parental support, coupled with a most meager need-based grant program.

This is not to say that a transfer of burden from parents to taxpayers will necessarily expand access. According to most observers, the socioeconomic bias observable in higher education in France, as in virtually all nations, is rooted deeply in sociocultural factors that sort young people out far before the time to attend an institution of higher education. Remediation must therefore look much more at access to secondary, than to higher, education. Also, the French system currently gives little attention to the nontraditional student (at least, relative to Sweden and the United States), and this potentially egalitarian program has little to do with parental support anyway. Furthermore, the total abolition or even the substantial reduction of the parents' obligation to support their children through higher education, while wonderfully simplifying and perhaps even egalitarian to some, would actually constitute an immediate and substantial transfer of income from current and prospective parents of students—overwhelmingly middle and upper-middle class, who are now supporting their children—to the general taxpayer and consumer. However, an easing of the means-testing of the *bourse*, and perhaps an expansion of the amount of the *bourse*, would at least target the transfer to the lowest-income parents—and would probably also have the greatest likelihood of inducing additional enrollment. Such an increase might even be paid for by raising fees or reducing some of the tax-deduction offsets that go now to the very wealthy. But an across-the-board reduction of the current parental share is not likely.

On the student side, many French students already work part time as much as is probably compatible with university studies. It would be possible to make the students' share more uniformly borne by the provision of a *generally available* and affordable loan program, which, in turn, would require either governmental capitalization or guarantees and probably some interest subsidy as well. Certainly, a generally available loan program would provide at least an opportunity for students who may now be discouraged from the very high expenses of, e.g., third-cycle or *Grandes Ecoles* studies, or from firstcycle studies as a resident in Paris, because of the inability of the parent to meet such expenses or because of the unwillingness of the students to impose such a burden on their parents.

The taxpayer burden is not likely to lighten, especially given the relatively low per-student cost of the universities themselves, compared to Northern European, or even to worldwide, standards. If anything, the taxpayer burden in France is likely to increase, both to improve the university operating budgets and to expand at least somewhat the *bourse* coverage, particularly if the recent governmental plans for enrollment increases are to be realized. At the same time, there is debate on the relative merits of direct aid (e.g., *bourse*) versus indirect aid (e.g., subsidized meals and tax relief). There have been mixed results from research into the relative efficacy of these two approaches, and the future debates are likely to continue on the most appropriate mix of taxpayer support in such forms as *bourse* and its possible expansion, the CROUS and their meal and lodging subsidies, the possibility of some modest tuitions as a supplement to direct institutional support, the continuation or modification of tax relief, and the possibility of a generally available, governmentally sponsored loan program.

5

SWEDEN

HIGHER EDUCATION IN SWEDEN[1]

Just as some of the policies and trends pertaining to student finance in Sweden can be better understood within a context of the overall enterprise of Swedish higher education, so can that overall enterprise be better understood when considered in light of some features of the nation as a whole. For example, Sweden may be characterized by its:

- small population (about 8,342,000 in 1984), especially relative to its large size (the fourth largest nation in Europe), making much of the country very sparsely populated and difficult to reach by "commutable" institutions of higher education;

- ethnic, religious, and cultural homogeneity, which does not rid Sweden of its share of the "disadvantaged" based on parents' social status and occupation, or, to a degree, on regional isolation, but makes Sweden freer than most countries from the additional complications of racial and ethnic disparities in setting policies with regard to, e.g., admissions criteria and student aid;

- political stability and a dominant sociopolitical ideology of democratic socialism, or "welfare-state capitalism," which manifests itself in the use of higher education as an instrument for the promotion of social mobility, equality, and economic growth

87

and in the imposition on universities, as on other institutions, of strenuous requirements for participatory governance;

- preference for social benefits for all, coupled with strongly progressive taxes on income and wealth, as opposed to programs of highly targeted welfare or assistance only to the very poor;

- strong central government, which enhances the authority of the Ministry of Education and which, in combination with the Social Democratic tradition, relative political stability, and highly advanced industrial and educational bases, elevates the role of planning in general, and manpower planning in particular, in the formation of higher education policy; and

- affluence, which, although by no means giving Sweden immunity from economic downturns or fiscal pressures on its public sector, has allowed an orderly and relatively well-financed expansion of the faculty and physical plant at the level of higher education and has kept Sweden thus far free from the most wrenching forms of downward adjustments or retrenchments that have affected higher education in the United States and the United Kingdom and that have seemed at least a potent threat in France and West Germany.

Lillemore Kim writes that: "Social equality as a goal has dominated in Sweden more than in most countries, [and] the originality of the Swedish approach to equality in higher education lies in its comprehensiveness and in the fact that the positions taken have been more radical than in other countries."[2] The most conspicuous targets of reform on behalf of greater equality in higher education in Sweden have been the nontraditional, mature student and females rather than, as in the United States, racial or ethnic minorities or the very poor. The general political and ideological stability—in spite of opposition parties, of course, and of several recent short periods of Center and Conservative government—has allowed Sweden to move very decisively and comprehensively in new directions, as in the higher education reforms of the mid-1970s, discussed below; but it has also made such changes on the whole slow to take form and very deliberate in execution, quite unlike either the United Kingdom or West Germany, where changes in governments have frequently lead to precipitous changes in governmental policies—or to paralyzing standoffs as, for example, in the issue of student loans in the United Kingdom.

Rune Premfors and Bertil Ostergren write that: "Among the industrialized nations of the West, Sweden has done the most in terms of organizing manpower planning."[3] The strong central government and the rational manpower approach to higher educational planning, although not nearly as dominant or as rigid as in the Socialist countries of Eastern Europe, has given a strong vocational orientation to higher educational development over the past two decades. In addition, the "manpower" orientation has buttressed a willingness to limit enrollments in Sweden in all of higher education beginning in 1979, as opposed to the years prior to that point when, as in West Germany and France, at least the university arts and science programs (i.e., the philosophical faculties of natural science, social science, and the humanities) were open to all graduates of the academic secondary school. Understandably, the juxtaposition of *numerus clausus* in all fields alongside a dominant goal of equality and expanded access, particularly for nontraditional students, has imposed a great burden on Swedish admission and aid policies.

U68 and the 1977 Reforms

Sweden, like most nations of the West, experienced in the 1970s a period of explosive growth in the demand for higher education coupled with equally great pressures for reform, which in Sweden sought to: (1) widen access to higher education, especially among nontraditional students; (2) diminish the status of the university vis-à-vis the nonuniversity sector; (3) diminish the authority of the senior professoriate vis-à-vis the authority of students, nonacademic employees, and publicly accountable officials; (4) inject more vocational relevance into the curriculum; (5) enhance efficiency and rational resource allocation; and (6) decentralize decision making. The major reforms were planned by a governmentally appointed commission that began in 1968 and that has been known by its acronym, U68. The principal changes recommended by U68, especially in admissions policies and in system-wide structure and governance, were finally enacted in the Higher Education Act of 1977. Among the major features of that act were:

1. The disestablishment of Sweden's former binary system, with a large, elite university component and a small, vocationally oriented, nonelite nonuniversity sector, and the formation of a unitary system of higher education, or *hogskola*, with a single structure for governance, admissions, planning, and budgeting in all units of higher education.

2. Ratification of an access experiment, begun in 1969, that established age and work experience as at least a partial alternative to academic credentials for admission to higher educa-

tion. This is the so-called 25/4 plan (originally 25/5) by which a certain quota of university places were held for those who met only minimal formal academic criteria but had attained the age of 25 and had at least four (originally five) years of work, military, or voluntary agency or club experience.

3. The establishment of six higher education regions, each anchored by a university, with at least some hoped-for decentralization of planning and decision making and an enhancement of services provided in the sparsely populated north.

4. The establishment of new governing units, including the Board of Directors of the National Board of Universities and Colleges, the national planning committees for undergraduate curricular areas, the regional boards, and the governing senates or councils of each insitution, each composed of a prescribed number of faculty, student, nonfaculty employee, and "public" representatives.

Structure and Governance

The Higher Education Act of 1977 established the unitary system, *hogskola*, with seven universities (including the University of Agricultural Sciences, under the Ministry of Agriculture); 28 other "university-type" institutions such as colleges of education and technology; and more than 30 additional schools and colleges, formerly of the nonuniversity sector, providing mainly nursing and paramedical studies, and administered locally.[4] The only private institutions of higher education in Sweden are the Stockholm School of Economics and a few schools of music and theological studies, all of which receive substantial public support.

Published figures on enrollments show 128,200 full-time equivalent undergraduates in 1982–83, with some 170,600 full- and part-time students enrolled in the fall of 1982, of whom 12,600 were postgraduate students.[5] Data for 1983–84 provided by the Central Study Assistance Committee show 195,200 full- and part-time registered undergraduates and 13,300 postgraduates.[6] Kim identified approximately 50,000 in the early 1980s as enrolled in those institutions that were formerly in the nonuniversity or nonacademic sector of tertiary education.[7] Sixty-two percent of all undergraduates in 1981 were 25 or older—a reflection of one of the major reform goals of the 1970s—but this percentage, while still very high compared to other nations, has fallen in recent years and was 58 percent in fall 1984.[8]

The governmental agency that directly supervises the higher educational system (with the exception of the Agricultural University) on behalf of the Cabinet is the National Board of Universities and Colleges (*Universitets-och Högskoleämbetet*, or UHÄ). The UHÄ is headed administratively by the Chancellor of the Swedish Universities and Colleges, who also chairs the Board of Directors, consisting of himself and 12 other members, most of them representatives of public interests rather than university or faculty interests directly.

The country has recently been divided into six regions, each with a board consisting largely of public (especially labor union) members and charged with planning and coordinating undergraduate higher education in the region—in ways not entirely clear as of 1985.

Governmental control of higher education, through UHÄ and its committees and extending ultimately to direct parliamentary action, reaches all the way to the curriculum (especially undergraduate) and the length of time for each of the 100 or so general undergraduate study programs, each of which can be revised by Parliament. These study programs are organized into five sectors, defined by the kinds of occupations or professions for which each program is appropriate: (1) technical; (2) administrative, economic, and social welfare; (3) medical and nursing; (4) teaching; and (5) cultural and informational. Planning for each of the five sectors is conducted by a committee of the UHÄ, and each committee is chaired by a member of the UHÄ board.

Admissions

The 25/4 principle was begun with several motives. By providing an alternative to formal academic secondary school credentials for admittance into the universities and other higher educational institutions, it encouraged further training that was of presumed benefit to the entire economy. It reduced intergenerational disparities in opportunity and educational attainment by giving a second chance to adults who passed through the system before the expansion of higher education, or whose family background had not been supportive of serious academic work in secondary school. It was, according to Kim, "primarily a way of modifying the social bias of academic achievement criteria."[9]

Admission was always restricted in the high-status advanced professional schools such as medicine, dentistry, and engineering by specific action of the government. Since 1979, enrollments in the other faculties have also been limited, although the principal form of governmental limitation to the liberal arts programs is through the provision of resources only according to an enrollment-planning target from which the individual institutions have some freedom to depart slightly, but which they have every incentive not to exceed by more than a little.

All admissions are handled centrally and totally impersonally, without contact between the institution and the applicant. Points are assigned for secondary school grades, attainment of 25/4 status, waiting time, and the like. From the start, a quota of places were set aside only for young people just out of academic secondary school with the highest grades. Some adjustments to the 1977 "25/4" policy (promoted especially by the periodic but short-lived conservative and center-coalition governments) have expanded this group and decreased the number of points to be gained from work experience or voluntary club activity alone. In addition, it is generally thought that the group of adults most ready to return to formal schooling and take advantage of the 25/4 opening have substantially already done so, and that the proportion of students admitted through this provision will level off at around the 1985 level of 7 percent of new university entrants.

For all the emphasis on access and equal opportunity in Sweden and the very real programs designed to further this goal, there remains a very high correlation between higher educational attainment and the socioeconomic status (SES) of the parents as measured by income, educational attainment, and occupational status. For example, of the 17- and 18-year-olds in 1980, using socioeconomic classes I (highest), II, and III (lowest), 65 percent of those in SES I were attending a three- or four-year *gymnasium* and preparing for the university, as compared to the 31 percent in SES II and only 18 percent in SES III. Twenty-five percent of the 17- and 18-year-olds in SES I were in nonuniversity, postsecondary higher education, compared to 51 percent of SES II and 53 percent of SES III. Only 10 percent of SES I youth were not in school, compared with 18 percent of SES II and 29 percent of SES III.[10]

The loss of participation from SES III youth occurs both at the point of entry into the academic secondary school track as well as at the point of transition from successful completion of academic secondary school to the university. Ruterberg and Svensson estimated that there were in 1983 only 13,000 17- and 18-year-olds from high socioeconomic status (SES I) families in all of Sweden, of whom 7,800, or 60 percent, could be expected to complete the *Gymnasium* with university entrance qualifications, and 5,400, or 69 percent, of the *Gymnasium* graduates and 42 percent of the original population who could be expected to start at a university. By contrast, of the 81,000 from the low socioeconomic-status families, only 16,200, or 20 percent, could be expected to complete the *Gymnasium* with university qualifications and only 8,900, or 55 percent, of the *Gymnasium* graduates and 11 percent of the original 81,000 could be expected to enter a university.[11]

SHARING THE COSTS AMONG PARENTS, TAXPAYERS, AND STUDENTS

Costs to the Student

There are no tuitions or fees to speak of in Sweden, so the expenses faced by the student and family are only the costs of living plus the costs of books, travel, and other expenses associated with study—as in France, Germany, and most of Europe. The major immediate difference between these costs in Sweden and the counterpart costs in France, Germany, the United Kingdom, or the United States is that the Swedish parent is not assumed to have any financial responsibility for them. Put another way, there is no official expected parental contribution in Sweden for the support of children in higher education. Although parents do help out (and some students claim that some parental assistance is unofficially expected by the Ministry, and may even be "forced," by what they claim to be inadequate state financial assistance), the official stance of the Ministry and of its Central Study Assistance Committee is that, in accord with Parliamentary policy, neither parental assistance nor student part-time work is expected or absolutely necessary in order to cover "adequate" maintenance costs, at least for the nine-month academic year. Thus, the total amount of the undergraduate "Study Means"—29,448 Skr [$3,926]* for 1984–85, and 31,627 Skr [$4,217] for 1985–86—which is mainly a student loan plus a small grant, can be taken as the official governmental estimate of students' academic-year maintenance costs.

The Central Study Assistance Committee (*Centrala Studiestödsnämnden*, or CSN), which is the agency of the Ministry responsible for all student financial assistance, acknowledges that even "minimum reasonable" expenses for nine months living away from home are greater than the available Study Means. A CSN-prepared budget for 1984–85, based on figures from the National Board for Consumer Policies, listed academic year expenses of 8,100 Skr [$1,080] for room, 14,400 Skr [$1,920] for board, and 11,250 Skr [$1,500] for all other expenses, for a total nine-month budget of 33,750 Skr [$4,500].[12] If

* All Swedish kronor (Skr) units in this chapter are followed by a U.S. dollar equivalent according to a 1985 purchasing-power ratio of 7.5 Skr = $1.00. See Appendix A.

TABLE 5.1
Cost to the Student, Sweden, Various Estimates for 1984–85 and 1985–86

	I Maximum Study Means (grant plus loan) for undergraduates[a]		II CSN estimated budget: living away from home[b]		III Estimated lower budget: living at home[c]		IV National Union of Students estimated budget: living away from home[d]	
	Skr	$	Skr	$	Skr	$	Skr	$
Tuition	—	—	0	0	0	0	0	0
Room and board	—	—	22,500	3,000	14,400	1,920	22,865	3,049
All other	—	—	11,250	1,500	11,250	1,500	11,092	1,479
Total 9 mos. 84–85	29,448	3,926	33,750	4,500	25,650	3,420	33,957	4,528
Est. 9 mos. 85–86[e]	31,627	4,217	36,885	4,918	28,033	3,738	37,111	4,948
Est. 12 mos. 85–86[f]	31,627	4,217	45,385	6,051	33,833	4,511	—	—

[a] These amounts are the maximum available; the grant portion is 2,178 Skr for both years; the loan is 27,270 Skr for 1984–85 and 29,448 Skr for 1985–86.

[b] Estimate from CSN, or *Centrala Studiestödsnämnden* (Central Study Assistance Committee), based on data from the National Board for Consumer Policies.

[c] Assume CSN "board" and "all other" budgets the same, but with no room cost.

[d] *Ekonomisk Budget för Ensamstående Högskolestuderande HT 1983*" (estimated budget for single student, Fall 1983) from the National Union of Students, presented to the author by incoming NSU President Thomas Persson, July 2, 1985; numbers increased 7.5 percent for 1984–85 as per Swedish retail price index.

[e] 1985–86 estimates are 8.5 percent above the 1984–85 figures. The full retail-price-index inflation is used because Swedish students have little parental or state-subsidized assistance to shield them from overall inflation.

[f] The 12-month estimates for the CSN and the estimated commuter budgets add 3 months of room and board and an additional 1,000 Skr of "all other costs" to the 9-month estimate; no 12-month estimate is attributed to the NUS.

TABLE 5.2
Study Means, Sweden, 1984–85 and 1985–86

Payable for 9-month academic year

	1984–85		1985–86	
	Skr	$	Skr	$
Grant portion	2,178	290	2,178	290
Loan portion	27,270	3,636	29,449	3,927
Total Study Means	29,448	3,926	31,627	4,217

Source: Central Study Assistance Committee (CSN).

the rise in Swedish prices of about 8.5 percent from 1984 to 1985 were to be fully reflected in the costs of student maintenance—and the Swedish student not living at home has little protection from the general retail price rise—a 1985–86 nine-month budget for the undergraduate student living away from home would be about 36,885 Skr [$4,918].

A commuter version of this budget, which omits only the 8,100 Skr [$1,080] estimated room costs, would be 25,650 Skr [$3,420] for 1984–85 and an estimated 28,033 Skr [$3,738] for 1985–86.

These estimates are very close to the budget prepared by the National Union of Students for 1983, which has been extrapolated to 1984–85 and 1985–86 by the Swedish retail price increases for these years: 7.5 percent and 8.5 percent respectively.[13] This budget, which we might assume to be more generous than "minimal," is, by extrapolation, 33,957 Skr [$4,528] for 1984–85 and 37,111 Skr [$4,948] for 1985–86. The unofficial CSN budget, the extrapolated CSN commuter budget, and the NUS budget are shown in Table 5.1 for both 9-month and 12-month periods, together with the 1984–85 and 1985–86 Study Means.

Study Means: Student-Borne Loans and Taxpayer-Borne Grants[14]

Each higher education student in good standing in Sweden is entitled to Study Means, which is a small grant and a much larger component of loan given to cover the student's cost of living for a nine-month study year. In 1984–85, the loan amount was 27,270 Skr [$3,636] and the grant amount, 2,178 Skr [$290], for a total Study Means of 29,448 Skr [$3,926]. In 1985–86, the grant component remained the same and the loan component increased to 29,449 Skr [$3,927] for a total of 31,627 Skr [$4,217] for the academic year for an unmarried undergraduate (see Table 5.2).

The Study Means program was begun in 1964 and implemented for the first time in 1965. At that time, the total Study Means was 7,000 Skr [$933] for a nine-month period, of which 1,750 Skr [$233], or 25 percent, was grant and the remaining 5,250 Skr [$700] was loan. Since that time, the grant component, which is raised only by the Parliament, has gone up a few times, but since 1980 it has remained at 2,178 Skr [$290], now down to 6.9 percent of the total. Since the total Study Means is indexed to inflation by the annual increase in the Swedish "base amount," which is a fundamental building block of Swedish pensions and benefits, this means that the total amount available to students has at least kept up with the cost of living in Sweden, although it has not increased in real terms at all, thus excluding students from a share of the real growth of the Swedish economy and, more importantly, the grant component, at about $290, has decreased to a nearly insignificant share.

Students must apply for the grant and loan combination. In 1983–84, there were 195,200 registered full- and part-time students. Of those, 118,000 received the grant portion of Study Means, with 15,500 of these taking only the grant portion and declining the loan. Of the 76,400 students who do not get grants, most are assumed to be either part-time and thus ineligible, had lost the right to Study Means because of unsatisfactory progress, were not eligible for Study Means by virtue of their own income, or were fortunate enough to be assured of support by their parents and thus not in need of a loan, and so did not even bother applying for the grant because it was so small.

The total amount paid out in 1983–84 was 210,000,000 Skr [$28,000,000] in grants, averaging 1,716 Skr [$229], and 2,559,000,000 Skr [$341,200,000] in loans, averaging 24,773 Skr [$3,303]. Of the 103,300 students receiving both a grant and a loan, between 13,000 and 14,000 had some reduction in this amount because of their own incomes.

In the application process, students request either the grant only or the grant plus the loan and then ask for either the maximum loan or some lesser amount. They must state their own income and assets in their application. Parental income is not taken into consideration at all in determination of Study Means;[15] neither is income of the spouse. (Income of the spouse is, however, relevant in connection with the ability to defer student debt repayment after graduation.)

The Study Means payout goes to students twice each semester. Their own declarations of income and assets are spot-checked, although income-tax forms do not need to be submitted along with the rest of the application. The Swedish information network on all citizens is apparently complete enough, and the population small enough (fewer than 200,000 registered students this year and only 550,000 students in the Study Means repayment stage for a program begun in 1965), that enforcement of accurate reporting seems not to be a major problem.

When students are first admitted to the university, they have a *right* to the Study Means, albeit with a possible reduction based on their own income and assets. After this, however, if students don't maintain satisfactory progress they can lose their Study Means, even though they may still remain in the university. "Satisfactory progress" is defined as 100 percent of normal progress in the medical fields, 75 percent in most open fields, and 67 percent in the engineering fields. Most undergraduate studies at the university level in Sweden take about three years, but they may range from two to six or seven years, with longer amounts for postgraduate doctoral study. The maximum duration of Study Means is six years, although it can be extended in exceptional circumstances. Approximately 5 percent of applicants are turned down because of lack of satisfactory progress, and CSN officials estimated that at least another 5 percent might know that their progress is unsatisfactory and therefore do not even apply.

The Study Means were reduced in 1984–85 by 50 percent of all of the student's own earnings in excess of 22,300 Skr [$2,973], increased to 23,980 Skr [$3,197] in 1985–86, and by 40 percent of all assets over 122,000 Skr [$16,267] in 1984–85, increased to 130,800 Skr [$17,440] in 1985–86. Fifteen percent of the total number of students have their Study Means reduced on the basis of their own income or assets.[16]

There are no child allowances or other tax advantages to families for having their children in universities. There is a special grant for families of those children who are still in upper-secondary school, even though they may be up to the age of 20, but this is because the family has responsibility for the child in Sweden through the upper-secondary level or to the age of 20, whichever comes first.

Indirect subsidies, such as those provided through the CROUS in France or the *Studentenwerke* in Germany, are very minimal in Sweden. There are student health clinics and a few special students services, but there is no subsidy to the student-run housing or food services.

Repayment Terms

Originally, the Study Means was expressed in terms of so many "pension units," sometimes called "base amounts"—the building block in Sweden for pensions and other benefits that need to have their nominal amounts in Kronor increased each year to maintain a constant real value. Prior to 1974, when the student completed studies, he or she would have accumulated so many pension units, or base amounts, of Study Means. Then as now, a portion of that total was considered a grant (25 percent in 1965 and a declining percentage ever since); the remainder had to be repaid over a period of years beginning the third year after completion of studies and extending, in most cases, through the year the student reaches the age of 50. The amount due each year was the total number of repayable pension units owed divided by the number of repayment years. The annual repayment obligation was thus some number or fraction of pension units, the dollar, or kronor, value of which depended on the value assigned to the pension unit in each particular repayment year. The effect was a loan that was interest free but that was linked to the cost-of-living-driven pension unit, so that the loan was paid back exactly in real terms of what had been borrowed.

This arrangement began to be criticized for several reasons, a major one being that the technical absence of an interest rate prevented students, many of whom were looking ahead to very high debts, from receiving the very lucrative tax deductibility of conventional interest, even though there was an effective interest rate equal to the rate of inflation. Therefore, a new rule was established in 1974 whereby a fixed adjustment index rate would be charged, serving as an effective, subsidized interest rate, although students would be guaranteed that they would receive the lower of that fixed adjustment index or, as in prior years, a rate based on the increase in consumer prices. That fixed rate in 1974 was 3.2 percent; it was raised in 1982 to 4.2 percent, where it stands in 1985–86.

Students pay 4.2 percent interest on their loans from the time of origination; there is, thus, no subsidy for the in-school years, although the interest is deferred during this period. At the end of study and a two-year grace period (during which interest continues to accumulate) the total amount borrowed, with accrued interest payments at 4.2 percent, is then normally divided by the number of years remaining through the student's fiftieth year (smaller debts are repaid more quickly) to determine the portion of principal to be repaid the first year. This first year's repayment is then increased by 4.2 percent each year, which provides a sloped repayment period rising at 4.2 percent per year but that also repays the loan at 4.2 percent interest.

There is a safety-net provision for the deferment of debts if the financial basis of the family falls below a fixed minimum, which in 1984 was 71,000 Skr [$9,467]—or 91,300 Skr [$12,173] if there are children under the age of 10. This financial basis includes one's own adjusted gross income, factors back in the tax advantage gained on the interest paid, and includes assets over 121,800 Skr [$16,240]. It also includes 40 percent of the spouse's earnings in excess of 20,000 Skr [$2,667], with that 40 percent rising as the spouse's income rises farther.

It is important to note that the repayment due that year, if the financial basis is low, is only deferred, not cancelled. Debts remaining after the age of 65 are, however, cancelled.

As an example of the repayment scheme, students graduating now who have had a normal Maximum Study Means loan will end up with a total amount borrowed of some 83,000 Skr [$11,081], which, with the accumulated interest, would lead to a debt at the initiation of repayment of 99,222 Skr [$13,230]. At that point, the first annual installment would be 4,961 Skr [$661], which amount would increase to 10,834 Skr [$1,445] in the twentieth year.

The True Loan and Effective Grant Components of Study Means

The loan portion of the Swedish Study Means is subsidized by virtue of its bearing a much lower rate of interest (4.2 percent) than money commands in Sweden's free market of commercial credit. The level of subsidy is clearly much less than in the German BAföG, which bears no interest rate at all, but is also clearly below the rate of interest even on risk-free investments. As explained in Appendix B, the "true loan" component of the Swedish Study Means can be thought of as the amount of debt that the actual repayment stream— that is, the approximately 20-year upward-sloping stream of payments returning 4.2 percent—would amortize at an appropriate discount rate, or a reasonable market-related rate of interest. The difference between this true loan principal, or the discounted present value of the repayment stream, and the actual principal amount borrowed is the "effective grant," or the present value of the stream of subsidies that keep the actual payments lower than they would have been at the market-related rate.

Table 5.3 shows the loan terms on 1,000 Skr of repayable Study Means and the present values of the repayment stream calculated with 8, 10, and 12 percent discount rates and assuming 20-year repayment periods. If 8 percent is an appropriate discount rate—that is, approximates what the unsubsidized rate of interest might be on the 1,000 Skr of student debt—then a 20-year repayment stream has a present value of only 594 Skr, or 59.4 percent of the loan, and a loan of 1,000 Skr carries an implicit grant of 406 Skr (1,000 – 594). If the discount rate should be higher, reflecting a higher true value of money and thus further diminishing the value of the subsidized re-

TABLE 5.3
Student Loan Terms and Present Value of Repayments on 1,000 Skr of Lending, Sweden

Initial loan (repayable portion of Study Means)	1,000 Skr
In-school period[a]	1.5 yrs
Grace period[b]	2.0 yrs
Interest rate, in-school and grace periods[c]	4.2%
Debt at beginning of repayment[d]	1,155 Skr
Interest rate in repayment[c]	4.2%
Repayment period[e]	end of grace period to age 51
Repayment mode[f]	graduated 4.2% rate of increase
Present value of repayments[g] { Discount rate 8%	594 Skr
Discount rate 10%	472 Skr
Discount rate 12%	380 Skr

[a] Period between origination of loan and end of schooling, assumed here to be 1.5 years for purpose of simplification and comparison.

[b] Period between end of schooling and beginning of first repayment period: two years.

[c] The "adjustment" index, or effective interest rate, is 4.2% or a rate based on the consumer price index, whichever is the lesser.

[d] Debt increases over in-school and grace periods by 4.2% compounded.

[e] Assuming studies ending at age 28, repayment beginning at age 31, and extending through age 50, for a 20-year repayment.

[f] The first year's payment, assuming a 20-year repayment, is 1/20 of total accumulated debt. This amount is increased at 4.2% annually, amortizing the debt in 20 years through payments graduated to approximate cost-of-living increases and thus to repay what was borrowed in approximate real kronor, effectively yielding a 4.2% rate of interest.

[g] See Appendix B.

payment stream, the present value, or true loan component, would be even smaller, and the effective grant component commensurately greater. At a 12-percent discount rate, for example, only 380 Skr of the original 1,000 Skr debt is true loan and 620 Skr represents an effective grant.

Costs Borne by the Student and the Taxpayer

With Swedish parents absolved from any official responsibility for their children's higher education expenses, the costs summarized in Table 5.1 are divided between the student and the taxpayer, with the parent at times assisting the student in meeting more-than-minimal expenses. The student's share in 1985–86 is reflected in:

- the true loan component of his or her repayable Study Means, calculated at a very conservative 8 percent discount rate at 594 Skr per 1,000 (Table 5.3), or 17,493 Skr [$2,332] on the 1985–86 repayable Study Means maximum entitlement of 29,449 Skr [$3,927], and

- term-time or vacation earnings up to 23,980 Skr [$3,197], which supplements the Study Means, as well as, for some students, additional earnings in excess of that amount, which reduce the Study Means entitlement 1 Skr for 2 Skr.

The taxpayer's share of the student's living expenses is reflected in:

- the grant portion of the Study Means, limited to 2,178 Skr [$290] for a normal nine-month academic year, and

- the effective grant component of the repayable Study Means, or the present value of the subsidies inherent in the terms of the loan—calculated, again, with a conservative 8 percent discount rate, at 406 Skr [$1,594] on the 29,449 Skr maximum repayable Study Means for 1985–86.

These shares are summarized in Table 5.4. The taxpayer's share is between 38 and 45 percent—in addition, of course, to the nearly 100 percent of the university's operating and capital costs. The share of the students is from 55 to 62 percent, depending both on their expenses and on what percentage, if any, of these expenses the parents are willing to assume, even while absolved of any official responsibility for the living and study costs of their children in higher education.

Trends, Issues, and Summary Observations

Like most European countries, but of course unlike the United States, the universities are public and "free"—that is, supported by the taxpayer and without tuitions or fees to students or families. Costs to students and families, then, are the costs of living, usually outside the parents' home, plus the costs of books, travel, and the like. Within this framework, the outstanding characteristics of the Swedish system of financial assistance are: (1) the absence of any officially expected parental contribution, that is, the financial independence of all students from their parents regardless of parental income and wealth,

TABLE 5.4

Sharing Higher Educational Living Expenses in Sweden among Parents, Students, and Taxpayers at Various Levels of Expense, 1985–86*

	Commuter budget, 9 months (28,033 Skr)		Low budget, 9 months: Full Study Means (31,627 Skr)		Moderate budget, 9 months (36,885 Skr)		High budget, 12 months (45,385 Skr)	
	Skr	$	Skr	$	Skr	$	Skr	$
Taxpayer-borne share of Study Means[a]	12,675	1,690	14,134	1,885	14,134	1,885	14,134	1,885
Student-borne share of Study Means[b]	15,358	2,048	17,493	2,332	17,493	2,332	17,493	2,332
Student earnings and/or parent-borne share of supplement	—	—	—	—	5,258	701	13,758	1,834
Total	28,033	3,738	31,627	4,217	36,885	4,918	45,385	6,051
Percent of total borne by taxpayer	45%		45%		38%		38%	
Percent of total borne by student or student/parent	55%		55%		62%		62%	

*Expense budgets taken from Table 5.1

[a] Taxpayer-borne share is the grant portion of Study Means, or 2,178 Skr, plus the effective grant portion of the repayable amount at an 8 percent discount rate, or 40.6 percent of the principal owed.

[b] The student-borne share is the true loan portion of the repayable grant, or 59.4 percent of the principal owed, assuming an 8 percent discount rate.

and (2) the heavy reliance on the students themselves, via moderately subsidized loans, to bear the expenses of student living. Among characteristics of lesser note, but still of significance, are (3) the inclusion of the great majority of students within the Study Means system (as opposed, e.g., to France, where the principal system, the *bourse*, involves only a small minority of students); (4) the essentially unitary nature of the system, without differentiation as to age or university status or commuting versus residential status; and (5) the financial independence from the spouse as well as from the parents in the determination of need for study means.

The Absence of an Expected Parental Contribution. An officially expected parental contribution has significance primarily as it reduces, or is offset against, what the student would otherwise get from the government (taxpayer) in the absence of the parental contribution. In practical terms, it reduces or eliminates taxpayer-borne aid to children of the well-off and instead targets available public resources to children of the supposedly needy. Means-tested, or need-based, aid as practiced in the United States, the United Kingdom, West Germany, and France is thought to (1) use public resources more cost effectively, on the assumption that the assistance makes a difference (i.e., generates new enrollment) among the poor and would make little or no such difference to the children of the affluent, who would almost certainly attend anyway; (2) provide another form of transfer payment to the poor, or at least to the poor who are fortunate enough to have children otherwise willing and able to attend the university; and (3) minimize the allegedly perverse transfer of wealth from the poor, who continue to pay taxes, but whose children are not so likely to benefit from the university, to the well-off, who pay not so very much more in taxes, but whose children are vastly more likely to continue in higher education.

Clearly, these supposedly egalitarian arguments in favor of targeting public student assistance at the poor and of continuing to expect parental contributions to the higher education expenses of their children carry little weight in Sweden, which is arguably the most self-consciously egalitarian nation in Western Europe. One answer to this apparent anomaly is that there must in fact be parental contributions, at least from those most able to help their children, in the form of in-kind provision of room and board to those who commute from home and in the form of cash to those students who are thus able to live at a higher standard of living. Another answer, although a bit tautological, is the previously mentioned Swedish preference for general social benefits and the concomitant distaste for benefits that require, any more than is necessary, the affixing of a "needy" label on any individual or family.

A similar and related reason for the disinclination in Sweden to tap parents for support of their children's higher education expenses is the generally flat distribution of Swedish salaries. The argument that students and parents should pay all because of the great monetary returns to higher education does not stand up to the facts of Swedish salary differentials. Similarly, the fact that the assistance given is overwhelmingly in the form of loans lessens both the burden on the taxpayer and the force of the argument that the "poor taxpayer" is subsidizing the middle- and upper-class student.

Finally, the most powerful argument in the United States or the United Kingdom in favor of preserving the principle of parental financial responsibility for at least some of the costs of their children's higher education (despite large and growing technical problems in enforcing this principle) is that the *abandonment* of the expected parental contribution would cause a sudden, substantial new burden on the general taxpayer, matched by an equally sudden and substantial effective tax relief flowing overwhelmingly to the middle and high socioeconomic classes. What makes the United States and other countries hold so fast to the principle of parental financial responsibility is not so much the inherent sanctity of that principle as it is the very great problem of abandoning it once it is in place. Thus Sweden, which has achieved a very considerable measure of socioeconomic equality through years of welfare measures, strong unions, and high taxes on income and wealth, does not need to *add* a new progressive measure in the form of a means-tested expected parental contribution and does not fear the loss of the parental responsibility principle, because it has been without it for many years. In summary, there does not seem to be any strong pressure in Sweden in the mid-1980s for shifting costs from either students or taxpayers onto parents.

The Extent of Student Debt. There is concern in Sweden about the large and rapidly growing level of student indebtedness.[17] The maximum annual borrowing in 1985–86 is 29,449 Skr [$3,927], and the past governmental practice of holding the grant portion of the Study Means constant, making the loan portion absorb the full brunt of inflation, threatens to continue to increase annual debt loads at a rate even faster than the prevailing rate of increases in costs and prices. At the start of 1985, there were 276,557 borrowers who had not yet entered into their repayment period, with average debts already of 42,860 Skr [$5,715].[18] Since many of these are still accumulating debt, the eventual final debt loads of these students currently still in the borrowing pipeline can be very substantial. Table 5.5 shows the levels of aggregate indebtedness of those expected to begin repayment in 1985. Thirty-five percent are beginning repayment with

TABLE 5.5
Levels of Indebtedness of Former Students Beginning Repayments in 1985

Level of indebtedness at beginning of repayment		No. of borrowers	Percentage of total	Cumulative percentage of total
Skr	*$*			
above 80,000	above 10,666	9,141	13%	13%
30,000–79,999	4,000–10,665	24,343	35	48
20,000–29,999	2,666–3,999	10,989	15.5	63.5
10,000–19,999	1,333–2,665	13,674	19.5	83
below 10,000	below 1,333	11,894	17	100
		70,041		

Source: "Studiestöd 1983/84," *Statistika Meddelanden*, 6 December 1985, Table 11.3, p. 63.

debts in excess of 30,000 Skr [$4,000], and 13 percent with debts in excess of 80,000 Skr [$10,666]. If a student entering the university in 1985 takes the maximum available Study Means loan of 29,449 Skr [$3,927] each year for four years and waits the normal two additional years before beginning repayment, all the while having interest compound at 4.2 percent annually, he or she will face an accumulated debt in 1991 of 140,715 Skr [$18,762]—a substantial loan in a country without great premium take-home salaries for university graduates.[19]

So far, defaults are very low: only about 2 percent. And concern about debt loads, *per se*, does not seem to be high on the list of priority concerns of the Swedish National Union of Students. At the same time, the maximum debt loads in Sweden are steep, even by U.S. standards for undergraduates, and are especially so by European standards; and there is also some concern (as yet without substantiating data) that the fear of high debts may be a disincentive to children of the poor, who, it is alleged, come out of a socioeconomic culture that resents and fears indebtedness. Stabilizing or actually reducing mounting debt loads, however, in the absence of the parent as a significant sharer of costs, will require an increase in the governmental share, either directly, through a larger proportion of Study Means given in the form of a grant rather than a loan, or indirectly, through more subsidization of the loans—e.g., making them interest free during the in-school years and grace period or reducing the rate of interest even below the current low 4.2 percent.

The Students' Agenda. The Swedish National Union of Students, or SFS (*Sveriges Förenade Studentkärer*), has at least five distinct goals with regard to the Study Means program, the first two having very significant resource implications and the other three having less major resource significance but carrying very important public policy significance. This agenda, as communicated to the author, is:[20]

1. Increase Study Means from its current level of 140 percent of the base amount to 200 percent of the base amount—that is, from 31,627 Skr [$4,217] to just over 45,000 Skr [$6,025].

2. Restore the grant portion of Study Means to its original 25 percent—which, in combination with goal 1, would yield a grant of 11,295 Skr [$1,506], or an approximately five-fold increase.

3. Prohibit the treatment of Study Means as income for the purpose of denying students means-tested social welfare benefits to which they would otherwise be entitled.

4. Increase the "free amount" of the students' own income (22,300 Skr [$2,973] in 1985–86) before beginning the reduction of allowable Study Means.

5. Defer loan repayments on the basis of the student borrower's own (low) income only, rather than, as currently, on the basis of the (low) income of the borrower and spouse family unit.

The first of the five—an increase in the total available Study Means—is not totally out of line with the unofficial government agenda, which seems to be cautiously in favor of some increase (not, however, to 200 percent of the base amount), but mainly for those students in greatest need (e.g., older students or those who must live away from home). The combination of the Student Union's first two goals has a very high price tag and is unlikely to be realized in Sweden's current (1985) political and fiscal climate.

Goal 3—treating Study Means as the loan it predominantly is rather than as income, which it clearly is not—seems on the surface to be only reasonable. However, access to income-supplement welfare programs that have been designed for the unemployed or the very poor—in addition to the grant and loan programs that have been designed to provide access to higher education—would conflict with the general policy of most governments, which is to assist students enough to remove the lack of money as a financial barrier to higher education but not to confuse the nature and financial problems of student life with those of poverty or unemployment. Furthermore, the policy of absolving even the wealthiest parents from any officially expected parental contribution makes it less likely that the Swedish Government would give the children of the wealthy who happen to be attending the university (and thus perforce "unemployed" and even, in a sense, "poor") access to the full range of welfare benefits that have been created to solve other problems.

The students' fourth goal—increasing the amount of money they can earn without having their Study Means reduced—is an excellent example of the rationing issue in student financial assistance. To the extent that student assistance is (1) a simple transfer of resources from taxpayers to students and (2) for the purpose of allowing or inducing university attendance, then needs testing is logical and even neces- ′ sary, and the assistance should be cut back as other resources become available. However, to the extent that the assistance is not just a simple transfer from taxpayer to student but is, at least in part, a loan, the burden of which is borne in substantial measure by the student, the need to ration the assistance is diminished. The fact that the Swedish Study Means is mainly a loan—with a subsidy, or an effective grant, to be sure, but still approximately one-half true loan—would seem to lessen the need for rationing it or for reducing the allowable Study Means as the student's own earned income rises beyond the current "free amount" of 22,300 Skr [$2,973]. Swedish student-assistance policy could, for example, treat the decisions to work and thus to earn income and to take Study Means and thus to assume debt as two independent decisions, each to be made by the student alone on the basis of his or her preferences: on the one hand, for extra (earned) income as opposed to more leisure time or more time for study, and on the other hand for extra (borrowed) income as opposed to less debt to be repaid later in life.

The Swedish Study Means, of course, is both grant, meaning the direct grant of 2,178 Skr [$290] plus the effective grant of approximately 50 percent of the loan inherent in the subsidized interest rate, and true loan. This may account for the ambivalence of governmental policy and the partial rationing of Study Means through the reduction in allowable amounts as own earnings rise beyond the current free-income limit. (This is not unlike the ambivalence in U.S. student loan policy that has led to such violent swings in the rationing of Guaranteed Student Loans according to the parents' income and the students' need.) In Sweden, a large increase in the students' free earnings limit seems unlikely as long as the Study Means is viewed primarily as a public expenditure that needs to be rationed. If, on the other hand, the grant and loan components were to be made more distinct and the latter less subsidized, the case for rationing might diminish further and the free earnings limit be raised according to the agenda of the National Student Union.

The Union's wish to defer and ultimately to forgive repayments on the basis of the student borrower's own income only is another example of an issue arising from the confusion between a grant and a loan. Present policy in Sweden is to defer and ultimately, if necessary, to forgive repayments when repayment would cause real hardship. In order to receive public assistance, which has been designed avowedly for those on the edge of hardship, it is generally thought legitimate to require demonstration of need or hardship. "Need" and "hardship" are, in turn, generally taken to be a function of the income (and sometimes also of the assets) of the individual and his or her spouse. If one member of the couple, generally the wife, chooses to withdraw for some time from the work force and to concentrate on child-rearing and/or other noncash-earning activities, that individual is not, for that reason only, automatically considered "poor" and entitled to public assistance. Such entitlement is considered to be a function of *family* needs and *family* earning power.

Sweden and the other Scandinavian countries have already established that one spouse's entitlement to Study Means is a function of his or her income and assets only, regardless of the income and assets of the spouse. In its most common practical application, this means that Study Means is just as available to the nonworking wife of a prosperous man as it is to a single nonworking man or woman or to the wife of an unemployed or nonprosperous man. This policy emerged from the women's movement of 1970s and is a public policy landmark in the quest for women's financial independence from their spouses: A woman in Sweden is thus assured of the means to return to school without having to rely on the permission or generosity of her husband.

From one perspective, then, the granting of debt forgiveness on the basis of own (low) income only could be seen merely as an extension of the granting of Study Means itself on the basis of own income or need only. As a practical matter, it would allow one spouse—clearly most often the woman, although not necessarily always—to escape repayment altogether if that spouse were not employed over the full repayment period of the loan. From another perspective, however, such a policy could be viewed as a substantial public (taxpayer) expenditure flowing overwhelmingly, albeit not exclusively, to families affluent enough to permit the wife the option of not having to be employed and yet advancing neither the goal of expanding educational opportunities nor that of promoting the greater freedom of women's choices by the simple fact that the education has already been partaken of. It is not clear, as of this writing, where the Government stands on the issue. What *is* clear, once again, is the complication and ambivalence arising out of the blurring on the one hand of a *grant*, which is a transfer of taxpayer's resources to the recipient, presumably on behalf of some public goal that would not be achieved in the absence of the transfer, and on the other hand of a *loan*, which, at least in its true (i.e., unsubsidized) form, is merely a voluntary shift of resource use from the future to the present, at whatever price is required to induce someone else to make a trade and to shift resource use from the present to the future.

The Government's Agenda. The Swedish Government has formed a national committee to overview the Study Means system. The ground rules are (1) "in principle" no new resources for the system, such that any proposed new expenses for one phase should be covered with proposed reduced expenses for another, and (2) a reaffirmation of the principal goal of Study Means, which is to extend higher educational opportunities to all groups. The committee, to begin in the fall of 1985, is to consider such possible changes as:[21]

- a differentiation of assistance according to living situations, e.g., a higher Study Means for the student living away from home;

- the trade-off between direct grants and effective grants through the level of subsidy in the loan plan;

- ways of lightening repayment burdens for borrowers with special needs; and

- "off-budget" ways of financing the loan component of Study Means.

The Student Union has adamantly opposed any differentiation among groups of students in the amount of Study Means to which they are entitled, presumably out of its fear of creating "advantaged" and "disadvantaged" classes of students and its reluctance to let government solve the problem of demonstrably inadequate resources for some (e.g., adult students) by taking something away from others (e.g., first-year commuting students). Returning to the rationing theme discussed above, it is almost certainly true that some students *need* more resources than others, and if the principal aim of Study Means is to make university attendance possible, presumably at or near the lowest possible cost to the taxpayer, then it follows that some students should receive more than others and that none should receive more than he or she needs. At the same time, "need" is not just an exogenous variable, to be inserted into a formula for the determination of the students' award. Rather, it is to a very considerable degree a function of the students' own choices and preferences. Thus, for example, should a student be rewarded for the additional need he or she may incur by choosing to go to a faraway university where in-kind help from parents is impossible, rather than to a nearby one, where commuting from home and all the commensurate cost savings are possible? Or, to take the opposite case, should a student be penalized for choosing to economize by living, taking meals, and doing laundry at home, thus paring down his or her absolute, minimal need? Or, as discussed earlier, should a student's decision to work and to be partially self-supporting be affected by the threat of a loss of assistance, that is, by a very high tax rate on the kronor earned?

As a general policy, it is easier to discriminate on the basis of some measurement of need when there is nothing the student can do to affect the measurement anyway, thus minimizing the chance of unintended incentives or distorted behavior. For example, greater need might be assumed, and more substantial assistance given, on account of criteria such as age or commuting distance from the nearest university, neither of which is easy for the student to alter. Also, as mentioned earlier, discrimination in the amount of assistance given is easier when the award is a clear case of a transfer from taxpayer to student, in which case either cost-effectiveness or fairness can justify a needs-based differentiation, than when the award is a loan, in which case the differentiation must also take into account the student's time preference for money and willingness to bear the debt and pay the interest. In short, some differentiation in award according to situation and need may well be coming and will appear as increased grants only for those in situations associated with greatest need.

The blurring of the distinction between loans and grants may be exacerbated in Sweden by 100 percent "on-budget" financing. That is, the full amount of all Study Means to be awarded in a given year is included in the government's current operating budget for that year as though it were all just like any other governmental expense, without the recognition that at least the true loan portion is much more properly viewed as a governmental investment and an asset. The inclusion of the full amount of repayable Study Means on the government's operating budget, without a clear offset to reflect the present value of anticipated repayments, overstates the cost to the taxpayer of the Study Means program, inflates the government's operating budget, and contributes to the view of Study Means as a grant that needs to be rationed rather than as a loan, the demand for which might find its own level in the exchange of time preferences between borrowers and lenders.

The U.S. Guaranteed Student Loan Program displays exactly the opposite phenomenon. Its capital is provided mainly through the private capital market, primarily banks, with the taxpayer obligation being an interest subsidy (the difference between the rate paid by the student borrower and the market rate received by the lender) and the guarantee (the total amount owed paid by the government to the lender in the event of default). By not budgeting the subsidies or guarantees until they become due, the U.S. Government can incur very large obligations in the form of future guarantee and subsidy commitments that are not reflected in the budget in the year they are incurred.

It can rightly be said that this issue is more one of appearance and accounting practice than it is of reality. But the Swedish practice of including all the Study Means in the budget as though it were an operating expense overstates the true cost to the taxpayer, just as the U.S. policy can understate it. The just-formed Overview Committee in Sweden can be expected to examine this issue and to consider ways, including private lending guarantees or anticipated repayment offsets, to reflect more accurately the cost of Study Means to the Swedish taxpayers—and perforce to the student borrower.

THE
UNITED STATES

HIGHER EDUCATION IN THE UNITED STATES

Higher education in the United States differs from its counterpart institutions and systems in Europe in a number of ways that are particularly germane to higher educational finance and the sharing of costs among parents, students, and taxpayers. The principal differences, constituting, in essence, the defining characteristics of American higher education in the mid-1980s, are: (1) its enormous size; (2) egalitarianism and the resulting diversity (e.g., in academic preparedness and socioeconomic status) of the student population; (3) a strong and diverse private sector; (4) the absence of a national ministry and the consequent relegation of all coordination and regulation to the states and to voluntary associations; (5) a revenue base that relies relatively less on the taxpayer and relatively more on students, parents, and philanthropists; and (6) aggressive marketing and price competition. This section will portray higher education in the United States by elaborating on each of these six points of difference.

The Size of the Enterprise

The enormity of the higher educational enterprise in the United States is more than a function of the nation's large size and considerable wealth. U.S. higher education is large not only in sheer numbers of students and institutions, but also in the proportion of youth going on to college, in the extent of part-time and nontraditional participation, in the size of its very large universities and the number of its very small colleges, in the cost per student, in research support per faculty member, and even in the proportion of GNP consumed by the enterprise. American higher education in 1985–86, for example, includes:

- an estimated 12,247,000 students;[1]

- 3,330 institutions (1,497 public and 1,833 private or independent);[2]

- 694,000 faculty (454,000 full-time);[3]

- $9.6 billion in campus-based research, more than 75 percent of which is sponsored;[4]

- more than $100 billion in total expenditures, counting institutional operating budgets and the costs of student maintenance;[5]

- approximately $18 billion in grants, loans, and work-study assistance from governmental and institutional sources to help students and parents (particularly low- and middle-income) meet the expenses of tuitions and student living costs;[6] and

- 63 percent of 1980 high school graduates in college by the spring of 1982;[7] 32 percent of all American adults in 1981 claiming to have had some college and 22 percent claiming to have degrees.[8]

Egalitarianism and Diversity of the Student Body

Probably no national character trait so epitomizes the United States as the belief in both the possibility and the desirability of bettering the socioeconomic station into which one was born. By hard work, right living, *and education,* it is believed that every American can and should make the very most of his or her natural abilities. Education, including college and even graduate school, is not just for the brilliant, but is, in some fashion at least, for nearly everyone. Education in the United States is thought to be the great engine of both social mobility and economic growth as well as the major cure for the ills of poverty, structural unemployment, idle youth, and mid-career boredom. It is considered a sound investment, even for its great cost, both for society (i.e., the taxpayer) and for the individual student and his or her family.[9]

There remains in the United States, as in all countries, an association between the socioeconomic status of the family and the higher educational participation of children as measured by entrance rates, completion rates, probability of postbaccalaureate study, and prestige of college attended. Young people from low socioeconomic backgrounds—which includes a large proportion of black, Hispanic, and Native American youth—are less likely to complete high school, and those who do are less likely to enter a four-year college, to graduate, or to go on to graduate study. Nevertheless, these associations are less pronounced than in most, if not all other, countries, if only because of the very great proportion of youth from all socioeconomic strata who finish secondary school with at least some college-preparatory work and the great percentage of those who go on to some form of higher education.[10]

Some part of American higher education is within reach of nearly anyone with a modicum of learning ability and enough interest to sign up for a course or two, perhaps in the evenings or on weekends only, with or without academic credit, related or unrelated to career aspiration. In fact, the idea of limiting the number of students to some governmentally predicted number of future openings in a certain kind of job is anathema to most Americans: better to give people a chance to win the available jobs, to create new jobs and opportunities unforeseeable by yesterday's manpower planners, or at the very worst to take a job for which they are educationally overqualified, with the satisfaction of the college education anyway, and with the enhanced ability to forge a new career sometime in the future.

Thus, there exists in American higher education the almost perpetual "second chance": the ability to try again, perhaps at a different and less rigorous college, in the event of failure. Similarly, there exists almost complete horizontal mobility, that is, the ability to transfer into a new academic field, even one so rigorous as medicine or law, at almost any point in an academic track, even from a totally unrelated field of study and with usually no more than some loss of time and academic credit.

With this great openness, accessibility, and mobility, of course, comes a great diversity in traditional academic preparedness and motivation. The United States has students in some colleges and even in some graduate schools who would not be admitted to, and probably would not succeed in, even the less selective institutions in most European higher education sectors. Academic failure and dropout rates among such students are high, and they tend to be found disproportionately in the least selective institutions, in the most vocational programs, and in the two-year programs. But America's egalitarian ethic and its great faith in education, coupled with special programs to enhance college-going among minorities and motivated by the financial need to maintain enrollments, combine to encourage students with a very wide range of abilities to try to find a place in American higher education.

The Importance of the Private (Independent) Sector

In the 1985–86 academic year some 1,833 colleges and universities, or nearly 50 percent of the total number in the United States, educating some 2,656,000 students, or just under 22 percent of the total fall 1985 enrollment, comprise that sector designated "private" or "independent." But the importance of this sector to American higher education is even greater than these statistics indicate. Many of the top-ranked research universities and nearly all of the most selective liberal arts colleges are private, and a disproportionate number of the nation's leading business executives, physicians, lawyers, and political and governmental leaders have come out of private higher education and have worked to keep the sector basically strong through charitable donations and public subsidies.

Although there is a relatively small but robust subsector of private proprietary, or for-profit, colleges and institutes, the term "private college" generally means a not-for-profit corporation, chartered under applicable state and federal laws and controlled by its trustees. The trustees are usually prominent alumni or other prominent citizens (often clergy in the case of a church-affiliated college), who serve without pay and who maintain fiduciary custody over the assets of the institution, select a president as chief executive officer to run the college, give and raise money, and select their successors according to the by-laws of the corporation. (Many such institutions prefer the designation "independent" to "private," in part out of a fear that the latter designation mistakenly suggests elitism and the absence of public accountability, and in part out of recognition that they, too, have become heavily reliant on taxpayer-borne subsidies as well as subject to a host of state and federal regulations that have blurred very substantially the difference between "private" and "public.")

The most significant characteristic of the private sector to this study is its dependence on tuition for nearly all the institution's basic operating expenses that cannot be met by endowment earnings, current annual giving, and, in a few states, unrestricted governmental grants for operating expenses. This does not, however, mean that tuition is lower in colleges with larger endowments and better fund-raising capability. Tuition, rather, is set more nearly according to what the market will bear, with the more prestigious colleges, generally also the more heavily endowed, usually able to charge higher tuition as well as to spend more nontuition revenue.[11] Thus, tuition in 1985–86 can range from $4,500 at a relatively low-cost, nonselective regional private college, which amount may also constitute 90 percent or more of the per-student instructional costs, to $10,000 or more at a prestigious college like Harvard or Stanford, which sum may also be supplemented by at least as much endowment income and current giving, reflecting actual per-student instructional costs of $20,000 or more.

At the same time, the very extensive financial aid available to students in the private sector, from both philanthropic and taxpayer sources, makes it impossible to determine who or what is actually bearing the cost from the figures on tuition alone. Grants from the state and federal government, both to the student directly and at times to the institution on the student's behalf, combined with the institution's own funds, either from endowment or current operations, can bring what at first glance may look to be the absolutely insurmountable cost of a private-college education down to within reach of some students from very low-income families.

Thus, the United States at both the state and federal levels has made public policy decisions to support financially the large and very diverse private/independent sector, not for the most part by direct institutional grants (as per the university grants in the United Kingdom, for example), but by grants to students on the basis of financial need, allowing (or forcing) such institutions to set a tuition rate high enough to bring in sufficient revenue but with the assurance that needy students will get some assistance in meeting these tuitions as well as room, board, and other expenses.

Decentralization and Autonomy

Education in the United States, insofar as government is involved, is reserved by the U.S. Constitution to the 50 states. Thus, with only a few exceptions such as the armed-services academies, the 1,500 public colleges and universities educating almost 9,600,000 students are owned and operated by the states, by municipalities under state regulations, or by special state-chartered public-benefit corporations. Furthermore, even at the state level, the existence of a large private sector, whose curriculums and degree standards are very nearly beyond governmental reach anyway, coupled with the traditions of lay boards of trustees, strong presidential offices, and a general political preference for decentralized government, have combined to assure that governmental control of higher education in the United States from any level of government is minimal by the standards of Europe or, for that matter, of most of the rest of the world.

This is not to say that the federal government is unimportant to higher education in the United States. Its importance, however, is overwhelmingly in the provision of financial support to students, including grants, loans, and work-study subsidies, and in the support of basic research, mainly to the top 100 or so research universities. Although there is now a cabinet-level Department of Education, the principal leverage it has over the nation's 3,330 colleges and universities is its ability to win sufficient congressional appropriations to maintain (and desirably, to increase) the federal student-assistance funds of approximately $8 billion. The significance to this study is that budgets, tuitions, grants, and nearly all the other basic ingredients that go into the cost of higher education and their impact on students and families, as well as many of the policies and programs of student financial assistance, are set by states, by individual institutions, by independent voluntary associations such as the College Scholarship Service of the College Board, and of course to some degree by the forces of supply and demand rather than by any central authority, as is the case in the European nations within this comparative study.

Use of Other-Than-Taxpayer Sources of Revenue

Compared to the other nations in this study, and probably to all other nations in the world, U.S. colleges and universities rely on more diverse sources of revenue and especially on more nongovernmental (or nontaxpayer) sources. Parents contribute very heavily at high income levels, although less than their French or German counterparts at low levels of income. Students contribute substantially, through both summer and term-time work and through borrowing. Philanthropy, from alumni, foundations, corporations, and friends, is a significant source of revenue to the private sector and increasingly to the public sector. Finally, businesses, sometimes through collective-bargaining agreements, are becoming a potentially significant "bearer of costs" for their own employees in further, or continuing, education and sometimes in undergraduate and graduate degree-oriented education as well.

Aggressive Marketing and Price Discounting

All U.S. colleges and universities are financially dependent on enrollments: private colleges because enrollments bring tuition revenue, and public colleges because enrollments drive their state budget formulas. The immediate financial threat is the sharp decline in the number of 18–22-year-olds—the traditional college-going age cohort—that began in 1978 and that will extend at least through the mid 1990s, ultimately reducing this traditional cohort by some 25 percent. This loss will exceed 40 percent in the Northeast, where the effects of declining birth rates in the 1960s are exacerbated by population out-migration in the 1970s and 1980s.[12]

Most industrialized nations are experiencing the same demographic phenomenon. What makes the downturn especially frightening to many U.S. colleges and universities is that this market may already be nearly saturated: that is, nearly all the young people who have the academic aptitude and interests appropriate at least to the more traditional, selective colleges are already college bound. Adult and part-time students have taken up much of the slack at many colleges; but this pool, too, certainly has a saturation point, even if that point is not yet known. To make matters even worse, the demand for the "bread-and-butter" traditional four-year liberal arts education has been softening for some time, quite apart from the diminution in the number of potential students. In short, most enrollment projections call for a decline in the number of students at U.S. colleges and universities and a very substantial decline at institutions that have little depth in their applicant pools, little access to adult and part-time students, and limited competitive advantage vis-à-vis other providers.

A nearly universal response to these pressures has been enhanced attention to marketing: research into the wants and preferences of potential students and of those, such as parents and school guidance counselors, who influence them; attractive college recruiting publications; radio, TV, and newspaper advertising; direct mail; and price discounting. Private institutions with high tuitions have always discounted their price via financial aid for those able students with demonstrated need—that is, whose parents are unable to cover the full costs—but have discouraged price cutting for marketing purposes only. By the mid-1980s, with enrollments beginning to turn down, with excess capacity driving the marginal cost of another student to the college down near zero, and with a burgeoning "excellence movement" craving symbols and gestures for the very able, the old college cartel is weakening, and price warfare seems imminent.

SHARING THE COSTS AMONG PARENTS, TAXPAYERS, STUDENTS, AND INSTITUTIONS/PHILANTHROPISTS

Costs to the Student and Family

Costs to the student and family in the United States vary principally by the magnitude of tuition and fees, which can range from a few hundred dollars at some public colleges to upwards of $10,000 at high-priced, selective private institutions. The variation in tuition and fee charges is almost as great among the institutions wholly within the private sector, with 6 percent of four-year private colleges reporting tuitions of less than $2,500, 44.3 percent less than $5,000, and nearly 4 percent more than $10,000.[13]

The other major source of variation is the difference between commuter and resident costs of room and board, which may be from as low as $1,000–$1,100 "out-of-pocket" to the family for a student living at home to well over $3,000 for a college residence with a complete meal plan, to far higher amounts for independent students, older students, and students supported more generously by their parents.

College costs for U.S. undergraduates are generally presented for the nine-month academic year only; most students still return home to live with parents for the three-month summer break. Adults and independent youths attending college must, of course, meet living expenses for summers and vacations, generally through summer employment.

A range of nine-month costs for 1985–86 is presented in Table 6.1, extending from costs for a low-cost public college in a commuting situation ($3,150), to the average costs of attending a public ($5,314) or a private institution ($9,659), to a high-cost example typified by an Ivy League college at $15,000.

The Parental Contribution

The U.S. system begins with an assumption of parental responsibility for meeting a portion of the costs of higher education, at least through the undergraduate years or until the child has left the house and become financially independent. The expected parental contribution is determined primarily by the family income, of course, but

TABLE 6.1
Cost Facing Undergraduate Students and Families, Nine Months, United States, 1985–86

	Low-cost public (commuter)	Average public (resident)	Average private (resident)	High-cost private (resident)
Tuition and fees	$ 800	$1,242	$5,418	$10,000
Room and board	1,030	2,473	2,781	3,400
All other	1,320	1,599	1,460	1,600
Total	$3,150	$5,314	$9,659	$15,000

Average public and private costs are from actual survey data as reported in the *The College Board News*, Fall 1985; also in *The Chronicle of Higher Education*, vol. 30, no. 24, 14 August 1985, p. 1.

The low-cost public commuter budget is based on the commuting students' "option two" expense estimate guideline for 1985–86 from the College Scholarship Service. The room-and-board estimate is for "at-home" costs only. See *CSS Need Analysis: Theory and Computation Procedures for the 1985–86 FAF* (New York: The College Board, 1984), pp. 52–53.

The high-cost private resident budget was drawn from catalogs of selective private colleges. Total costs at such institutions reach $17,000 for the highest-cost undergraduate institutions.

also includes an expected contribution from some portion of assets, including home equity. Special considerations that diminish the ability of a family to contribute to the costs of college and that are not immediately controllable by the family—such as number of dependent children and their educational expenses, if any, unusually high medical and dental bills, and taxes—as well as the ages of the parents and the number of parents working are factored into the calculation of the expected parental contribution.[14]

The expected contributions from a two-parent family with one child in college and another not yet of college age, with no net assets and no unusual expenses, is shown in Table 6.2 as a function of adjusted gross income. Expected contributions begin when the annual income reaches about $15,000, taking about 15 percent of annual income above $15,000, with what is in effect a "marginal tax rate" increasing to about 25 percent on income in excess of $35,000. Since the median income of families with college-age children is close to $30,000, it is clear that U.S. parents contribute very substantially to the costs of their children's higher education, with contributions of $10,000 a year and up common for more affluent parents of children attending high-priced private colleges.

TABLE 6.2
Expected Parental Contribution for Academic Year 1985–86 as a Function of 1984 Family Income (Adjusted Gross)

Assume a family of four with two parents, the student, and one additional dependent child.

Adjusted gross income	Expected contribution
$15,000	0
20,000	700
25,000	1,430
30,000	2,230
35,000	3,210
40,000	4,500
45,000	5,890
50,000	7,270
55,000	8,540
60,000	9,810
65,000	11,060
70,000	12,230
75,000	13,410
80,000	14,580

Based on 1985–86 uniform methodology and excluding any special considerations or home equity. The expected contribution at the adjusted gross income level of $15,000 by CSS suggestion is actually a *minus* $60, but the federal government does not recognize negative expected parental contributions. See College Scholarship Service, *CSS Need Analysis: Theory and Computation Procedures for the 1985–86 FAF* (New York: The College Board, 1984). See also *Federal Register*, vol. 50, no. 67, April 1985, pp. 13,919–13,923.

The American system of need analysis assumes that parents can and should devote a noticeable proportion of their current annual income, requiring some sacrifices, as well as some proportion of their net discretionary worth (net assets less a provision for retirement) to the costs of their children's higher education. For most families, this means cutting back substantially on discretionary spending, perhaps forgoing or deferring vacations, entertainment, new autos, home improvements, and the like. Most expected contributions, particularly if based to any substantial degree on assets, will also involve either liquidation of a portion of these assets or else the assumption of new debt, perhaps in the form of a second mortgage or a home equity loan, to preserve intact the primary asset holdings. Finally, a family may prefer to meet the expected contribution not just by cutting current consumption and depleting savings, but by extending the burden into the future through a PLUS loan (Parent Loan for Undergraduate Students), available to a maximum of $3,000 per year per student, guaranteed by the state and federal governments and carrying an interest rate of 12 percent.

The Student Contribution

The U.S. student is also assumed to bear some responsibility for the costs of his or her college education through summer and term-time work and subsidized loans, as well as through a portion of his or her own assets or savings. This expectation, termed self-help, is considerably higher for students at high-priced private or independent colleges, particularly where little aid is available, but it exists at all colleges and is expected of students from all socioeconomic backgrounds.

Loans. Undergraduate students borrow through two principal governmentally sponsored programs: Guaranteed Student Loans (GSLs) and National Direct Student Loans (NDSLs). Guaranteed Student Loans are made by private lenders, usually banks, and are guaranteed by the federal government. Undergraduates can borrow up to $2,500 a year and up to $12,500 for all undergraduate years. Students whose parents earned less than $30,000 in the preceding year can borrow up to the cost of education, not to exceed the limit. Students whose parents earned more than $30,000 must show a remaining financial need after the expected family contribution and other sources of income have been subtracted from the total cost of attendance at the particular college.

The interest rate to the student is zero percent while in school (or in certain other endeavors) and during a six-month grace period; for new borrowers in 1985–86, it is 8 percent during the 10-year repayment period. The private lenders are paid the 8 percent by the government (taxpayer) while the borrower is in school, plus an additional interest supplement designed to bring the total return to the lender up to a market rate, set every 180 days by the federal government. (The supplement for the quarter ending 30 September 1985, on GSL loans made after October 1981 was 2.84 percentage points, bringing the return to the lender at that time to 10.84 percent [8 + 2.84]).

National Direct Student Loans are made by the college from a revolving loan fund that has been capitalized by direct appropriations from the federal government and supplemented increasingly by repayments. As in the GSL program, NDSLs carry no interest during the in-school years or the six-month grace period after graduation. The interest rate thereafter is 5 percent. Because of the greater subsidy and easier access of these loans, they are to be targeted at low-income students.

Considering all forms of student loans—GSLs, NDSLs, and the several much smaller state and federally sponsored student loans,[15] it has been estimated that more than 3.3 million students in 1985–86 will borrow nearly $9 billion, with new loans averaging almost $2,300.[16] This amount of lending is up from 1.5 million students borrowing $3 billion in 1979, reinforcing the conclusion that the past decade has seen a substantial shift of higher educational costs from parents and taxpayers to the student, largely in the form of more students borrowing larger amounts. The College Board in 1984 reported ". . . the continuation of a trend that began in the mid-1970s: the ever-increasing emphasis on loans over grants"—an observation buttressed by the decline of grants from 80 percent of all federal student assistance in 1975–76 to just under 45 percent in 1984–85, with the proportion of federal assistance in the form of loans increasing in those years from 17 percent to 52 percent.[17] Total accumulated debts at the end of four years of undergraduate education are being reported commonly in the neighborhood of $10,000, and debts for students completing medical and other advanced professional schools can easily top $30,000.

As explained in Appendix B and in the earlier chapters on the German and Swedish loan plans, a subsidized loan can be divided into a true loan and an effective grant, the former being the present value of the actual repayment stream at some appropriate discount rate and the latter, the difference between this present-value calculation and the actual principal amount borrowed—or, equally valid, the present value of the stream of subsidies measured as the differences between each payment and what the payment would have been had the loan carried a more realistic rate of interest. Table 6.3 shows the present value of the repayment stream for a $1,000 Guaranteed Student Loan to be $854 with a discount rate of 8 percent, $753 discounted at 10 percent, and only $667 discounted at 12 percent. The corresponding effective grants are thus $146, $247, or $333 per $1,000 borrowed. By this perspective, if a student takes a $2,000 GSL toward the annual cost of his or her college education, and if 10 percent is an appropriate discount rate, that student may be credited with $1,506 in true loan, or a real student-borne contribution to costs, with $494 being credited to the taxpayer, who will bear the cost of the loan subsidies.

Another adjustment that can be made to refine the actual burden of U.S. student loans is an estimate of that proportion of student lending that is actually repaid by the parents and that in some cases was originally a substitute for a portion of the expected parental

TABLE 6.3
Student Loan Terms (Guaranteed Student Loan Program) and Present
Value of Repayments, United States

Initial loan	$1,000
In-school period[a]	1.5 years
Grace period[b]	0.5 years
Interest rate, in-school and grace periods	0%
Debt at beginning of repayment	$1,000
Interest rate in repayment[c]	8%
Repayment period[d]	10 years
Repayment mode	equal quarterly payments of $36.56

Present value of repayments[e]	Discount rate 8%	$854
	Discount rate 10%	$753
	Discount rate 12%	$667

[a] Period between origination of loan and end of schooling; assumed here to be 1.5 years for purposes of simplification and comparison.

[b] Period between end of schooling and beginning of first repayment period: six months by law, but extensions are possible for, e.g., military service.

[c] For loans taken out since 1984; earlier loans carry other rates.

[d] Ten years maximum.

[e] See Appendix B.

contribution. Particularly during the late 1970s and early 1980s, when prime interest rates in the United States were above 15 percent and when the 1978 Middle Income Student Assistance Act opened the federally subsidized GSL program to all students regardless of need, and before a series of amendments in the mid-1980s began to "close the loan window" to children of very affluent parents, it was legal and clearly rational for parents to substitute their children's borrowing (at effective annual interest rates below 5 percent) for their own contribution (which could earn 12 percent in any bank) to the maximum extent possible. In addition, some parents believe that their children should end at least their undergraduate years debt free and therefore formally or informally assume some or all of the repayment burdens on undergraduate student debt. In 1981, however, the GSL program guidelines changed and began to require that all students from families earning more than $30,000 a year borrowing under the GSL program must show need—that is, a gap in funds required to meet the costs of college *after* assuming a full expected family contribution. The reauthorization of the basic GSL legislation expected to take place in 1986 may well extend this needs test to all students applying for federally guaranteed student loans. Thus, we will not in this chapter attribute any part of new student borrowing to parents, but readers may be alert to the possibility that student debts accu-

mulated during the period of the "open GSL window" may in fact
represent a combination of student and parental debt, with the federal
subsidy effectively shifting a portion of each over to the federal taxpayer.

Summer and Term-Time Employment. "Working one's way
through college" is almost legend in the United States. Christoffel
reports a study of high school seniors who began college in the fall
of 1980: Two-thirds of the part-time and 52 percent of the full-time
students had jobs. By 1981, 75 percent of the part-time and 55 percent
of the full-time students were working during term time. Eighty percent of adult part-time students in 1981 were employed. In 1983–84,
some 850,000 students worked part time through the assistance of the
federal College Work Study Program, which picks up 80 percent of
the expenses of hiring college students. In summary, Christoffel's
findings suggest that a majority of American students work at least
part time.[18]

Amounts earned vary widely. The uniform methodology for determining financial need assumes a summer savings contribution of
$700 for new students and $900 thereafter. A work-study job during
the course of the academic year can earn $1,200 or more, and many
students earn a great deal more, particularly if they hold down an
outside, non–work-study job.[19] Term-time earnings above $1,500,
however, would be discouraged by most campus financial aid officers
as encroaching too much on study time. However, earnings of $2,000
and even much higher are not at all uncommon, particularly for older
students and for students at less selective, community-oriented institutions where students frequently maintain both a full-time job and
full-time (i.e., 12 credit-hours) study or else alternate between se-
mesters of full-time study and part-time work and then part-time study
and full-time work. Counting both summer savings and term-time
earnings, U.S. students commonly earn in the range of $1,000–$2,000.

The Taxpayer's Contribution

Because the European countries in this comparative analysis for
all practical purposes charge no tuition, the costs of higher education
that have been distributed among the British, French, German, and
Swedish parents, students, and taxpayers have been almost entirely
the students' costs of living plus those costs of education such as
books, travel, and equipment that are typically met by the student or
his or her family, even with the assistance of governmental or institutional grants. The *full* taxpayer-borne costs, of course, would be the
taxpayer's share of these expenses, on a per-student basis, plus the

per-student direct costs of undergraduate instruction as might be revealed in the institutions' operating budgets were such data to be available.[20]

The U.S. situation is considerably complicated by the fact that the costs faced by students and their families include both the costs of student living and that portion of institutional, or instructional, costs that are passed on as tuition or fees. It is even further complicated by the great variation within the United States in actual unit costs of instruction among different institutions as well as the very great difference in the taxpayer's share of these costs, as between the public and the private sectors. To the student and his or her family, there is probably no significant difference between their share of instructional costs as reflected in tuition and their share of the costs of student living as reflected in the charges for room and board and other expenses, less whatever aid is received to defray these costs. Nor do government grants distinguish, for most purposes, between tuition and other costs. However, the need for students and parents in the United States to meet some portion of instructional costs, as well as all student maintenance costs, with or without assistance from government or from the institution itself, means that taxpayer-borne, need-based grants in the United States will be inflated relative to similar grants in Europe—only slightly in the case of public institutions, for which tuitions and fees typically constitute only 20–30 percent of the actual costs of undergraduate instruction, but very greatly in the case of private institutions, in which tuitions may constitute 70 to 90 percent of such costs.[21] (This does not, of course, mean that the total per-student taxpayer contribution in the United States is necessarily higher. On the contrary, because all the tuition revenue goes to support university operations, the taxpayer contributions to the institutions' operating budgets are reduced by the presence of tuitions—at least those that can be paid by more well-to-do parents or industrious students and that therefore do not need to be covered by a taxpayer-borne grant.)

With these caveats in mind, the principal, generally available, taxpayer-borne, need-based grants to undergraduates (excluding work study and the true value of loans, which are considered in this analysis to be student-borne revenues) are Pell Grants, Supplemental Education Opportunity Grants, the implicit grants of the subsidized loan programs at the federal level, and various need-based grant programs at the level of the 50 states.

Pell Grants. These are awarded to students on the basis of need as determined by their own and parents' income and assets. Except for the requirement to show satisfactory progress toward the degree and at least a half-time course load, the Pell Grant is given as an entitlement without regard to ability, achievement, the particular institution attended, or the major program of study. The maximum award in 1985–86 by the authorizing statute is $2,600, but the Pell Grant Program is not an automatic entitlement, and the actual awards depend upon the amount appropriated by the Congress each year and the number and needs of potential recipients. In 1985–86 the actual maximum award is $2,100, which is given to students from families (two parents and one additional nonstudent dependent child) with incomes of about $9,860 and below; the minimum grant is $250, just before the awards phase out entirely at a 1984 family income of about $26,500. Pell Grants cannot be more than 60 percent of the federally determined cost at a particular institution. At the low-cost institution portrayed in Table 6.1, for example, with a tuition of $800, the government allows a consideration of an additional $1,100 for a commuting student's room and board plus only $400 for all other costs, for a total allowable cost of education of $2,300, 60 percent of which is $1,380—the maximum Pell Grant for a student of such an institution. The Pell Grants rise as tuition and the actual room-and-board charges rise up to the maximum award for the particular income and number of dependents. Beyond this point, Pell Grants are insensitive to increases in tuition and give no more to a student at a very high-priced private college than to a student from a similar family financial background in residence at an average-cost public college. In 1984–85, some 2,853,000 students received Pell Grants at an estimated average award of $1,105.[22]

Federal Supplemental Educational Opportunity Grants. These are awarded to needy students at the discretion of the college financial aid office, whose allotment of federal SEOG funds is determined by the number of students from low-income families enrolled in recent years. SEOGs range from $200 to $2,000 and may take into account the student's full need, including tuition charges. Supplemental grants, together with the subsidies inherent in the governmental loan programs, represent the principal contribution of the federal government toward the goal of bringing more expensive private higher education more nearly into reach for young people from low-income families. In 1984–85, some 655,000 students received SEOGs, averaging an estimated $550.[23]

State Need-Based Grants: All states provide some form of need-based financial aid to undergraduates, although there is wide variation in generosity and mechanics. The total state grant dollars for 1984–85 were estimated at $1,257 billion—almost 40 percent of the combined general federal grant programs of Pell and SEOG.[24] Some states provide "portable" grants, good for attending colleges out-of-state as well as in-state; other grants are good only in-state. Most state grant programs are designed avowedly to provide some extra assistance to needy students attending private colleges, thereby reducing somewhat the so-called tuition gap between the lower-tuition public sector and the higher-tuition private sector.

The most generous of the state need-based financial aid programs is New York State's Tuition Assistance Program, or TAP. TAP provides a maximum academic-year undergraduate grant of $2,700 or tuition, whichever is less (i.e., reducing the maximum grant to undergraduate students in New York's public colleges and universities to the State University tuition, or $1,375), with the maximum award reduced according to parents' income, beginning the reduction at a net taxable annual income of $5,000 and phasing out the award altogether for net taxable incomes above $29,000 (equivalent to an adjusted gross income of $34–$35,000). New York State TAP awards for full-time undergraduates in private nonprofit and public colleges are shown in Table 6.4. Awards are reduced by $500 if the college attended is private proprietary, or profit-making. There are also TAP awards for graduate and advanced professional study, as well as special schedules for students who can prove financial independence from their parents. A state need-based grant program such as New York's TAP thus supplements the federal Pell Grant Program for students for a wide range of college costs, and it also goes beyond Pell in providing some additional aid to cover the higher costs of attending a private college.

Federal Loan Subsidies: As explained above and in Appendix B, governmentally subsidized and guaranteed loans can be viewed as being composed of a true loan, which is that principal amount that the expected repayment stream would actually amortize at a rate of interest closer to the market rate, and an effective grant, or subsidy, which is the difference between the principal amount received and the true loan. As shown in Table 6.3, a conservatively assumed discount rate of 10 percent suggests that at least 25 percent of the amount borrowed under federal GSL terms should be considered an effective grant from the taxpayer to the student, realized in the stream of subsidies that lower the eventual repayments. In 1984–85, an estimated 3,403,000 students took out Guaranteed Student Loans averaging $2,326, for an average effective subsidy of $580, or about 25 percent of the principal amount borrowed, and an average true loan of $1,746, assuming the 25–75 division suggested by the 10-percent discount rate assumption.[25]

Other Federal and State Assistance to Students: In 1975–76, veteran's education benefits and education benefits to children of

TABLE 6.4
New York State Tuition Assistance Program (TAP) Grants for
Undergraduates at New York State Public and Private Colleges, 1985–86

New York State net taxable income of family[a]	Estimated TAP award at private college	Estimated TAP award at public college[b]
$29,000	$ 300	$ 300
27,500	453	300
25,000	740	300
22,500	1,015	300
20,000	1,290	300
17,500	1,565	300
15,000	1,840	515
12,500	2,100	775
10,000	2,330	1,005
7,500	2,525	1,200
below 5,000	2,700	1,375

Source: *Standard Descriptions of State and Federal Student Assistance Programs for Use by Postsecondary Institutions in Complying with Part 53 of the Regulations of the Commissioner of Education* (Albany: The State Education Department, April 1985).

[a] Net taxable income is adjusted gross income less exemptions and deductions, or appropriately 15–20 percent under adjusted gross.

[b] The public-college award uses the 1985–86 State University tuition and college fee of $1,375 as the maximum TAP award for the public sector. Upon receipt of four or more semester payments, the annual award is reduced by $200. The provisions in the legislation allow for a minimum award of $300 per year.
The actual award is $2,700 minus:

Net taxable family income	Reduction
$ 5,000 or less	no reducton
5,001 – 8,000	7% of excess over $5,000
8,001 – 11,000	$210 + 8% of excess over $8,000
11,001 – 14,000	$450 + 10% of excess over $11,000
14,001 – 25,000	$750 + 11% of excess over $14,000
25,001 – 29,000	$1,960 + 11.5% of excess over $25,000
29,001 or more	no award

social security recipients (i.e., persons drawing federal retirement or disability allowances) totaled 5.273 billion dollars: nearly one-half of all federal higher education assistance and more than 80 percent of all federal grant aid. Strictly speaking, neither program was need-based or means-tested, although it was assumed that most of these benefits went to students who were either independent from parental support (e.g., veterans' education benefits) or whose parents' resources would have been limited anyway (e.g., dependent children of social security recipients). By the mid-1980s few veterans were still drawing on higher education benefits, and grants to children of social security recipients had been phased out as allegedly duplicative of the Pell Grants and other truly need-based programs. Federal benefits, thus, are estimated by Wagner to have fallen to about $746 million in 1985–86, or less than 5 percent of all federal student assistance.[26] Other federal and state assistance includes special state grants to educationally and economically disadvantaged students and to Native American students, special grants to students in certain underserved professions (e.g., nursing), and various smaller state- and federally subsidized loan programs to supplement the major Guaranteed Student Loan Program. These federal and state awards are not, however, generally available to U.S. undergraduates and are not considered further in this analysis.

Summarizing the Per-Student Taxpayer Contribution to the Costs of Higher Education. Taxpayer-borne assistance to students in the United States is difficult to summarize because the range of awards is so great and because each student's total taxpayer-borne assistance, from both federal and state sources, is a complex function of:

- parents' income;

- own income;

- "family factors," such as the number of other dependent children both in and out of college;

- the tuition charges at the particular college attended, which may range from a few hundred to ten thousand dollars; and

- decisions of the campus financial aid officers in awarding federal supplemental grants.

Consequently, average awards derived by dividing total expenditures by the estimated number of recipients are not particularly useful because they ignore this range. Furthermore, published federal- and state-aid data is always by program, and program averages are not additive. Empirical studies that take aided students themselves as the units of observation and that then determine, by student and/or parental reports, the grants that have actually been obtained are much more useful for our purpose. Unfortunately, such studies often aggregate dissimilar types of aid (e.g., Supplemental Educational Opportunity Grants and Campus Work Study) and contain such variation, and probably such reporting error, that they are also not particularly useful for an international comparative study, such as this one, that must compare similar data.[27]

Therefore, this study employs the concept of "representative" awards, based on financial aid practices and consistent with empirical data but not drawn from any single source. Such representative taxpayer-borne awards—for low- and middle-income students at high and low-cost colleges—are shown in Table 6.5. Note that the Pell Grants, except for a reduction at the very lowest-cost colleges, do not vary by the cost of the college for a given family income. On the other hand, federal SEOGs, which are awarded by the campus aid officers, and the state grants, most of which are also tuition sensitive, do reflect the variation in costs, particularly in tuitions and living costs. By design, the federal and state taxpayers provide larger awards to equally needy students at more expensive institutions. However, these awards lessen but do not eliminate the cost (price) differentials, particularly between the private and public sectors.

Institutional/Philanthropic Contributions

Historically, some students and their families have been given financial assistance in meeting the costs of college by the institution itself from funds made available through philanthropic donations, principally by alumni. Institutional, or philanthropic, support comes from three sources. The first is endowment, or income from past philanthropy. The second is current donations from alumni, businesses, and friends of the college. The third, found only in private colleges and much less prevalent, is generated by charging and getting tuitions from some students and families that are above and beyond the amounts necessary to cover all costs, thus generating some budgetary surpluses with which to grant aid in the form of tuition discounts to some needy students.

Institutionally awarded student aid, mainly originating with one of these philanthropic sources, was reported to total $2,634,000,000 in 1984–85—or just under the total of all federal Pell Grants.[28] This total, however, includes some graduate fellowships as well as undergraduate aid and includes both merit aid, given without regard to need and mainly for the purpose of attracting a particular student to a particular campus, and need-based or means-tested aid, given for the ostensible purpose of supplanting funds that the family is financially unable to provide and thus making the selection of a particular college at least financially feasible. The Miller and Hexter studies reported that about 40 percent of low-income students and more than 50 percent of middle-income students at private colleges receive college-provided aid averaging around $2,000; only 4 percent of low-income students and 5 percent of middle-income students at public colleges received any college-provided aid, and the average awards

TABLE 6.5

Representative Taxpayer-Borne (Federal and State), Need-Based Assistance to Students in the United States for Low- and Middle-Income Students Attending High- and Low-Cost Institutions, 1985–86[a]

Principal federal and state grant programs	Maximum award	Students from low-income[b] families at:				Students from middle-income[c] families at:			
		Lowest-cost public ($3,150)[d]	Average-cost public ($5,314)	Average-cost private ($9,659)	High-cost private ($15,000)	Lowest-cost public ($3,150)	Average-cost public ($5,314)	Average-cost private ($9,659)	High-cost private ($15,000)
Federal Pell grants[e]	$2,100	$1,290	$1,650	$1,650	$1,650	$ 0	$ 0	$ 0	$ 0
Federal supplemental grants	2,000	0	450	800	1,000	0	0	900	1,200
State need-based grants[f]	2,700	500	800	1,500	1,500	0	200	300	300
Subtotal taxpayer-borne cash grants	$6,800	$1,790	$2,900	$3,950	$4,150	0	200	$1,200	$1,500
Federal loan subsidies[g]	625 +	125	375	550	800	125	375	625	800
Total taxpayer-borne assistance[h]	$7,425	$1,915	$3,275	$4,500	$4,950	$125	$575	$1,825	$2,300

a The figures in Table 6.5 are "representative," i.e., are consistent with U.S. financial aid policies and with available data, but do not come from any particular empirical study or single source. The chart considers only those costs that are faced by the student and the family—not the instructional costs that, particularly for public colleges, are also borne in part by the taxpayer.

b The "low-income" range is approximately $10,000–$15,000 taxable (adjusted gross) income.

c The "middle-income" range is approximately $30,000–$35,000 taxable (adjusted gross) income.

d The four representative cost figures are from Table 6.1.

e An adjusted gross family income of $15,000 with no assets gives a family of four a Pell index of 490 and a maximum grant of $1,650. The low-cost public commuter situation described in Table 6.1, however, presents a cost-of-education ceiling, for the purpose of grant calculations, of only $2,150 ($800 tuition, $1,100 maximum allowable room and board, and $400 maximum allowable "all other"), 60 percent of which is $1,380.

f The maximum generally available, need-based state grant is New York State's TAP maximum. Most states are considerably smaller, however, and the estimates here seek a representative-size state grant program.

g The federal-loan-subsidy estimates assume a 10-percent discount rate per Table 6.3, or 75 percent "true loan" and 25 percent subsidy or "effective grant." It is assumed that borrowing reaches the maximum $2,500 GSL at the "average private" college but is supplemented by as much as $700 NDSL, for a total of $3,200, at the "high-cost private" college.

h Federal College Work Study is an important component of the total federal student assistance program, but is not included in these totals on the grounds that the costs are borne by students and that the recipients of the taxpayer-borne subsidies are the institutions which receive the labor, rather than the students.

were under $800.[29] Given the reasonable assumption that the combination of low tuition and public need-based grants (e.g., Pell, SEOG, and state grants) have removed the financial barrier to attending the nation's public colleges even for children from the lowest-income families, it is likely that most of the institutionally awarded grants in the public sector are based on criteria other than need and provide the student with some extra purchasing power rather than supplant or relieve any other source of financial support. In the private sector, however, the role of philanthropically originated, institutionally awarded grants is very significant for most students from low- or middle-income families faced with yearly college costs ranging from $7,500 to $15,000 and up. Institutionally awarded aid in most cases makes up the difference between the total costs faced by the student and his or her family and the sum of all resources available from the three primary sources of family (i.e., the expected family contribution as revealed by need-analysis procedures), taxpayer or government (e.g., Pell, SEOG, and state grants), and the student (through savings, term-time work, and loans). This institutionally awarded grant may be less than $1,000 or may, at a well-endowed expensive college, and particularly for a student whom the college wishes very much to enroll, be in excess of $5,000.

The Financial Aid Package

The cost of higher education faced by students and families in the United States—tuition and fees, room and board, and all other expenses—is shared by the parents of dependent students, to the extent of their financial abilities; by the students themselves, through their own assets, through summer and term-time earnings, and through governmentally subsidized loans; by the taxpayers, through federal and state grants and through loan subsidies; and by philanthropists or donors, through gifts to particular (primarily private) colleges that in turn allow those colleges to grant scholarships to needy students. Except for those students and families whose resources are sufficient to meet all expenses without the need for governmental grants, subsidized loans, or college grants, each student's mix of resources is individually "packaged" by the financial aid officer of his or her particular college. This packaging proceeds essentially through the following steps:

Step 1. The total expenses faced by the student and his or her family are determined. These would correspond to the expenses illustrated in Table 6.1 and generally represent a "modest-but-adequate" budget, exceeded by those students whose parents contribute more than the minimum expected or needed, or who contribute more themselves through savings, earnings, or loans.

Step 2. Governmental grants to which the student is entitled (i.e., apart from any decision by the college's financial aid officer) are estimated, and the student is assumed to have applied for them and to receive them. These principally include federal Pell Grants and any state entitlement aid.

Step 3. The parents' expected contribution is calculated, generally through one of the independent need-analysis agencies (e.g., College Scholarship Service or American College Testing Program) or through a procedure of the college's own choosing. Students may apply to be considered financially independent of their parents. Such status generally requires three conditions for both the current and the prior year: (1) living no more than six weeks a year with the parents; (2) not being claimed by parents as an income-tax exemption; and (3) receiving no more than $750 in support from parents. (Independent status for the purpose of qualifying for institutionally given aid is granted by the college at its own discretion. Eligibility for independent status for the purpose of receiving federal Pell or state need-based grants is similarly based, but is an entitlement should the student qualify.)

Step 4. A student self-help expectation is added, composed of expected prior summer savings and some combination of term-time work (often subsidized in part by the federal government's College Work Study Program) and loans, including either a National Direct Student Loan offered by the college or a Guaranteed Student Loan that the student must secure from a private lender with the college certifying need. This self-help total may be $3,000 to $5,000 or even more at an expensive private college where the parental, institutional, and taxpayer-borne shares fall far short of meeting the full need. The self-help expectation may be a great deal lower, however, at a less expensive college, or where the parental contribution is sufficient to meet most of the need, or where a college wants so much to attract a particular student that it is willing to make up the shortfall from a very low self-help by a very high institutional grant (Step 5).

Step 5. The remaining need—that is, the difference between the budget and all the revenue sources assumed in Steps 2–4—

must be made up by institutional sources, at the discretion of the college financial aid officer. Some of these sources, such as the federal Supplemental Educational Opportunity Grant, are taxpayer-based. Others are from endowment earnings or current gifts from donors earmarked for aid. Some may come from college operating budgets, constituting a kind of "differential pricing."

Step 6. Should the amounts still be inadequate (which would be the case only for private colleges and generally for those without substantial endowments), the college may help meet the gap either by providing a bit more self help (e.g., a larger NDSL loan or more assured work study) than was originally assumed or by admitting the student but passing the problem of seemingly inadequate assistance on to the student and his or her family. (Some states, for example, have established special nonfederally guaranteed loan programs to help parents borrow more than the officially expected parental contribution.) In fact, although some aid officers might deny the practice, students whose needs are too great and who lack special highly sought-after qualities may be denied admittance on the grounds that the student's academic credentials are not strong enough to warrant the devotion of more institutional resources and the further belief that there is no point in admitting a student who could not attend without extraordinary personal and family hardship.

The resulting aid packages are almost infinitely variable. They cannot be predicted precisely from governmental or college policies, discerned from published averages, or necessarily revealed by student or family self-reporting. Representative aid packages can, however, be illustrated, disaggregated by the cost of the college (e.g., as typified by the range of costs in Table 6.1) and by the income level of the family. Such representative packages are shown in Table 6.6. Student shares, including summer savings, term-time earnings, and loans, range from $800 for a student from a high-income family at a low-cost college to a $5,300 gross, or a $4,500 net, contribution for low- and middle-income students at a high-cost private college. Parental shares, a function of income, assets, and other considerations, range from a low of no contribution at all to a high of an estimated $12,800 for the high-income family with a student at a high-cost college. Taxpayer-borne grants—counting only the taxpayers' share of tuition, room, board, and other expenses, and omitting their share of direct instructional or institutional expenses—range from a low of

TABLE 6.6
Sources of Revenue to Meet College Costs at High- and Low-Cost Institutions for High-, Middle-, and Low-Income Families, United States, 1985–86

Sources of revenue	Lowest-cost public ($3,150)[a] Family income[b]			Average-cost public ($5,314)[a] Family income[b]			Average-cost private ($9,659)[a] Family income[b]			High-cost private ($15,000)[a] Family income[b]		
	low	middle	high	low	middle	high	low	middle	high	low	middle	high
Student:												
Term-time and summer work	$ 860	$1,075	$ 800	$ 914	$1,114	$ 600	$1,659	$1,600	$1,000	$ 2,100	$ 2,100	$ 1,100
Loans	500	500	0	1,500	1,500[c]	600	2,200	2,500	0	3,200	3,200	1,100
Total gross student contribution	1,360	1,575	800	2,414	2,614	0	3,859	4,100	1,000	5,300	5,300	2,200
(less loan subsidies)[d]	(125)	(125)	0	(375)	(375)	0	(550)	(625)	0	(800)	(800)	(275)
Total net student contribution	1,235	1,450	800	2,039	2,239	1,200	3,309	3,475	1,000	4,500	4,500	1,925
Parents: from current income, savings, and Loans	0	1,575	2,350	0	2,500	4,114	150	2,759	8,659	150	3,200	12,800
Taxpayer:												
Federal and state need-based grants	1,790	0	0	2,900	200	0	3,950	1,200	0	4,150	1,500	0
plus loan subsidies[d]	125	125	0	375	375	0	550	625	0	800	800	275
Total net taxpayer contribution	1,915	125	0	3,275	575	0	4,500	1,825	0	4,950	2,300	275
Institutional/philanthropic: College grants	0	0	0	0	0	0	1,700	1,600	0	5,400	5,000	0
TOTAL	$3,150	$3,150	$3,150	$5,314	$5,314	$5,314	$9,659	$9,659	$9,659	$15,000	$15,000	$15,000

a This chart considers only those costs faced by the student and the family—not the institutional costs that, particularly for the public institutions, are also borne in part by the taxpayer. Actual numbers are "representative" and conform in total to the cost estimates from Table 6.1, but the numbers are derived as explained below and do not come from any one empirical study.

b "Low" family income would be in the $10,000–$15,000 adjusted gross annual income range; "middle income" is in the range of $30,000–$35,000, or just within reach of some college-based federal aid at private institutions, but not at public ones; "high income" is more than $75,000.

c The taxpayer's share is from Table 6.5; "subtotal taxpayer-borne cash grants." The parent's share from the low-income family is assumed to be zero, with very small amounts, however, to help with very high private college costs. Parents' share from the middle-income family is from Table 6.1, with a bit extra for the high-cost, a bit less for the average public, and exactly one-half the total cost for the low-cost public college. Parents' share from the high-income family is the remaining need after some minimal self help. The student's share and the institutional and philanthropic share balance to cover the rest of the costs, with loans and work being essentially interchangeable, and with total "self-help" rising to a maximum of $5,300 at the high-cost private college, assuming a $3,200 loan package made up of $2,500 GSL and $700 NDSL.

d The taxpayer-borne loan subsidy estimate is 25 percent of the principal, per Table 6.3 with a 10 percent discount rate assumption. The subsidy estimate is netted out of the student's gross contribution and added to the taxpayers' share.

zero for most high-income families and even for middle-income families at low-cost colleges to a high of more than $4,000 for low-income students at high-cost colleges.

Trends, Issues, and Summary Observations

The 1980s in the United States have seen an erosion of both the parental and the taxpayer share and a resulting increase in the share borne by the student. These three trends are obviously related, yet are also to some degree independent of one another.

The Erosion of the Parental Contribution. The erosion of the parental contribution is due to three principal factors. First is the increasing proportion of undergraduate students who are adult and genuinely independent financially from their parents, the increasing proportion who want to establish a claim of financial independence, plus some whose parents refuse to support them and who have thus forced the issue of independence. Second is the increasing proportion of students, even in the traditional college-going age group, whose parents have divorced or separated, greatly complicating the process of determining need or ability to pay, not to mention actually getting the expected contribution from the estranged parent. A final factor is the apparent diminution of parental willingness to sacrifice for their children's college education, perhaps akin to the growing American disinclination to save, give, or be taxed even for supposedly worthy goals.

The expected parental contribution works best with reasonably affluent parents who have never been divorced, who value higher education for their children and are willing to sacrifice to make it possible, and whose children enter college right after high school and attend full time for four years until graduation. Unfortunately, this no longer describes the overwhelming majority of student-family situations, and the expected parental contribution, while far too significant to be abandoned, may continue to be strained and even eroded.

A Lessening of Taxpayer (Especially Federal) Support in the Form of Need-Based Grants. Federal grant aid has declined both in real value and as a proportion of total financial resources available to students during the 1980s. From 1980–81 to 1984–85, federal student aid of all sorts declined 18.9 percent in constant dollars, while federal loan aid and state aid of all forms was increasing.[30] A report by the National Institute of Independent Colleges and Universities on student aid packages between 1979–80 and 1983–84 found the Pell Grant aid to students at independent colleges, for example, falling by 34.5 percent in constant dollars.[31]

Much of the decline in federal grants has been in entitlement programs that were not necessarily need-based, e.g., the phasing out of federal aid to dependent survivors of social security contributions and the phasing down of veteran's benefits. But the need-based grants—principally Pell and Supplemental Educational Opportunity Grants—have also declined in real terms: by 5.7 percent and 17.2 percent respectively.[32] Reasons for the decline in federal student aid, and in grant aid in particular, may be partly economic—that is, a need to reduce all public expenditures in the face of soaring federal budgets—but are more fundamentally ideological. The conservative sentiment represented by the administration of President Ronald Reagan and the Republican majority in the U.S. Senate (and shared by some fiscally conservative Democrats and by others who are otherwise strong supporters of measures to help the truly needy) is that federal need-based aid had become excessive, wasteful, and beyond the levels necessary to assure higher educational opportunities for the children of the needy. Such a sentiment assumes that a diminution of federal aid may indeed lead to a restoration of some lost parental support, to a curtailment of higher educational costs, to more appropriately frugal student living standards, to more student self help, to a greater role for the states vis-à-vis the federal government, or at worst to a return to the work force of those who may not be particularly academically prepared or inclined anyway—any or all of the above consequences being quite acceptable to American conservative ideology.

On the other hand, the erosion of federal grant aid is directly related to the increase in student-debt levels and may be a partial cause of the decline in the proportion of low-income youth, especially minorities, beginning, and especially continuing in, college. College attendance and completion rates for black students, for example, actually dropped between the mid-1970s and the mid-1980s, despite the fact that their high school graduation rates continued to improve.[33]

Increasing Reliance on Student Loans. The Guaranteed Student Loan Program increased from 1980–81 to 1984–85 by nearly 20 percent in number of loans, 8.4 percent in size of average loan, and (with other loan programs) from 40.7 to 51.7 percent of all aid in those two benchmark years.[34] This increasing reliance on loans was reported with alarm by Frank Newman in his 1985 report sponsored by the Carnegie Foundation for the Advancement of Teaching. Although corroborating evidence is very thin, Newman echoed concerns held by many American higher education observers as he speculated that the increasing reliance on loans might:

- affect career choices by driving students toward high-paying jobs and away from socially important but less remunerative ones

- discourage students, particularly from low-income and minority backgrounds, from entering or continuing in college

- undercut traditional values such as working one's way through college (with the help of family, philanthropy, or taxpayer) and then starting a career or profession "even" and relatively unburdened, and

- prove to be economically inefficient for the government, which incurs repayment subsidy commitments far into the future, and economically damaging to the private sector, which must compete with students in the capital market and which will find future student purchasing power diminished by repayment obligations.[35]

Newman's speculations about the possible detrimental effects of heavy loan burdens have been disputed by other researchers.[36] Definitive answers are unavailable in 1986. Clearly, though, debt loads, by any historic comparison, are getting very high for some students, and there is as of 1986 no reason to predict any change in this trend.

The Increasing Practice of Awarding Grants and Price Discounts without Regard to Need. Not long ago, nearly all American colleges operated under one or more formal or informal compacts that agreed, in essence, to avoid price warfare and to concentrate available aid resources on bringing college within financial reach of the needy rather than to compete for students through offers of financial aid. Like any cartel, these compacts survived as long as the members controlled the supply and as long as demand was high. However, as enrollments in the United States are finally beginning to fall in response to the declining number of college-bound high school graduates (with worse yet to come), and as the marginal cost of educating a student in an underenrolled college falls to near zero, colleges are beginning to cut prices through selective discounts—not just to the needy, who pay relatively little anyway, but to those families who could probably afford to pay all costs but who might be induced to alter their choice of college with a relatively small grant. In addition, the United States in the mid-1980s is in the midst of an "excellence" movement in education that looks with favor on rewards for merit and with disinterest, at best, on public money spent on the nonmeritorious poor. Although the amount of so-called merit aid is still small relative to the amount given on the basis of need, such expenditures do divert resources that might otherwise go either to needy students, to additional operating expenditures, or to curbing the next round of tuition increases. More serious to the critics of non-need-based aid is the observation that any enrollment-altering effect must be short-lived at best, as institutions are forced to match the price discounts of their competitors. "The result," writes Wagner, "is that an increasing proportion of resources will be devoted to price inducements that do nothing to increase access to higher education generally, let alone enrollments at individual institutions."[37]

Cost Sharing in U.S. Higher Education.[38] Despite continuing downward pressures on all public expenditures, and despite the increasing proportion of nontraditional college students who may no longer have access to parental resources, it is difficult to imagine a fundamental, massive shift away from the current balance of cost sharing in the United States among parents, taxpayers, and students. To begin with, it is unlikely that the next decade will see any significant change in the underlying cost of instruction, that is, the production function that links inputs such as faculty, staff, books, laboratories, and classrooms with outputs such as students served, research produced, or learning added. Without such a change, these costs must still be borne by the same three or perhaps four parties that bear them today: students, parents, taxpayers, and to a lesser extent institutions or philanthropists. Any further diminution of the taxpayers' share must, then, be taken up by a commensurate increase either in the students' share, which for many students is already the heaviest of any nation, or in the parents' share, which is also already very high by most comparative measures and which is furthermore exceptionally visible and thus vulnerable—either shift being increasingly unpopular politically and thus increasingly unlikely.

It is true that the taxpayer burden could be lessened and the student and parental burdens at least not increased through a significant reduction in the size and cost of the overall higher educational enterprise itself. For example, if the proportion of youth going on to college, already far higher than in any of the other nations in this study, could only be stabilized, the extension into nontraditional populations ceased or even rolled back, and the amount of time spent in college and graduate school also frozen or even reduced, then enrollments—and presumably costs—could be reduced very significantly, if only temporarily, just by the decline in the number of 18–22-year-olds in the United States over the next decade. However, the nation's commitment both to education and to equal opportunity is far too high, and the nation's wealth too great, to permit such a significant abandonment of the principles that underlie the public taxpayer support of higher education. A continued shift of the taxpayer burden from the federal to the state level is possible, although even that trend may soon run its course. The students' share may continue to broaden to embrace even more students than it does now, but it is unlikely to increase significantly when it is now the heaviest. Parents will continue to have a primary and substantial obligation. In short, the costs of U.S. higher education will almost certainly continue to be borne by students, parents, taxpayers, and donors, with each segment alert to resist any attempt on the part of another sector to shift the burden onto it.

7

SUMMARY OBSERVATIONS ON SHARING AND SHIFTING THE COSTS OF HIGHER EDUCATION

The five systems studied are very different and yet very alike. They are quite different (more so than had been anticipated) in the basic costs faced by the student and the family. They differ greatly in their approaches to what Americans would call "financial aid," and the resulting shares borne by parents, students, and taxpayers differ considerably for students and families from similar circumstances. But the countries are substantially alike in their dependence for meeting these costs upon parents (except for Sweden), students (except for the United Kingdom), taxpayers, and institutions/philanthropists (mainly the United States). They are also alike in that they all profess to bring higher education into the reach of all who are qualified, without regard to family socioeconomic status. And most employ concepts and tools familiar to the field of student finance: need analyses, expected parental contributions, governmentally sponsored student loans, and the like. This concluding chapter will summarize and analyze these similarities and differences, attempting as much as possible to control for differences in family income.

THE COSTS TO THE STUDENT
AND FAMILY

The great difference between the United States and most of Europe with regard to costs and student financial assistance is that the students in the United Kingdom, France, Germany, and Sweden pay almost no part of the costs of instruction—that is, pay zero or minuscule tuitions and fees—whereas U.S. students pay a small but noticeable portion of these costs in the public sector and a very large portion in the private, or independent, sector. Because the principal interest of this study was in the policies and policy instruments that fall within the concept of "financial assistance," the unit of observation was those costs faced by the student and his or her family.

In the United Kingdom, the Federal Republic of Germany, France, and Sweden, this meant only the costs of student living (except for some tuition-paying *Grandes Ecoles* students in France). In the United States, the costs faced by the student and family include, of course, the costs of student living plus tuition and fees.

Figure 7.1 shows a variety of cost estimates for each of the five countries in the study. There is considerable variation both within each country and among the five countries. Within-country variation can be attributed to commuter-resident status, to the amount of tuition or fees paid (in the United States and to a limited degree in France), and to individual student living standards, which in turn are probably very largely a function of resources available to the student-family unit. Between-country variation can be attributed to the presence or absence of tuition, to the general cost of living, to the extent of governmentally subsidized room and board, and to the prevailing cultural sense of how well a student ought to live—in comparison, say, with his or her nonstudent age peers.

For example, discounting tuition, costs among the five countries studied are highest in Sweden, reflecting the general high cost of living in that country, the absence of governmental subsidization of living expenses, and a cultural view that would have a 21-year-old student live at about the same standard as a 21-year-old worker. The costs in Germany are also quite high and would be higher were it not for some savings made possible by the governmentally subsidized *Studentenwerke*, which provide low-cost meals and some low-cost housing. French costs are the lowest, due to lower living costs generally (compared to Sweden, the United States, or Germany); to the subsidized meals and housing available from the local *Centre Regional des Oeuvres Universitaires et Scolaires*, or CROUS; and finally to a tradition in which living either at home or in genteel academic poverty continues to be a more accepted condition of student life than, say, in England, West Germany, or Scandinavia. The United Kingdom estimates are low partly because of its lower living standards in general and possibly because the only estimates available were either from the Ministry, which may have some incentive to estimate low in order to restrain the growth of grant expenditures, or actual survey results from the National Union of Students, which may also err on the downside as expenditure surveys often do. However, taking all factors into consideration, incuding inevitable errors in estimation, and controlling especially for commuter-resident status in each country and for the presence of tuition and fees in the United States, the costs faced by students and families in the five countries portrayed in Figure 7.1 are quite similar.

THE PARENTAL CONTRIBUTION

Comparative expected parental contributions are shown in Figure 7.2 as a function of income and also in Figures 7.3, 7.4, and 7.5 as a proportion of total revenues for different parental income assumptions. Among the five countries studied, only in Sweden (but also elsewhere in Scandinavia) are parents not officially expected to contribute toward the direct living expenses of their children in higher education. Some contributions are still common from middle- and higher-income parents, either to provide their children with higher student living standards or to lessen some of their children's dependence on loans, but the direct burden of higher educational costs on parents in Sweden is the lightest at all income levels.

In fairness to Swedish parents, who may not feel their burdens so light, carrying as they do the greatest overall tax burden of the five countries studied, the cost of higher education weighs on all parents as taxpayers as well as upon those parents who have themselves attended the university, many of whom will be paying off their own Study Means loans for many years—not unlike paying an annual surtax for the privilege of having attended the university. Also in fairness to Sweden's social welfare system, the nation has achieved such a level of equality in the distribution of income that it is not considered necessary or even appropriate to charge the system of financing higher education with the additional task of further redistributing the nation's income. With these caveats, however, the Swedish parents *qua* parents, particularly those with higher incomes and with several university-bound children, clearly benefit vis-à-vis parents in the other countries in this study, with the student especially and also those taxpayers without children in college carrying a commensurately heavier burden.

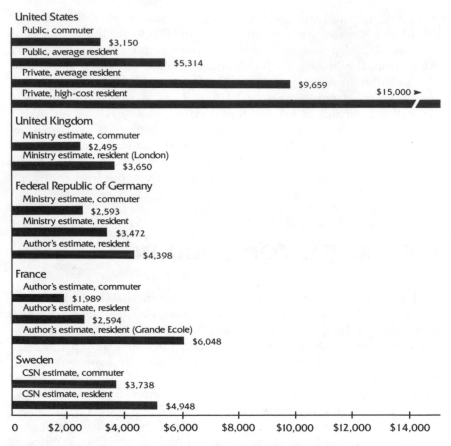

FIGURE 7.1 Costs faced by students and their families, United States, United Kingdom, Federal Republic of Germany, France, and Sweden, various estimates, 1985–86.

The greatest burden on the low-income parents seems to be in France, where Figure 7.2 shows the need-based grant reduction (and hence the implicit expectation of a parental contribution) beginning at a very low income. The cash costs of university attendance in France tend to be low, but the proportion of those costs borne by parents among low-income families, as shown in Figure 7.3, is quite high.

The Federal Republic of Germany also begins its expected parental contributions at a rather low annual income, at least in comparison to the United Kingdom and the United States (and of course to Sweden, with its absence of any expected parental contribution). Both the French and German expected parental contributions rise in

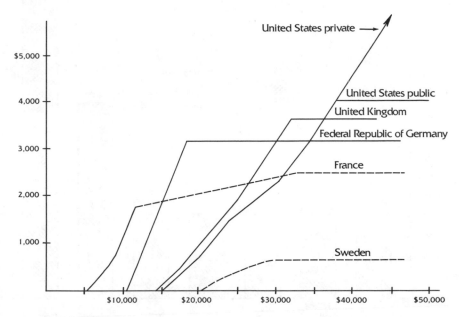

FIGURE 7.2 Higher education expenses borne by parents as a function of family income, United Kingdom, Federal Republic of Germany, France, Sweden, and the United States, 1985–86 (see notes below).

United Kingdom: From Table 2.3, based on prior year's "residual income," assuming one additional nonstudent dependent. $1 = £.593.

Federal Republic of Germany: From Table 3.4, based on two years' prior net taxable family income, assuming one additional nonstudent dependent. $1 = DM2.16.

France: From Table 4.5, based on two years' prior taxable income, assuming one additional nonstudent dependent and 13 points and a total expense limit of 13,000F [$1,747] over the income range of *bourse* eligibility, or an income of up to approximately 85,000F [$11,425], after which both expenses and parental contributions are assumed to rise until an expense limit of approximately 20,000F [$2,688] per Table 4.6. $1 = 7.44F.

Sweden: There is no officially expected parental contribution. Parents do frequently supplement the Study Means, however, particularly at middle and upper incomes; the estimates above assume that parents and students split supplementary expenses, per Table 5.4. $1 = 7.5 Skr.

United States: From Table 6.2, based on prior year's adjusted gross income, assuming one additional nonstudent dependent and no substantial home equity or other assets. The contribution to high-cost private colleges may rise as high as $12,000–$13,000. Contributions to public colleges generally cap at $4,000–$4,500.

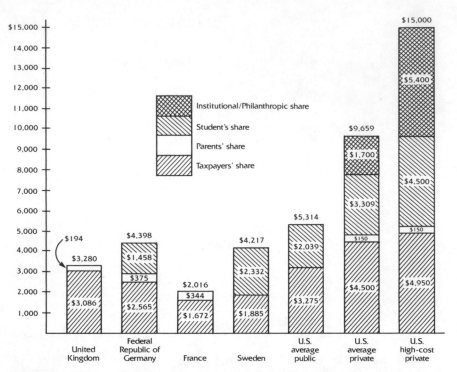

FIGURE 7.3 Sharing the costs of higher education for low-income families in the United Kingdom, Federal Republic of Germany, France, Sweden, and the United States, 1985–86 (see notes below).

United Kingdom: "Low income" is under £8,520 [$14,368], which is the start of the expected parental contribution per Figure 2.1. Total cost is NUS estimate of £1,945, per Table 2.1. The taxpayer portion is the "elsewhere-than-London" mandatory grant of £1,830 [$3,086]. The remaining need is assumed to be a family contribution, per Chapter 2.

Federal Republic of Germany: "Low income" is under DM23,820 [$11,028], which is the start of the expected parental contribution per Figure 3.1. Total cost is the "more adequate budget" estimate of DM9,500 [$4,398], per Table 3.1. The taxpayer portion is the "effective grant" within the 10-month maximum BAföG with an 8 percent discount rate assumption per Table 3.3, or DM7,880 [$3,648] × (1.00 − 0.297) = DM5,539 [$2,565]. The student contribution is the "true loan," or DM7,880 [$3,648] × .297 = DM2,340 [$1,083] plus one-half of the remaining need of DM1,620, or DM810 [$375]. The parental contribution is the remaining DM810 [$375].

France: "Low income" is 50,000F [$6,720], which is still high enough for a 12-point family to be eligible for only the third largest grant. Total cost is assumed to be $15,000F [$6,720], per Table 4.6. The taxpayer contribution is a *bourse* of 10,440F [1,468] plus 2,000F tax relief for a total of 12,440F [$1,672]. Net (after tax relief) parental contribution, cash and in-kind, is 2,560F [$344] per Table 4.6. No student contribution is assumed for *bourse* recipients, per text.

Sweden: "Low income" is assumed to be approximately 90,000 Skr [$12,000], a level at which the Swedish parent, who is not officially expected to contribute anything at any income level, would probably be unable to supplement the Study Means total of 31,627 Skr [$4,217]. The total cost is assumed to be the Study Means, per Table 5.1. The taxpayer and student portions are per Table 5.4.

United States: "Low income" is assumed to be in the $10,000–$15,000 range. The total cost and the taxpayer, parental, student, and institutional shares are all per Table 6.5.

148

a very steep functional relationship to annual income, constituting in effect a very high marginal tax rate on income beginning with the modest income at which a contribution is first expected (and the *bourse* or BAföG begins to be reduced) and continuing as incomes rise until that income at which the *bourse* and BAföG are phased out altogether and parental contributions have presumably taken their places. Such a severe means testing supports the general French and West German proposition that the expenses of student maintenance are fundamentally and properly *family* expenses (shared, perhaps, by both parents and students) and that the principal taxpayer responsibility is only for a sharply targeted program of assistance to the very poor.

The U.K. and the U.S. public-college expected parental contributions are very similar, as shown in Figure 7.2. Both begin at higher income levels than in either France or Germany, thus placing less burden on low- and lower-middle-income families, and both rise in less steeply sloped relationships to income, reaching maximum parental contributions (and phasing out the taxpayer-borne contributions) at parental incomes in the $30,000–$40,000 range. For the United Kingdom, this means that the great majority of families are eligible for grants and that a substantial number, even from the lower middle class, need make no contributions at all to the higher educational costs of their children. In contrast to the French and West German systems, which leave student living expenses to the parents and students except when incomes are very low, the U.K. system leaves at least the bulk of them to taxpayers (i.e., governmental grants) except when parental incomes are high.

The parental contribution in the United States is very light at low and lower-middle incomes but becomes very substantial at upper-middle and higher incomes, as shown in Figures 7.3, 7.4, and 7.5, for families with children attending private colleges because of the need to pass on instructional costs, via tuition, to both parents and students. Part of this heavy parental burden reflects the higher cost of instruction at U.S. colleges, most of which have much more extensive physical plants, nonacademic student support services, and administrative support than do their European counterparts. In addition, however, the heavy parental burden at upper-middle and higher incomes reflects a public policy decision in the United States (albeit more historically derived than consciously decided upon) to allow much of higher education to be both operated and financed privately, thus implicitly relieving the public sector and the taxpayer of what would otherwise have been their burdens, and instead to pass on more of these actual instructional costs to students and parents as the presumed prime recipients and beneficiaries. While the low-income parents in the United States continue to be relieved of this burden even

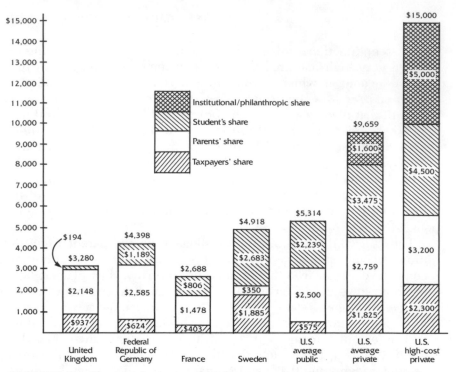

FIGURE 7.4 Sharing the costs of higher education for middle-income families in the United Kingdom, Federal Republic of Germany, France, Sweden, and the United States, 1985–86 (see notes below).

United Kingdom: "Middle income" is assumed to be £15,000 [$25,290]. Total cost is N.U.S. estimate of £1,945 [$3,280] per Table 2.1. The parental contribution is £1,274 [$2,148] per Table 2.3. The taxpayer portion is the mandatory grant (elsewhere than London) of £1830 [$3,086] minus the expected parental contribution, or £556 [$937]. The student contribution is the remaining need, or £115 [$194].

Federal Republic of Germany: "Middle income" is assumed to be DM36,000 [$16,667]. Total cost is the "more adequate" budget of DM9,500 [$5,398] per Table 3.1. The parental contribution is DM5,583 [$2,585] per Table 3.4. The maximum BAföG is assumed to be DM7,500 for 10 months, DM1,917 [$888] of which (7,500–5,583) would be awarded. The taxpayer contribution is the "effective grant" of 1,917 × (1.00 − 0.297) = DM1,348 [$624] per Table 3.3, assuming an 8-percent discount rate. The students' portion is the "true loan" of DM1,917 × 0.297 = DM569 [$263] plus the gap of DM2,000 [$926] between the total cost and the maximum BAföG, or DM2,569 [$1,189].

France: "Middle income" is 125,000F [$16,801] per Table 4.6. Total cost is 20,000F [$2,688] per Table 4.6. The taxpayer contribution is 3,000F [$403] of tax relief; the parental contribution, net of tax relief, cash, and "in-kind," is 11,000F [$1,478]; the student contribution, 6,000F [$806] in earnings, all from Table 4.6.

Sweden: "Middle income" can be anywhere in the range of 150–225,000 Skr [$20–30,000], as there is no means testing or expected parental contribution. The total cost is the "moderate budget" per Table 5.4. The taxpayer contribution is 14,134 Skr [$1,885]. Students pay their portion of study means and split the needed supplement of 5,258 Skr [$701] with their parents, for net contributions of 2,629 Skr [$350] and 20,122 Skr [$2,683] for parent and student respectively per Table 5.4.

United States: "Middle income" is assumed to be in the range of $30–$35,000. The total cost estimates and the estimated taxpayer, parental, student, and institutional shares are all per Table 6.5.

when their children are attending the high-cost private colleges, thus reflecting the use of need-based grants in the United States as a general economic welfare tool, the upper-middle- and high-income parents of college-going children, enjoying a lighter overall tax burden than their West European counterparts, pay a "user charge" via college tuitions that is extremely high for those electing to send children to private colleges and by comparison even for those whose children attend the public colleges and universities. This perspective contrasts most sharply with the Swedish viewpoint, which assumes the costs of higher education to be the joint responsibility of the student and the general taxpayer and which rejects not only the concept of parental responsibility but also the use of need-based, or means-tested, grants as a tool of general social welfare or income redistribution.

THE STUDENT CONTRIBUTION

Student contributions are shown in Figures 7.3, 7.4, and 7.5 for students for low-, middle-, and high-income families. The students' share of costs is highest in the United States for low- and middle-income students attending higher-cost private colleges, but it is most consistently high, particularly as a share of total needed revenues, in Sweden. It is also relatively high in the Federal Republic of Germany, although the high initial debt burden of German youth from low- and lower-middle-income families is greatly reduced by the extent of repayment subsidies within the BAföG system. In all three countries, governmentally sponsored programs make student loans available at subsidized rates, with long repayment periods and without any tests of credit worthiness *per se*. The United States is the only country among the five studied that encourages part-time student employment to the extent of subsidizing colleges, universities, and other public agencies for hiring students.

The students' share of higher education costs is relatively low in France, which lacks a generally available, governmentally sponsored loan program, although students who are not *bourse* recipients (thus excluding those from the poorest families) are allowed and even encouraged to take part-time jobs, and there are many small, unsubsidized loan programs available at least to special (e.g., *Grandes Ecoles*) students.

The students' share is by far the lowest among these five nations in the United Kingdom, which not only has no governmentally sponsored loan programs (and the students and the opposition clearly

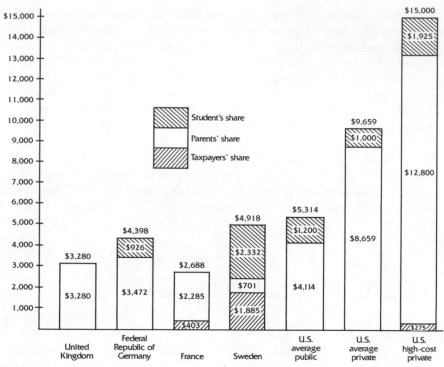

FIGURE 7.5 Sharing the costs of higher education for high-income families in the United Kingdom, Federal Republic of Germany, France, Sweden, and the United States, 1985–86 (see notes below).

United Kingdom: The total cost is the NUS estimate of £1,945 [$3,280] per Table 2.1. High-income families are ineligible for taxpayer-borne contributions, and students are discouraged from working or borrowing, so the entire cost is assumed to be borne by parents.

Federal Republic of Germany: The total cost is the "more adequate" budget of DM9,500 [$4,398] per Table 3.1. High-income families are ineligible for BAföG, so there is no taxpayer contribution. Parents are assumed to contribute what would have been the BAföG, or DM7,500 [$3,472]; students contribute DM2,000 [$926] to make up the full budget.

France: The total cost is 20,000F [$2,688] per Table 4.6. The taxpayer contribution is 3,000F [$403] of tax relief. High-income parents are assumed to provide the remaining net 17,000F [$2,285].

Sweden: The total cost is the "moderate budget" per Table 5.4. The taxpayer and student contributions are 14,134 Skr [$1,885] and 17,493 Skr [$2,332] respectively per Table 5.4. The parents are assumed to contribute the needed supplement of 5,258 Skr [$701].

United States: "High income" is beyond the range of either taxpayer or institutional/philanthropic assistance at the high-cost colleges. The parent and student contributions are per Table 6.6.

intend to keep it that way), but also actively discourages students from working part time.

Although this study did not examine extensive trend data, it has been shown that the students' share of expenses has been increasing over the past decade or so in the United States and in Sweden, and it can certainly be said to have increased in the Federal Republic of Germany with the 1984 conversion of the BAföG from a mainly grant to an all-loan program. This trend is of concern in part because of the possible problems in connection with rising student debts, e.g., rising defaults, declining respect for obligations, or the alleged distortion of career choices. Of equal concern is the shift of costs from parents and taxpayers onto students, seemingly without public awareness and thus perhaps with neither rationale nor intent.

STUDENT LOANS AND CHOICE

The rationale for a student loan program follows the rationale for the student bearing a portion of the cost of higher education: Whatever that portion is to be, there must be generally available loans so that students with no current income or assets of their own can meet their share of expenses and repay when they are finished with schooling, are earning a living, and presumably are reaping some of the monetary benefits of their higher education. Because most students have neither established credit nor collateral, it is essential that a policy requiring the student to pay a portion of the costs be supported either by governmental guarantees, as in the U.S. Guaranteed Student Loans, or by direct provision of governmental capital, as in the Swedish Study Means, German BAföG, or U.S. National Direct Student Loans.

There are no generally available, nongovernmentally sponsored student loans in any country. Hence, where there is no such governmentally sponsored loan program—as in the United Kingdom or in France—it is very difficult to sustain a policy that assumes any substantial portion of costs being borne by the student. This, of course, is the cornerstone of the students' position in the United Kingdom that no student loan program of any type whatsoever be allowed to be formed: once in place, it is feared that it would be all too easy to shift costs from the taxpayer or parent or both to the student. With no available loans whatsoever, the government remains under great pressure to maintain its grants, to the obvious benefit of the students.

However, student loans also serve, on a much smaller basis, a function quite apart from support of an overall policy of student cost sharing. This is the provision of choice to students who, for whatever reason, are excluded by public policy from the taxpayer grants that would have been available or who for some reason are denied the otherwise expected contribution from their parents—but who, were loans to be available, would be willing to borrow in order to supplant the missing taxpayer or parental contribution and to invest in their own higher education. Were student loans even available in the United Kingdom, for example, students denied the Mandatory Grant or the parental contribution offset would at least have a chance to proceed on their own—with no change in the fundamental, underlying policy of no student share for the regular student. Similarly, the French student who had been denied help from his or her parents, or who wished to live away from home, would also be able to do so with the assistance of a generally available student loan program, again with no diminution of the current commitment to taxpayer-borne assistance, which is very minimal anyway.

A similar observation may be made where student loans are available, but at such enormous subsidy and cost to the taxpayer that they must be rationed according to some standard of need. For example, what of the German student who is denied a BAföG loan because of his or her parents' income, but who very much needs to borrow to enable a certain living standard or to make up for a shortfall in the parental contribution (in lieu of taking them to family court)? Or what of the Swedish student needing or wanting to borrow a bit more than the maximum Study Means in order to make up for what is generally believed to have been an erosion over time of the real purchasing power of that assistance? Were student loans to be generally available at a rate of interest not far below the true cost of money, such borrowing could easily take place with no more justification than the understandably high present value placed on money by students with no alternative means of receiving a higher education. However, the strict need-based rationing of these loans, made necessary by their very high subsidies, precludes them from being easily used either to fill in for shortfalls in the parental contribution or simply to provide a somewhat-higher-than-minimal standard of student living. Such loans of choice or convenience are thus available altogether in the United Kingdom or France and are virtually unavailable in Sweden and West Germany. Only in the United States, and only with the supplement of the relatively high-cost, market-rate Auxiliary Loans to Assist Students (ALAS), are students able to borrow as much as they reasonably need purely as an expression of their time preference for money and their faith in sufficient private returns to their investments in education.

SHARING THE COSTS: WHO SHOULD PAY?

The aim of a comparative study is to deepen and broaden our understanding of why countries have developed their particular responses to their similar challenges, how and why one's own country has developed as it has, and what it might take to change a given system in a particular way. The fundamental question of who should pay has been faced in all the countries of this study. Answers have been provided from the perspectives of economic theory, political ideology, and culture. Let us examine each perspective.

The Economic, or Human Capital, Perspective: Who Benefits? Who Should Pay? The appropriate share of costs to be borne by the student as opposed to the taxpayer is a favorite question of economists, many of whom believe the answer to lie in the proper apportioning of benefits between the student and society. The students' benefits, or the private returns, are thought to be revealed in higher lifetime earnings for university graduates or in some monetary expression of the nonpecuniary advantages to college such as more occupational options or a greater power over one's own life—benefits that should make the student willing to invest in his or her own higher education if the investment capital (i.e., student loans) were only available. The public benefits, on the other hand, are those such as more enlightened civil discourse, lower crime rates, or a more stable economy that benefit those other than the student himself or herself. The sum of all of the strictly private decisions to invest in higher education will, by definition, have ignored all the strictly public benefits and is thus likely to lead to an overall investment in higher education at a level below that which is socially optimal. By this public finance perspective, the general taxpayer-borne subsidy of higher education is the mechanism by which the price of the product is dropped below its true cost in order to increase the sum of the private investment decisions to a level at which the full social (public and private) benefits and the full social costs are in balance.

The public benefit rationale for taxpayer-borne subsidies applies more to the basic costs of instruction and to the presence or absence of tuition than to the extent of student maintenance grants, which have been the focus of much of this study. By their provision of essentially tuition-free higher education, at least to most students, the European nations in this study are treating higher education as though its benefits were overwhelmingly public; and the United States, through its low-tuition public sector, implicitly acknowledges substantial public benefits.

The taxpayer-borne subsidies targeted upon students from low-income families via need-based, or means-tested, grants or loan subsidies have an altogether different theoretical rationale. The case for additional subsidies (i.e., beyond free or low tuition) to students from low-income families is not just because such students, being from poor families, would not be able to afford the student-maintenance expenses of university life—indeed, there are many things that the children of the poor cannot afford to buy—but because this particular thing, "a higher education," is so terribly important to individual and social well-being that its distribution to the young must not be a function of the family's ability to pay.

Such an argument goes far to explain why student maintenance expenses cannot simply be left to the parents. It is not altogether clear, however, why the taxpayer and not the student, via loans and part-time earnings, needs to bear these expenses. By one argument, the student from a low-income family has just as much chance to earn a good income and to repay a loan as does the student from a middle- or high-income family. On the other hand, it is commonly asserted in the United States, West Germany, Sweden, and undoubtedly elsewhere that students from low-income backgrounds have a cultural fear of, or aversion to, debt, and may be less ready to seize the opportunity presumably offered by a student loan program than would be the typical middle-income student. Buttressing this argument for at least some taxpayer-borne grant support to students from low-income families is the pervasive, disquieting fact that higher education, with or without need-based grants, is disproportionately partaken of by middle- and upper-income youth in all countries in this and every other study. While the causes for this phenomenon are almost certainly deeply rooted in cultural expectations, peer rewards, and the impact of family on success in early schooling, and while "loans versus grants" may play a relatively minor role in socioeconomic transmission of college attendance, the seriousness of the issue and the apparent intractability of the more fundamental causes has led a number of countries, probably the United States foremost, to place great weight on need-based grants to induce more college-going from the children of low socioeconomic families.

In fact, the economic theories underlying public subsidies to higher education have done little to enhance our understanding of what policies exist or should exist. Those who are inclined to favor substantial taxpayer-borne grants seem to discern many social benefits. Those inclined to favor free markets, low taxes, and private colleges tend to see few. In the end, policies toward parental contributions, grants, loans, student employment, or loan subsidies seem to be edified scarcely at all by such constructs as the mix of public and private benefits to higher education. In fact, the human capital concepts of public and private returns to public and private investments in higher education seem to be of little interest to policymakers anywhere and to be of declining interest to researchers and policy analysts.

The Political Perspective: The Effect of the Immediately Dominant Political Ideology. To some degree, the apportioning of the burden of costs of higher education follows traditional Western socio-economic-political ideology. The left, with its more favorable inclination toward a larger public sector and toward increased transfer payments to the poor, could be expected to favor a high proportion of taxpayer-borne costs. The right, on the other hand, could be expected to favor smaller taxpayer-borne expenditures and more reliance on "free choice" and a market-oriented apportioning of costs. To be sure, the conservative Reagan, Thatcher, and Kohl governments in the United States, the United Kingdom, and Germany have all attempted in the mid-1980s to lower if not the absolute amounts, then the recent rates of increase in direct grants to students, and to shift some additional costs to parents (at least to those who can afford to pay) and students in the form of higher loan burdens and even the possible introduction in Europe of tuition. At the same time, all three of these conservative governments have failed to make substantial changes in the systems they inherited from their more liberal predecessors. The massive cuts in federal student aid proposed by the first and subsequent Reagan budgets never materialized. The Thatcher government's trial balloons of means-testing the tuition grants and of introducing even a limited loan program were violently opposed by her own as well as the opposition parties. And the Kohl government's conversion of a grant to a loan program ended up with a loan so heavily subsidized that it changed the ultimate division of burden between students and taxpayers very little.

In the meantime, France, nominally run from 1981 to 1986 by a Socialist-dominated coalition, has one of the least generous programs of aid to the children of the very poor. Sweden, arguably the most consistently egalitarian nation of Western Europe, has almost no grants at all (beyond, of course, the traditionally free public higher education), and it provides no special financial assistance to the children of poor parents.

In short, the immediately dominant political ideology may point the way or apply pressure toward some shift in the apportioning of cost burden among parents, students, and taxpayers. Knowledge only of the ideology, though, at least as represented by the party or coalition in power, does little to predict the cost-sharing characteristics of a particular system. Furthermore, a fundamental change in that system is not much easier to effect through a mere change in government than it is through the arguments of the human capital economist.

A Cultural Perspective: Sharing the Costs of Higher Education. Policies and instruments for apportioning the costs of higher education are functions of traditions and beliefs with roots far deeper and more complex than either party ideology or economic sophistication. In the United States, for example, the college years, or at least the undergraduate portion thereof, may be viewed more nearly as an extension of childhood than as a beginning of adulthood. The typical U.S. undergraduate begins college at age 17 or 18, incompletely educated even in the most general sense, still in almost complete financial dependence on his or her parents, and very often with no clear occupational goal and little sense of adult civic and social responsibilities. Little wonder that the United States has built a system of sharing the costs of higher education on the primacy of the parental contribution. And no wonder, too, that this system is becoming increasingly strained as more and more U.S. undergraduates are *not* 17-to-22-year-olds from two-parent households, but are mature adults and/or are not living with both natural parents.

In most of Europe, higher education may be more easily construed as the start of adulthood rather than as the end of childhood. European undergraduates are a bit older than their traditional American counterparts. They are more likely to have completed their general education in academic secondary school and to be entering the university for the start of specific professional studies. They may look upon university studies not so much as something they are especially fortunate to be able to do and for which privilege they should be pleased to live under the twin burdens of collegiate poverty and parental dependency, but as their proper calling at this stage of their lives, not unlike the workplace for their age peers who are not in higher education. Funds should be made available to those whose calling is the university, whether as a "study wage," a student grant, or a repayable grant, to enable them to live more-or-less like others of their age—and, desirably, not in any prolonged state of dependence on their parents (the French notwithstanding).

Much social welfare tradition in both the United States and the United Kingdom is built on the principle of means testing or targeting, in which certain goods or services are made available at public expense but only upon demonstration of need, which generally means some degree of poverty and dependency. Financial assistance in the United States and the United Kingdom, then, begins with the premise that parents should pay as much as they can afford in support of their children's higher education. But public and philanthropic assistance steps in if the parents declare their inability to pay all that is necessary. In this sense, need-based financial assistance, coupled with the underlying expected parental contribution, are parts of the underlying U.S. and U.K. systems of income redistribution that subsidize for poor people certain otherwise expensive but so-called essential goods and services like food, rent, and health care, as opposed to systems of income maintenance or outright transfer payments that redistribute income without regard to expenditure or use. In contrast, the Swedish welfare state has achieved such relative wage parity that poverty *per se* is held to be a relatively insignificant factor in accounting for the low higher educational participation of working-class and rural youth, and the Swedish Social Democratic agenda has therefore concentrated more on improving retention at the secondary level and on alternative criteria for admittance (e.g., the 25–4 rule) rather than on enhancing taxpayer-borne grant aid for higher education. At the same time, Sweden has achieved a very high degree of income equalization through progressive income taxes, high minimum wages, high employment, and the absence of any significant nonproductive underclass. Sweden thus has no need of targeted income transfers—to parents of university students or to other categories of "worthy poor"—to even further redistribute income. In fact, there is some thought in Sweden that targeting aid and requiring some families to declare their need would be demeaning as well as unnecessary.

In France, too, academic streaming by socioeconomic class occurs overwhelmingly before and during the academic secondary level, and the sons and daughters of the poor who make it through the rigorous French *lycée* are highly motivated for university life and apparently find the combination of subsidized meals, family assistance, and grants, minimal though they may be, generally sufficient to sustain them. In the United States, by contrast, large numbers of young people from low socioeconomic backgrounds graduate from comprehensive high schools with minimal academic preparedness and great ambivalence toward further schooling; for them, the difference between a small grant and a large one or between a grant and a loan may be a much more significant factor in deciding between the alternatives of college or the workplace. Similarly, attributing withdrawal or academic failure to the lack of adequate finances is a socially acceptable explanation for not pursuing a college degree in a country where college attendance has become the norm rather than the elitist exception.

In short, the proper apportioning of costs between parents, students, and taxpayers is not easily arrived at through a traditional division of benefits thought to be "public" or "private." Nor is a country's generosity with taxpayer-borne grants—or, conversely, its readiness to pass the burden on to students through loans—predictable merely from the general socioeconomic ideology of the party in political power. Rather, the sharing of the costs at any one time and the underlying policies and programs of need-based grants, expected parental contributions, student loan programs, and the like are linked to such social, political, and economic factors as: the balance of national concern for equality versus meritocratic rewards, the prevailing wage differentials between the graduates of the secondary and tertiary educational levels, the political power of students, the general economic climate and in particular the status of the public treasury, etc. In fact, what is probably more interesting and useful is not one or another particular apportioning of these costs at a point in time, but rather the probable consequences of proposed changes or shifts in one or another share, to which this concluding chapter now turns.

SHIFTING THE COSTS: THE DYNAMICS OF COST SHARING

The beginning premise of this study was that the costs of higher education have to be met by three principal sources: parents, students, and taxpayers, with institutions or philanthropists a fourth source of some significance at least in the United States. A basic corollary to this premise is that a change in the share borne by one party must either mean a change in the shares of one or both of the others, or else a change in something even more fundamental, such as the living standards of students or the socioeconomic profile of the student body. For example, a significant decline over time in taxpayer-borne, need-based grants must mean either a corresponding decline in the standard of student living, a decline in the proportion of students judged to have need, an increase in the contributions of at least some parents, or an increase in the contributions of at least some students—or some combination of the above.

The most important benefit from a comparative study such as this may be the greater understanding that can emerge from an array of examples of the intended and unintended consequences of changes in one or another of the policy tools of higher educational finance. For example:

Decreasing the average size of need-based grants (as in the United States since 1980)

- may, but probably will not because of the income levels involved, lead to increased parental contributions;

- may lead some students to reduce their overall expenses by choosing a lower-cost (priced) public college rather than a higher-cost (priced) private one; and

- may lead to higher annual and aggregate student debts.

Increasing taxpayer-borne grants to needy students (as is proposed by students in most countries in most years)

- maintains the standard of student living, assuming the increase to be commensurate with the rising costs of student life;

- gives the student options (e.g., to attend a higher-cost institution or one farther from home); and

- may lessen the need to borrow or to work part-time or both.

Beginning a program of taxpayer-borne grants, or tax credits, to students and/or families on bases other than financial need (as has been proposed by the Reagan Administration in the United States)

- allows the student to increase his or her standard of living;

- allows the student to borrow less or work fewer part-time hours; or

- allows the parents to reduce their contributions accordingly, in which case neither of the other two possibilities will happen and parents of bright young people will become the prime beneficiaries.

Reducing taxpayer-borne grant benefits dollar-for-dollar for student earnings (as in France)

- will discourage part-time work and thus reduce student living standards, but only for the very lowest-income students who have a chance at a grant anyway.

Opening up the availability of highly subsidized student loans without regard to need (as in the United States in 1978)

- encourages all students to borrow to the maximum allowed, with much of the resulting borrowing either displacing what would otherwise have been the parental contribution or allowing the student to reinvest the borrowed funds at a higher rate of interest.

Maintaining very low interest rates and high subsidies within the student loan program (as in Germany and Sweden, especially)

- increases the taxpayer-borne share of costs; and

- incurs the phenomenon listed immediately above; or

- requires all loans to be rationed strictly according to need, which in turn precludes a student from choosing to borrow in lieu of a parental contribution.

Making student loans generally available where they now are not (as might be done in United Kingdom or France)

- may begin a steady erosion of taxpayer-borne grants and parental contributions as both other sources see relief from their burdens in the expansion of student loans; and

- would give at least the choice of higher education, at some personal cost, to students otherwise ineligible for grants or unsupported by their parents.

Introducing tuitions where there currently are none (as might be the case in France, West Germany, or Sweden)

- in Sweden, would increase student debts even more, as well as the taxpayer-borne subsidies thereof;

- in Germany, could lead to tuition sharing in almost any desired proportion by: (1) BAföG recipients, through higher debts; (2) parents of BAföG recipients, through higher parental contribution; (3) non-BAföG recipients and their parents, in whatever way expenses are now shared, presumably mainly by parents; and (4) taxpayers, through BAföG subsidies; and

- in France, would increase mainly the parental-borne costs, which would place considerable hardship on low-income families, for whom the *bourse* is now barely adequate.

Covering tuitions with taxpayer-borne grants only in cases of need, i.e., making the tuition grant means tested (as was proposed in the United Kingdom in late 1984)

- would increase costs paid by the highest-income parents; and

- would reduce slightly the taxpayer-borne burden, or else allow the increased net tuition revenues to be retained and spent by the institutions.

There are few right or wrong policies in the comparative study of almost any field. To most Americans, the U.K. system looks a bit odd because of the absence of a student contribution; the Swedish system because of no parental contribution; the French system because of such a seemingly meager taxpayer-borne contribution and all the disincentives to studying away from home; and the German system because of the political blood that was shed over a student-loan program so heavily subsidized that the true costs are still borne overwhelmingly by the taxpayer. The U.S. system, if it may be called that, must in turn look odd to colleagues from these other countries because of the aggressive competition on the part of institutions for students; the coexistence of public, private not-for-profit, and proprietary for-profit institutions of postsecondary and higher education; the high tuitions paid in the private sector and yet the competitive robustness of most of that sector vis-à-vis the lower-priced public sector; the bewildering array of grant and loan programs; and the almost total individualization of the ultimate price to the student and his or her family. In its own way, though, each national system is trying to assure equality of opportunity; to provide necessary funding for the universities; to become no more, and perhaps even a bit less, of a burden to the taxpayers; and to avoid undue political antagonisms on the part of either parents or students.

APPENDIX A

CONVERSION OF NATIONAL CURRENCY UNITS TO U.S. DOLLARS

Any comparison of money amounts—such as family incomes, grants, or loans—across countries, where such amounts are, perforce, originally expressed in units of the national currencies, requires a conversion to a common currency for purposes of comparison. For this study, for example, we want to express the size of the 1984–85 U.K. mandatory grant of £2,100 and the two-child family income of £8,100 at which point grant reductions begin to be made, the total maximum Swedish study means of 29,448 Skr and the student income of 22,300 Skr above which the study means is reduced, and the other critical grant and income indices from France and Germany all in U.S. dollars so that they are comparable to one to another (for which purpose, of course, any common-denominator currency would suffice) and also meaningful to the U.S. reader, for whom a family income in Germany or a student loan in Sweden will have real meaning only when expressed in U.S. dollars of comparable purchasing power.

Such comparisons, then, require converting national currencies to U.S. dollars, an experience familiar to anyone who has traveled abroad and had to buy British pounds, French francs, or German Deutschmarks. In theory, the exchange rates at which currencies are freely bought and sold should reflect what each currency can purchase in goods or services in its own country. If three Deutschmarks trade freely for one American dollar, then *in theory* one could presume that DM300 should be able to command in Germany what $100 commands in the United States.

However, freely floating exchange rates are affected by factors other than the relative purchasing powers of the currencies within their home countries. Interest rates, political considerations, and other factors may give a particular currency a value in exchange for another currency that at least in the short run does not reflect the relative purchasing powers of the two currencies in their respective countries. Thus, the U.S. dollar in 1984 and 1985, largely because of the continuing high real interest rates in the United States, had a value relative to other free European currencies considerably greater than its purchasing power *in the United States* relative, say, to the purchasing power of the Deutschmark *in the Federal Republic of Germany*. Specifically, the market exchange rate of the dollar to the Deutschmark on 1 July 1985 was DM3.04. However, at that very time, DM3.04 in Germany were worth a good deal more than $1 was worth in the United States in comparable purchasing power, and if we need to compare grant or income levels in Germany to those in the United States, we need a *purchasing power parity index* rather than a *market exchange rate*.

Purchasing power parities are actually ratios of prices of particular goods and services in different countries. As in any price index, the particular set of goods and services must be stipulated: all consumption goods and services, total national products, governmental expenditures, etc. The most commonly used purchasing power parity (PPP) takes into account the set of goods and services that make up all final expenditures. Like a consumer price index, which is similarly an average of a great many prices, a PPP is useful for making general comparisons of the purchasing powers of several currencies in their respective nations even though they may not always accurately reflect the relative purchasing powers for particular sets of goods and services.

A different but related complication enters into the comparison of family incomes across countries that may have quite different public provisions for certain family needs like medical care, rent, and higher education. Thus, to compare in the fullest sense German with American family incomes, we need to know not only what the two currencies can purchase in the respective countries, but also whether basic goods and services are provided free of charge or are heavily subsidized in one or the other country, or whether other tax or, for example, child-allowance policies differently affect the family living standards in the two countries even beyond the purchasing powers of their respective family incomes.

A full consideration of all of these factors was quite beyond the scope of this research. Nevertheless, the literature on purchasing power parities was examined, and the most recent data, from the Organization for Economic Cooperation and Development, was employed. The OECD work, by Peter Hill in 1984, covered the United States, France, Germany, and the United Kingdom. A purchasing power parity conversion for the Swedish kronor was estimated by converting the German Deutschmark and Danish kroner purchasing power parities to the Swedish kronor via current exchange rates be-

TABLE A.1
Purchasing Power Parity and Exchange Rates, 1984 and 1985, in National
Currency Units Per $U.S.

	1985		1984	
	Purchasing power parity	*Exchange rate*	*Purchasing power parity*	*Exchange rate*
France franc (F)	7.44	9.27	6.74	8.55
Germany, Federal Republic Deutschmark (DM)	2.16	3.04	2.33	2.78
Sweden kronor (Skr)	7.5	8.75	7.2	8.19
United Kingdom pound (£)	0.593	0.768	0.549	0.737

Purchasing power parities and exchange rates for France, Germany, and the United Kingdom are from Peter Hill, "Real Gross Product in OECD Countries and Associated Purchasing Power Parities," OECD Economics and Statistics Department Working Paper no. 17, December 1984. Figures for Sweden were derived as explained in the text. Exchange rates for 1985 are as of 1 July as reported in the *International Herald Tribune*; PPP estimates for 1985 from France, Germany, and the United Kingdom were extrapolated from 1984 figures given OECD retail price indices 1 April 1984 and March 1985 as reported in the *Employment Gazette* May 1985, p. 553 (London).

tween those countries. Purchasing power parity estimates for 1985 were extrapolated from the 1984 OECD data according to the formula:

$$PPP_{85} = PPP_{84} \frac{1 + \inf_C}{1 + \inf_{U.S.}}$$

where $\inf_C$ is the 1984–85 increase in consumer prices in country C and $\inf_{U.S.}$ is the 1984–85 increase in U.S. consumer prices, drawing on OECD retail price indices, measured from March 1984 to March 1985.

The purchasing power parities for the United Kingdom, France, West Germany, and Sweden for 1984 and 1985 in U.S. dollars are summarized in Table A.1.

APPENDIX B

THE PRESENT VALUE OF LOAN REPAYMENTS AND THE CALCULATION OF TRUE LOAN AND EFFECTIVE GRANT COMPONENTS OF STUDENT LOANS IN THE UNITED STATES, THE FEDERAL REPUBLIC OF GERMANY, AND SWEDEN

The Concept of Present Value

Any sum of money to be either paid or owed at a specified future time can be expressed as an equivalent *present value*, given only an appropriate *discount rate*. Thus, the value now—the present value—of $1,000 to be paid or owed one year from now is $909.09, if discounted at 10 percent. The calculation of discounting is simply the reverse of the process of growing a sum at interest: $909.09 invested for one year at 10 percent becomes $1,000.

The appropriate discount rate is generally a function of the prevailing rate of interest for a particular sum of money for a particular period of time. Thus, the promise of $1,100 a year from now is worth no more to one than $1,000 right now because that $1,000, invested for one year at 10 percent, would yield $1,100 in a year. If 10 percent is the correct rate, and ignoring special cash-flow needs, one should be indifferent between the $1,000 in hand today and the certain promise of $1,100 a year from today.

Naturally, as interest rates go up, the advantage of having money in hand (to invest) is enhanced, and the more promise of a certain sum in the future is diminished; a higher discount rate is appropriate, say 12 percent, and the $1,100 a year from today takes on a present value of only $982.14.

A flow of future sums, such as the payments to amortize a loan, can also be given an equivalent present value. Naturally, the full flow of payments required to amortize a $1,000 loan over, say, 10 years at 8 percent interest, discounted at 8 percent, is the amount of the original loan, or $1,000. But if we had a flow of payments in fact only amortizing the loan at 3 percent (i.e., ten annual payments of $117.23) and continued to believe 10 percent to be a more appropriate discount rate, reflecting more nearly the real value of the money lent, the present value of the flow of payments would be only $720, or $280 less than the amount of the loan. If one were to be so fortunate as to be given $1,000 with an obligation to repay over 10 years on only a 3 percent amortization schedule, when the money is actually worth 10 percent, it could be said that one was actually given a true loan of only $720—the present value of the repayments discounted at 10 percent, or the amount that the repayments actually amortize over 10 years at 10 percent—with the remainder, or $280, being the present value of a flow of subsidies, or the effective grant component of the original $1,000.

The Present Value of Student Loan Repayments

It is precisely in this way that the *true loan* and the *subsidy*, or *effective grant*, components of student loans under U.S., German, and Swedish repayment provisions have been calculated using alternative discount rates of 8, 10, and 12 percent. It was assumed in all cases that the average student loan is taken out 1.5 years before the completion of studies. This is probably a conservative "in-school" assumption (i.e., working to depress the ultimate calculation of the subsidy component) at least for the United States, where so many students go on to graduate work; but we also expect higher borrowings in the later years, so an assumption of 1.5 years to the end of studies seemed reasonable.

For each country, there is a prescribed grace period between the completion of studies and the beginning of the repayment obligation. At that point, the debts to be amortized are the same as the amounts originally borrowed in the United States and the Federal Republic of Germany where there is no interest charged during either the in-school or grace periods, but have increased in Sweden, where interest is charged and accrued during both the 1.5-year assumed in-school period and the 2-year grace period.

The prescribed repayment schedules are then stipulated: 10 years at 8 percent for the United States; 20 years at 0 percent for the Federal Republic of Germany; and a 20-year, 4.2 percent repayment schedule for Sweden that is graduated at a slope, or rate of increase, of the same 4.2 percent annually.

All payments were then discounted back to the assumed origins of the loans at discount rates of 8, 10, and 12 percent. The results are summarized in Table B.1. At the 10 percent discount rate, for example, the repayments on a U.S. student loan of $1,000 have a present value of $753, suggesting an effective grant component of $1,000 − $753, or $247. If we assume a 12 percent discount rate, the present value of the repayments is $667 and the effective grant is $333.

For the Federal Republic of Germany, the combination of the very long 5-year grace period, the long 20-year repayment schedule, plus the absence of any interest reduces the present value of repayments on an original loan of DM1,000 to DM227 or DM175, with corresponding effective grant components of DM773 and DM825 on discount rate assumptions of 10 and 12 percent respectively.

For the 30 percent of German student borrowers who have their loans reduced by one-quarter at the outset by virtue of being in the top 30 percent of their classes, the present values of repayments fall to DM170 or DM131, with effective grant components of DM830 or DM869 under discount rate assumptions of 10 or 12 percent respectively. Clearly, there is very little "true loan" in the German BAföG repayment obligation.

The Swedish repayment provisions fall midway between the U.S. and West German plans in the resulting effective subsidy. The grace and repayment periods are longer and the interest rate is lower than in the United States. But the 4.2 percent rate is much higher, of course, than the German rate, and the fact that Swedish student loans accrue interest during the in-school and grace periods tends to reduce that element of subsidy relative to the United States. On discount rate assumptions of 10 percent and 12 percent, the repayments on a Swedish student loan of 1,000 Skr have present values of 472 Skr and 380 Skr, with corresponding effective grant components of 528 Skr and 620 Skr.

The discount rate assumptions of 8, 10, and 12 percent were selected to reflect something conservatively approximating the prevailing costs of money in the United States, the Federal Republic of Germany, and Sweden. Relatively lower rates for Germany and Sweden could be argued on the bases either of slightly lower prime interest rates or of probable lower unsubsidized student loan rates were there to be a comprehensive student loan program without the benefit of taxpayer subsidies. At the same time, a truly unsubsidized student loan program available to all students without credit examination would have an astronomical rate of interest in any country, especially in the United States with its high default experience, and attempting to estimate a market rate for student loans as a guide to an appropriate discount rate is probably not a useful exercise. If anything, the assumptions of 8, 10, and 12 percent are on the low side, particularly for the United States, but the purpose of the present

TABLE B.1
Present Value of Repayments on 1,000 Units of Initial Lending, United States, Sweden, and Federal Republic of Germany, Assuming 1.5 Years In-School, and Using Discount Rates of 8, 10, and 12 Percent

	United States	Sweden	Federal Republic of Germany
Repayment period	10 years	(a)	20 years
In-school assumption	1.5 years	1.5 years	1.5 years
Grace period	0.5 years	2.0 years	5.0 years
Interest during in-school	0 percent	4.2 percent	0 percent
Interest during grace period	0 percent	4.2 percent	0 percent
Interest during repayment	8 percent	4.2 percent	0 percent
Original loan	$1,000	1,000 Skr	DM1,000
Period from origination to repayment (in-school plus grace)	2 years	3.5 years	6.5 years
Debt at start of repayment	$1,000	1,155 Skr	DM1,000
Mode of repayment	equal quarterly	graduated annual	equal quarterly
Amount each payment	40 @ $36.56	(b)	80 @ DM12.50
Present value of repayments at 8% discount rate	$853.59	593.84 Skr	DM296.88
at 10% discount rate	$753.25	471.90 Skr	DM226.62
at 12% discount rate	$667.11	380.46 Skr	DM175.05

[a] The repayment period in Sweden is normally the number of years between the initiation of repayment and age 51; a 20-year repayment period is most often used for illustration.

[b] The first annual payment on the Swedish debt of 1,155 Skr would be 57.76 Skr, which payment would increase each year for 20 years at a 4.2 percent annual rate of increase, and which repayment stream would amortize the starting debt at an annual interest rate of 4.2 percent.

value of repayment calculations is to illustrate the too-often-unappreciated subsidy, or effective grant, that is contained within all student loans; and some conservative assumptions, which tend to err on the side of minimizing the effective grant component, were thought to be more appropriate to this study.

Finally, it is important to note that these calculations have not included any provision for loan losses or administrative costs borne by the government. This study focuses on the allocation of the costs faced by the student, family, and government at the outset of studies, and it is not designed to reflect the total or average per-student cost to the taxpayer of maintaining a student-support system. For this reason, the effective grant component that is borne by the taxpayer should not be viewed as a calculation of average total cost to the taxpayer per 1,000 units of student lending. Such an amount would be considerably higher than the effective grant calculated for the purpose of this study, particularly for the United States, and, if charged to the student by assuming a reduced average repayment flow, would substantially further lower the true loan component.

NOTES

1. Cost Sharing in Higher Education

1. Maureen Woodhall, *Review of Student Support Schemes in Selected OECD Countries* (Paris: Organization for Economic Cooperation and Development, 1978).
2. Maureen Woodhall, *Student Loans as a Means of Financing Higher Education: Lessons from International Experience* (Washington, D.C.: The World Bank, 1983). See also Woodhall, "Student Loans: Lessons from Recent International Experience" (London: University of London Policy Studies Institute, 1981). Also, Woodhall, *Student Loans: A Review of Experience in Scandinavia and Elsewhere* (London: George Harrap, 1970).
3. Michael Vorbeck, "Financial Aid to Students in Europe: A Summary Analysis," *International Journal of Institutional Management in Higher Education*, vol. 7, no. 3, November 1983, pp. 289–305.

2. The United Kingdom

1. Sources for the section on "Structure and Governance" include: *The Development of Higher Education into the 1990's* ("The Green Paper"), presented to Parliament by the Secretary of State for Education and Science, the Secretary of State for Scotland, the Secretary of State for Wales, and the Secretary of State for Northern Ireland (London: Her Majesty's Stationery Office, May 1985; Keith Fenwick and Peter McBride, *The Government of Higher Education* (Oxford: Martin Rubertson, 1981); Alan Matterson, *Polytechnics and Colleges* (Essex: Longman House, 1981); Michael Shattock, "British Higher Education Under Pressure: Politics, Budgets and Demography, and the Acceleration of Ideas for Change," *European Journal of Education*, vol. 19, no. 2, 1984, pp. 201–16; *Excellence in Diversity: Towards a New Strategy for Higher Education* (The Leverhulme Report) (Guilford, Surrey: The Society for Research into Higher Education, 1983); *A Strategy for Higher Education into the 1990's: The University Grants Committee's Advice* (London: Her Majesty's Stationery Office, September 1984).
2. The 46 publicly funded universities include the Open University, which has university powers but is not under the funding purview of the University Grants Committee. The UGC considers the University of Wales as seven separate entities for funding purposes and also funds two advanced schools of business, giving rise to another defendable total, 54, for the number of U.K. universities. There is also one chartered private university, The University of Buckingham.
3. The term "academic drift" was used by John Pratt and Tyrrell Burgess in their 1974 report on the polytechnics and is given recent, comprehensive attention by Guy Neave in "The Dynamics of Integration in Non-Integrated Systems of Higher Education in Western Europe," in Harry Hermanns, Ulrich Teichler, and Henry Wasser, eds., *The Compleat University* (Cambridge, Mass.: Schenkman Publishing Co., 1983), pp. 263–76.
4. *Report of the Committee on Higher Education* (The Robbins Report) (London: Her Majesty's Stationery Office, 1963).
5. *The Development of Higher Education into the 1990's* ("The Green Paper"), 1985.
6. The mandatory- and discretionary-award program described in this section and used as a basis for the analysis of sharing costs in the United Kingdom is actually

the program applicable to England and Wales. Scotland and Northern Ireland have similar programs, but the fullest measure of accuracy would have this entire section limited to England and Wales.

7. Clive Booth, "DES and Treasury," in Alfred Morris and John Sizer, eds., *Resources and Higher Education* (Guilford, Surrey: The Society for Research into Higher Education, 1982), pp. 46–47. Also, House of Commons Library Research Division, "Student Grants, Fees, and the Parental Contribution," research note no. 213, 10 January 1985.

8. The increase of tuitions to full cost to overseas students has been a policy of enormous controversy and the subject of much discussion and some emerging analysis. It is, however, essentially extraneous to the scope of this study.

9. See *The Development of Higher Education into the 1990's* ("The Green Paper"). For attempts to reduce access to nonstudent benefits, see "Changes in Student Benefit Entitlement," Social Security Advisory Committee press release 7 January 1986. For NUS response, see "Proposed Changes in Student Benefit Entitlement" (London: National Union of Students, February 1986).

10. John Saxby, *Undergraduate Income and Expenditure: Survey 1982/83* (London: National Union of Students, February 1984), pp. 32–43.

11. *Ibid*, p. 42.

12. Sources of information on the United Kingdom (England and Wales: see n. 6 above) student grant program include: Department of Education and Science, *Grants to Students: A Brief Guide* (London: DES, July 1984); "Student Awards in 1982–83: England and Wales," *DES Statistical Bulletin*, January 1985; *The Education (Mandatory Awards) Regulations 1984, Statutory Instruments 1984 No. 1116* (London: DES); Maureen Woodhall, "Financial Support for Students" in Alfred Morris and John Sizer, eds., *Resources and Higher Education* (Guilford, Surrey: The Society for Research into Higher Education, 1982); Department of Education and Science, "Student Grants for 1985–86," news release 31 May 1985; House of Commons Library Research Division, "Student Grants, Fees, and the Parental Contribution" (Kay Andrews). Research Note No. 213, 1 January 1985.

13. Department of Education and Science, "Student Awards in 1982–83: England and Wales," *Statistical Bulletin*, January 1985.

14. Maureen Woodhall, "Financial Support for Students" in Morris and Sizer, eds., *Resource Use*, p. 98.

15. DES, "Student Awards in 1982–83: England and Wales," *Statistical Bulletin*, January 1985, fn. to Table 4.

16. DES, *Grants to Students: A Brief Guide*; also John Saxby, *Undergraduate Income and Expenditure Survey 1982/83* (London: National Union of Students, February 1984), pp. 15–16.

17. The case for a loan program in the United Kingdom is argued most consistently and persuasively by Maureen Woodhall. Recent statements of her position include "Try Banking on Student Loans," *The Times*, 2 April 1986 and "The Role of Selectivity in Alternative Patterns of Financial Support for Students," University of London Institute of Education, April 1986. See also Mary Farmer and Ray Barrell, "Why Student Loans Are Fairer than Grants," *Public Money*, 12 June 1982, pp. 19–24.

18. See "In Praise of Grants," *The Times Higher Education Supplement*, editorial 29 October 1982, p. 32.

19. Woodhall, "The Role of Selectivity," pp. 9–10.

20. See publications by the National Union of Students; "The Case Against Loans," 1965; "No to Loans," 1967; "Why We Don't Need Loans: Some Current Questions Answered," 1971; and *Student Loans: The Costs and The Consequences*, 1985.

21. "Grant Us a Living: A Discussion Document on Student Financial Support," London: National Union of Students, February 1985, p. 10.

22. National Union of Students, *Student Loans: The Costs and The Consequences* (London: NUS, 1985), p. 4.

23. *Ibid*, p. 6.

24. See "Thatcher Faces Revolt on Student Aid," *Chronicle of Higher Education*, 12 December 1984; and "British Government, Faced with Party Revolt, Retreats on Proposed Cuts in Student Grants," *Chronicle of Higher Education*, January 1985.

25. Delivered to the House of Commons 12 November 1985, as reported in *Education*, 22 November 1985, p. 462.

26. House of Commons Library Research Division, *op. cit.*, p. 13.

3. The Federal Republic of Germany

1. For general descriptions of the West German higher educational system, see Hansgert Peisert and Gerhild Framheim, *Systems of Higher Education: Federal Republic of Germany* (New York: International Council for Educational Development, 1978); Ulrich Teichler and Bikas Sanyal, "Higher Education and the Labour Market," in R. Avakov *et al.*, eds., *Higher Education and Employment in the USSR and in the Federal Republic of Germany* (Paris: UNESCO International and Institute for Educational Planning, 1984); and Claudius Gellert, "Politics and Higher Education in the Federal Republic of Germany," *European Journal of Education*, vol. 19, no. 2, September 1984, pp. 217–232.

2. Teichler and Sanyal, "Higher Education," p. 99 and Table 5.

3. For a history and evaluation of the German comprehensive university, see Harry Hermanns, Ulrich Teichler, and Henry Wasser, eds., *The Compleat University* (Cambridge, Mass.: Schenkman Publishing Co., 1983).

4. *Basic and Structural Data: 1984–85* (Bonn: Federal Ministry of Education and Science, November 1984), p. 66.

5. A comparison of The University of Dortmund and the Fachhochschulen Dortmund is instructive, with each institution providing similar programs in, e.g., architecture, engineering, informatics, and business, albeit with greater theoretical and mathematical content within the university curriculums.

6. See "Studentenwerke: Social Welfare Organizations at the Universities in the Federal Republic of Germany" (Bonn: Deutsches Studentenwerke, September 1984).

7. For a conservative viewpoint on this era, see John W. Chapman, ed., *The Western University on Trial* (Berkeley: University of California Press, 1983).

8. Interview with Dr. Ruediger Juette of the West German Rector's Conference, Bonn, 11 July 1985.

9. See Peisert and Franheim, *Systems of Higher Education*, pp. 74–79; also, Gellert, "Politics and Higher Education in the Federal Republic."

10. The mid-1970s figure is from Peisert and Franheim, *Systems of Higher Education*, p. 155; the 1981 figure is from "Student Awards: Office Note Outlining Student Aid Arrangements in Other Countries" from the U.K. Committee of Vice Chancellors and Principals, mimeographed, May 1985. The 1984–85 estimate was given by Ministry officials, although the published governmental data now report a higher figure due to a more restricted denominator.

11. Gellert, "Politics and Higher Education in the Federal Republic."

12. Teichler and Sanyal, "Higher Education and the Labour Market," p. 103.

13. This conclusion is based on reading such as Teichler, Gellert, and Peisert, cited above, as well as interviews with Ministry officials and others cited in the Acknowledgments.

14. Interviews with B. Hoffmeister of Vereinigte Deutsche Studentenschaften (National Union of Students) on 10 July 1985 and with D. Iversen of the Studentenwerke Bonn on 11 July 1985.

15. Interview with Hoffmeister.

16. Information supplied by Ministry of Education and Science through Messrs. Brenner and Schmidt-Bens, interview 24 June 1985.
17. Correspondence with Karl Roeloffs, 15 March 1985.
18. The early BAföG program is described in Maureen Woodhall, *Review of Student Support Schemes in Selected OECD Countries* (Paris: Organization for European Cooperation and Development, 1978), pp. 53–58; and in Peisert and Franheim, *Systems of Higher Education*, pp. 155–56. For recent information in English, see *Basic and Structural Data: 1984–85* (Bonn: Federal Ministry of Education and Science, November 1984); in German, see *BAföG '84–85* (Bonn: Der Bundesminister für Bildung und Wissenschaft, Autumn 1984).
19. The information on offsets was provided in the interview with Brenner and Schmidt-Bens.
20. Reported in the Hoffmeister interview and corroborated by the most recent surveys of actual expenditures and income sources.
21. Reported in the Iverson interview.
22. Table 3.2 shows the present value of payments discounted at 8 percent equal to DM297 on an initial principal of DM1,000, i.e., 29.7 percent. See also Appendix B.

4. France

1. Sources used for this section include Alain Bienaymé, "The New Reform in French Higher Education," *European Journal of Education*, vol. 19, no. 2, 1984; Alain Bienaymé, *Systems of Higher Education: France* (New York: International Council for Educational Development, 1978); Alain Bienaymé, "Efficiency and Quality in Higher Education" (English translation of "Efficience et qualité de l'enseignement supérieur" published in *Chroniques d'Actualités de la SEDEIS*, 15 June 1984); Louis Levy-Garboua and François Orivel, "Inefficiency in the French System of Higher Education," *European Journal of Education*, vol. 17, no. 2, 1982, pp. 153–160; Pierre Goldberg, "The University System in France," in Lyman Glenny, ed., *Funding Higher Education* (New York: Praeger Publishers, 1979); and Manfred Stassen, *Higher Education in the European Community: A Handbook for Students* (Brussels: Commission of the European Communities, 1979).
2. Bienaymé, "The New Reform in French Higher Education" p. 153.
3. See Bienaymé's *Systems of Higher Education: France*, pp. 1–13, for a discussion of the counting difficulties; see also his "Efficiency and Quality" p. 29, for 1982–83 enrollment estimates.
4. The number of institutions properly labeled "university" apparently depends partly on who is beholding and counting. Manfred Stassen counted 69 "in the general sense of the term" in 1979 (in *Higher Education in the European Community*); Alain Bienaymé in 1984 cited "roughly 80" ("The New Reform in French Higher Education," p. 154); and the author counted 71 in a listing of universities and their budgets prepared by the Ministry in 1985.
5. *Grandes Ecoles* enrollments are also elusive. Bienaymé identified nearly 63,000 in 1982–83 in the schools of engineering and commerce. The total nonuniversity sector, excluding IUTs, higher technical streams, and *classes préparatoires*, enrolls 100,000–115,000 students. See Bienaymé, "Efficiency and Quality in Higher Education," p. 28 (Table).
6. "French Election Threatens Research Agency," *Chronicle of Higher Education*, 12 February 1986, p. 36.
7. The information on CROUS is from *Infos-Etudiants: 1984* and from an interview with the Paris CROUS director, M. Moha, 19 June 1985.
8. Bienaymé, *Systems of Higher Education: France*, pp. 30–41; also Bienaymé, "The New Reform in French Higher Education," pp. 154–55.
9. See Guy Neave, "On the Road to Silicon Valley: The Changing Relationship

Between Higher Education and Government in Western Europe," *European Journal of Education*, vol. 19, no. 2, 1984.

10. Bienaymé, "New Reforms in French Higher Education," p. 155.
11. Bienaymé, *Systems of Higher Education: France*, pp. 35–36.
12. Bienaymé, "New Reforms in French Higher Education," p. 156.
13. "France's New Conservative Government Is Split over University Reforms," *Chronicle of Higher Education*, 23 April 1986, pp. 39–40.
14. *Infos-Etudiants: 1984*, pp. 7–10.
15. The 1984–85 CROUS Handbook (*Infos-Etudiants: 1984–85* (cited costs of 15,800F–16,900F [$2,124–$2,272]. The range of 16,000F–19,000F is based in part on extrapolations from student surveys reported in Nabil Abboud and Philippe Cazenave, "Budgets des Etudiants," *Education et Formations*, no. 2, 1983, p. 69; Benoit Millot and François Orivel, *L'Economie de L'Enseignement Supérieur* (Paris: Cujas, 1980), p. 261.
16. The technical information on the 1985–86 *bourse* is contained in Ministry of Education "circulaires" no. 85–206, 4 June 1985, and no. 85–130, 9 April 1985.
17. Some 155,000 *bourses*, including the graduate-level *bourses de licence* and *bourses à caractère spécial*, as well as the undergraduate need-based *bourses d'enseignement supérieur sur critères sociaux*, were given in 1984–85 out of a total student population of over 1,000,000. Interview with M. Chevason, chief of the Bureau de Bourse, Ministry of Education, 17 June 1985.
18. *Ibid.*
19. It should be reiterated that the need-based grants that are the subject of this chapter, the *bourses d'enseignement supérieur sur critères sociaux*, are designed for first- and second-level studies only. The graduate-level grants, *bourses à caractère spécial* and *bourses de license*, for 1985–86 will be from 12,744F to 14,670F [$1,713–$1,972] for the regular grants and from 13,698F to 15,624F [$1,841–$2,100] for those having completed Military or other National Service.
20. Jean-Pierre Jarousse, "les Contradictions de l'Université de Masse Dix Ans Aprés (1973–83)," *Revue Français de Sociologie*, vol. XXV, 1984, p. 194.
21. Maureen Woodhall, *Review of Student Support Schemes in Selected OECD Countries* (Paris, Organization for Economic Cooperation and Development, 1978), p. 48.
22. See Nabil Abboud and Philippe Cazenave, "Budgets des Etudiants," p. 69. Abboud and Cazenave counted both the *exoneration fiscale*, or "income-splitting" privilege, which lowers the marginal tax rate for a family with an 18-to-26-year-old child who is a student (estimated in 1982–83 to be worth on average 1,270F [$171]) and the *caisses d'allocation familiales*, or family allowance, estimated to be worth 1,442F [$174]. We have used a conservative estimate of 2,000F–3,000F as a range of tax-advantage offsets.
23. *Ibid.*, pp. 77–79.
24. *Infos-Etudiants: 1984*, p. 15.
25. Interview with M. Chevason, 26 June 1985.
26. Sophie Ozgun, "Etudiants, l'argent des banques vous interesse!" *Le Monde de l'Education*, March 1984.

5. Sweden

1. General background information on Swedish higher education came principally from the following sources: "Higher Education and Research in Sweden 1984–85: Some Facts and Figures" (Stockholm: National Board of Universities and Colleges, 1984); Lillemor Kim, "Admission to Higher Education in Sweden and Its Implications for Integrated Higher Education," and Rune Prenfors, "Integrated Higher Education: The Swedish Experience," in Harry Hermanns, Ulrich Teichler, and

Henry Wasser, eds., *The Compleat University* (Cambridge, Mass.: Schenkman Publishing Company, 1983), pp. 101–28 and 129–48; Rune Premfors and Bertil Ostergren, *Systems of Higher Education: Sweden* (New York: International Council for Educational Development, 1978); Lillemor Kim, *Widened Admission to Higher Education in Sweden: The 25/5 Scheme* (Stockholm: The National Board of Universities and Colleges, 1982); Sixten Marklund and Gunnar Bergendal, *Trends in Swedish Educational Policy* (Stockholm: The Swedish Institute, 1979); various issues of *Fact Sheets on Sweden* published by the Swedish Institute; and various issues of *Brief Survey of Higher Education in Sweden,* published (mimeographed) by the National Board of Universities and Colleges.

2. Lillemor Kim, "Admission to Higher Education in Sweden," p. 110.
3. Rune Premfors and Bertil Ostergren, *Systems of Higher Education: Sweden,* p. 81.
4. *Ibid.,* pp. 33–36.
5. "Higher Education and Research in Sweden 1984–85: Some Facts and Figures," p. 8.
6. Data supplied by Central Study Assistance Committee, or CSN (*Centrala Studiestödsnämnden*), to the author, May 1985. See CSN, *Studiestöd 1983–84* (Stockholm: Statistics Sweden, 6 December 1985).
7. Kim, "Admission to Higher Education in Sweden," p. 113.
8. "Age Distribution of Students," published by Statistics Sweden, 1981 and 1984.
9. Kim, "Admission to Higher Education in Sweden," p. 106.
10. Allan Svenssen, "Rekrytering till högre uthildning," Göteborg University Department of Education, 1983.
11. Sven-Eric Reuterberg and Allan Svenssen, "Studiehjälpens betydelse för eleverna igymnasieskolan," Göteborg University Department of Education, 1985.
12. Written reply from Central Study Assistance Committee (CSN) to the author, dated 30 May 1985.
13. The National Union of Students' budget is a one-page document entitled *Economisk Budget för Ensamstående Högskolestuderande,* presented to and translated for the author by Thomas Persson, incoming vice-president of the Swedish National Union of Students, on 2 July 1985. The retail price data is from OECD Main Economic Indicators, reported in *Employment Gazette* (London), May 1985, p. S53.
14. Most of the material in the following section was provided directly to the author by the Central Study Assistance Committee (CSN) in written form and by the CSN representative, Gabriella Hansson, in interviews 1 and 2 July 1985. Published accounts may be found in *Studiestöd 1983–84* (Stockholm: Statistics Sweden, 6 December 1985); "Swedish Study Assistance" and the "1985–86 Appendix" (Sundsvall: Centrala Studiestödsnämnden); "Higher Education in Sweden," *Fact Sheets on Sweden,* published by the Swedish Institute, January 1983; "A Survey of National Benefits for Students" (Sundsvall: Centrala Studiestödsnämnden, June 1981); and Maureen Woodhall, *Review of Student Support Schemes in Selected OECD Countries* (Paris: OECD, 1978), pp. 81–86.
15. The upper-secondary-school aid, called "Study Assistance," is partly linked to family income, at least through the age of 20. Also, the means-tested grant amount for "Study Assistance" can be a much larger proportion of the total than it is for the higher education "Study Means." At age 20, however, even if the student is still in the upper-secondary track, he or she goes on to Study Means and becomes independent of the parent. In fact, most parents are reported to continue helping at the upper-secondary level until students have reached the age of 21. (In Sweden, as in many European countries, upper-secondary education generally lasts until age 18 or 19 and can more easily extend even beyond these ages, particularly for

children of families from more remote geographical areas from which they may have to travel and board in order to attend an upper-secondary *gymnasium*.)

16. Data from Central Study Assistance Committee (CSN) to the author, July 1985.
17. Donald Field, "Student Debt Prompts Growing Concern in Scandinavia," *Chronicle of Higher Education,* 9 October 1985, p. 39.
18. *Studiestöd 1983–84,* p. 61.
19. This sum assumes loan installments of 14,724 Skr twice a year for four years, all loans accumulating and compounding interest at 4.2 percent annually until the end of the sixth year.
20. The agenda summarized here was presented to the author by Thomas Persson, incoming SFS vice-president; it does not necessarily constitute an official agenda of SFS.
21. From an interview with Gabriella Hansson of the Central Study Assistance Committee (CSN), 1 July 1985.

6. The United States

1. Estimates are by the National Center for Education Statistics as reported in Robert L. Jacobsen, "The New Academic Year: Signs of Uneasiness Amid Calm and Stability on Many Campuses," *The Chronicle of Higher Education,* vol. 31, no. 1, 4 September 1985 (Special Report).
2. *Ibid.*
3. *Ibid.*
4. *Ibid.*
5. *Ibid.*
6. The Washington Office of the College Board, *Trends in Student Aid: 1980 to 1984* (New York: College Entrance Examination Board, 1984).
7. National Center for Education Statistics data, reported in *Higher Education and National Affairs,* vol. 34, no. 3, February 1985.
8. Census data reported in *New York Times,* 20 October 1985, p. 39.
9. See Howard R. Bowen, *Investment in Learning* (San Francisco: Jossey-Bass Publishers, 1977).
10. See, for example, Valerie Lee, "Access to Higher Education: The Experience of Blacks, Hispanics and Low Socio-Economic Status Whites" (Washington, D.C.: American Council on Education, May 1985); *Two Years After High School* (Washington, D.C.: National Center for Educational Statistics, 1984); or Linda Darling-Hammond, *Equality and Excellence: The Educational Status of Black Americans* (New York: College Entrance Examination Board, 1985).
11. See Howard R. Bowen, *The Costs of Higher Education* (San Francisco: Jossey-Bass Publishers, 1980) for both theory and empirical evidence behind this proposition.
12. David W. Breneman, *The Coming Enrollment Crisis* (Washington, D.C.: The Association of Governing Boards of Universities and Colleges, 1982). See also Breneman, "The Coming Enrollment Crisis: Focusing on the Figures," *Change,* vol. 15, no. 2, March 1983, pp. 14–33.
13. College Board data cited in Jean Evangelanf, "Students' Costs Will Rise 7 Pct., Nearly Twice Inflation Rate," *The Chronicle of Higher Education,* 14 August 1985, p. 1. See also Scott E. Miller and Holly Hexter, *How Middle Income Families Pay for College* (Washington, D.C.: American Council on Education, July 1985); also *How Low Income Families Pay for College* by the same authors and publisher.
14. College Scholarship Service, *CSS Need Analysis: Theory and Computation Procedure for 1985–86 FAF* (New York: College Entrance Examination Board, 1984), pp. 9–13.
15. There are additional governmentally sponsored student loan programs either for

students ineligible for GSL or NDSL by virtue of non-need or for students in special programs such as nursing or other health professions. There are also some small privately financed loan programs. The overwhelming majority of student borrowing, though, is through GSL and NDSL.

16. Jonathan Friendly, "Rising Debt to Repay Student Loans Is Causing Concern," *New York Times*, 1 October 1985, p. C-1.

17. Donald A. Gillespie and Nancy Carlson, *Trends in Student Aid: 1963 to 1983* (Washington, D.C.: The Washington Office of the College Board, December 1983), and *Trends in Student Aid: 1980 to 1984 Update* (Washington, D.C.: The Washington Office of the College Board, 1984).

18. Pamela Christoffel, *Working Your Way Through College: A New Look at an Old Idea* (New York: College Entrance Examination Board, October 1985).

19. Miller and Hexter, *How Middle Income Students Pay*, reports 45 percent of aided middle-income students at independent colleges averaging just over $1,000 in CWS earnings. High-priced independent colleges assume $1,200–$1,300 in their packaging calculations. A new dimension to student earnings is the growing cooperative education movement through which students maintain virtually full-time, frequently well-paying jobs while pursuing higher education degrees. Joseph Cronin of the Massachusetts Higher Education Assistance Corporation reports 100,000 U.S. students in this mode (private correspondence 16 April 1986).

20. Truly comparable, complete, and up-to-date institutional cost data is extremely difficult and perhaps impossible to obtain. Jean-Pierre Jallade has published some comparative budget studies, for example, but much of his data base is UNESCO, whose data in turn are notoriously both old and suspect: see Jallade, "Expenditures on Higher Education in Europe: Past Trends and Future Prospects," *European Journal of Education*, vol. 14, no. 1, 1980, pp. 35–48. See also Lyman Glenny, ed., *Funding Higher Education: A Six Nation Analysis* (New York: Praeger Publications, 1979).

21. The proportion of costs covered by tuition depends on what institutional expenditures are included as "costs." Gillespie and Carlson used all educational and general expenditures plus scholarship and fellowship expenditures, all as reported by the National Center for Educational Statistics, and got proportions of 16.3 percent for public and 51.6 percent for private colleges (*Trends in Student Aid: 1963 to 1983*, New York: College Entrance Examination Board, 1983, p. 10.) However, many educational and general expenditures, and arguably all scholarship and fellowship expenditures, should *not* be included as direct costs of undergraduate instruction. A smaller and more appropriate true-cost estimate as a denominator would probably yield proportions in the range of 20–30 percent for public and 70–90 percent for private colleges.

22. *Student Financial Aid . . . Making a Difference* (Washington, D.C.: National Association of Student Financial Aid Administrators, 1985), p. 10.

23. *Ibid.*

24. Washington Office of the College Board, *Trends in Student Aid: 1980 to 1984* by Lynn Quincy and Donald A. Gillespie (New York: College Entrance Examination Board, 1984). pp. 3–5.

25. NASFAA, *Student Financial Aid*, p. 11.

26. Alan P. Wagner, "Student Financial Aid in the 1980's," to be published in American Education Finance Association, (1986) Yearbook (Cambridge, Mass.: Ballinger, forthcoming).

27. The Miller and Hexter Studies (*How Middle Income Students Pay for College* and *How Low Income Students Pay for College*) exhibit those problems, although they also provide some useful benchmarks of aid packages. Other examples of financial-aid packages can be found in Scott E. Miller, "College Costs: How Do Families

Pay," *Educational Record*, vol. 66, no. 3, Summer 1985, pp. 40–43; College Scholarship Service, *CSS Need Analysis: Theory and Computation Procedures*; Dolores E. Cross, "Utilization of Financial Aid and Family Resources in Meeting College Costs," published by the New York State Higher Education Services Corporation, August 1983; "I Love New York Guide to Independent Colleges and Universities," prepared by the Commission on Independent Colleges and Universities (Albany, New York) and distributed by Chase Lincoln First Bank, September 1985; and various college catalogs, most of which give representative packages of financial assistance.

28. *Trends in Student Aid: 1980 to 1984*, p. 3.
29. Miller and Hexter, *How Low Income Families Pay*, pp. 25–28, and *How Middle Income Families Pay*, pp. 17–18.
30. *Trends in Student Aid: 1980–1984*, p. 6.
31. Julianne Still Thrift, *Paying for College: Trends in Student Financial Aid* (Washington, D.C.: National Institute of Independent Colleges and Universities, 1985).
32. *Trends in Student Aid: 1980–1984*, p. 6.
33. Darling-Hammond, *Equality and Excellence: The Educational Status of Black Americans*. See also Edward B. Fiske, "Minority Enrollment in Colleges Is Declining," *New York Times*, 27 October 1985, p. 1; and Gaynell Evans, "Social, Financial Barriers Blamed for Curbing Blacks' Access to College," *The Chronicle of Higher Education*, vol. 30, no. 23, 7 August 1985, p. 1.
34. *Trends in Student Aid: 1980–1984*, pp. 7–8.
35. Frank Newman, *Higher Education and the American Resurgence* (Princeton: The Carnegie Foundation for the Advancement of Teaching), 1985, pp. 72–79.
36. The issue of student debt-load manageability is examined in some depth in Theodore Marchese, "Fullfilling the Institution's Obligations to Student Borrowers," and Dwight Horch, "Determining Student Capacity to Borrow," both in *Proceedings: College Scholarship Service Colloquium on Student Loan Counseling and Debt Management*, 24 December 1985, Denver, Colorado. See also W. Lee Hansen and Marilyn Rhodes, "Student Debt Crisis: Are Students Incurring Excessive Debt?" University of Wisconsin–Madison: Wisconsin Center for Educational Research, October 1985. An excellent analysis portraying potential major problems in the trend toward more reliance on student debt is Martin A. Kramer and William D. Van Dusen, "Living on Credit," *Change*, May/June 1986, pp. 10–19.
37. Alan Wagner, "Student Financial Aid in the 1980's," p. 30.
38. These observations draw upon D. Bruce Johnstone, "The Future of Financial Aid: Principles, Problems, and Probable Outcomes," *College Board Review*, No. 141, Fall 1986.

BIBLIOGRAPHY

General

Chapman, John W., ed. *The Western University on Trial.* Berkeley: University of California Press, 1983.

Cronin, Joseph M. "Student Financial Aid: An International Perspective." *College Board Review*, No. 141, Fall 1986.

Gaines, Adam, and Turner, Nigel. *Student Loans, the Costs and the Consequences: A Review of Student Financial Support in North America and Scandinavia.* London: The National Union of Students, September 1985.

Glenny, Lyman A. *Funding Higher Education: A Six Nation Analysis.* New York: Praeger, 1979.

Hermanns, Harry; Teichler, Ulrich; and Wasser, Henry, eds. *The Compleat University: Break From Tradition in Germany, Sweden, and the U.S.A.* Cambridge, Mass.: Schenkman Publishing Company, Inc., 1983.

Hill, Peter. "Real Gross Product in OECD Countries and Associated Purchasing Power Parities." Paris: OECD Economics and Statistics Department Working Paper No. 17, December 1984.

International Association of Universities. *International Handbook of Universities and Other Institutions of Higher Education* (8th ed.). London: The MacMillan Press Ltd., 1981.

Jallade, Jean-Pierre. "Financing Higher Education: The Equity Aspects." *Comparative Education Review*, June 1978, pp. 309–25.

Neave, Guy. "On the Road to Silicon Valley? The Changing Relationship Between Higher Education and Government in Western Europe." *European Journal of Education*, vol. 19, no. 2, 1984, pp. 111–19.

Perkin, Harold. "Redesigning the University for the 1980s and Beyond: An International Perspective." *The College Board Review*, no. 134, Winter 1984–85, pp. 10–18.

Stassen, Manfred, ed. *Higher Education in the European Community: A Handbook for Students.* Brussels: Commission of the European Communities, 1979.

Vorbeck, Michael. "Financial Aid to Students in Europe: A Summary Analysis." *International Journal of Institutional Management in Higher Education*, vol. 7, no. 3, November 1983, pp. 289–305.

Woodhall, Maureen. "The Links Between Finance and Admissions Policies in Higher Education." *Policies for Higher Education in the 1980's.* Paris: Organization for Economic Cooperation and Development, 1983, pp. 188–205.

Woodhall, Maureen. *Review of Student Support Schemes in Selected OECD Countries.* Paris: Organization for Economic Cooperation and Development, 1970.

Woodhall, Maureen. *Student Loans as a Means of Financing Higher Education: Lessons from International Experience.* Washington, D.C.: The World Bank, 1983.

The United Kingdom

Becker, Tony; Embling, Jack; and Kogan, Maurice. *Systems of Higher Education: United Kingdom.* New York: International Council for Educational Development, 1977.

Department of Education and Science. "Demand for Higher Education in Great Britain 1984–2000." DES Report on Education no. 100, July 1984.

————. *Grants to Students: A Brief Guide*. London: DES, July 1984.

————. "Student Grants for 1985/86," DES news release, 31 May 1985.

The Development of Higher Education into the 1990's ("The Green Paper"), presented to Parliament by the Secretary of State for Education and Science, the Secretary of State for Scotland, the Secretary of State for Wales, and the Secretary of State for Northern Ireland. London: Her Majesty's Stationery Office, May 1985.

Edwards, Tony; Fitz, John; and Whitty, Geoff. "Private Schools and Public Funding: A Comparison of Recent Policies in England and Australia." *Comparative Education*, vol. 21, no. 1, 1985, pp. 29–45.

Hexter, Holly. *Grants Versus Loans: Recent Proposals for Change in Student Aid in Great Britain*. Washington, D.C.: American Council on Education, June 1985.

House of Commons Library Research Division (Kay Andrews). "Student Grants, Fees, and the Parental Contribution." Research Note No. 213, 1 January 1985.

Matterson, Alan. *Polytechnics and Colleges*. Essex: Longman House, 1981.

Morris, Alfred, and Sizer, John, eds. *Resources and Higher Education* (Publication 8 in the Leverhulme Programme Study into the Future of Higher Education). Guilford, Surrey: The Society for Research into Higher Education, 1982.

National Advisory Body for Local Authority Higher Education. "Report of the Continuing Education Group." London: NAB, August 1984.

National Union of Students. "Grant Us A Living: A Discussion Document on Student Financial Support." London: National Union of Students, February 1985.

————. "Proposed Changes in Student Benefit Entitlement." (Submission by the National Executive Committee of the National Union of Students to the Social Security Advisory Committee.) London: National Union of Students, February 1986.

Saxby, John. *Undergraduate Income and Expenditure: Survey 1982/3*. London: National Union of Students, February 1984.

Shattock, Michael. "British Higher Education Under Pressure: Politics, Budgets and Demography and the Acceleration of Ideas for Change." *European Journal of Education*, vol. 19, no. 2, 1984, pp. 210–16.

Steedman, Hilary. "Recent Developments in Higher Education in the United Kingdom." *European Journal of Education*, vol. 17, no. 2, 1982, pp. 193–203.

University Grants Committee. *A Strategy for Higher Education into the 1990s: The University Grants Committee's Advice*. London: Her Majesty's Stationery Office, September 1984.

Urrows, Elizabeth, and Urrows, Henry. "Hard Times, Dropped Expectations: The Impact of Budget Cuts and Raised Fees on British Universities and Students." *The College Board Board Review*, no. 132, Summer 1984, pp. 17–23.

Woodhall, Maureen. "The Role of Selectivity in Alternative Patterns of Financial Support for Students." University of London Institute of Education, April 1986.

Federal Republic of Germany

Basic and Structural Data: 1984/85. Bonn: Federal Ministry of Education and Science, November 1984.

BAföG '84/85. Bonn: Der Bundesminister für Bildung und Wissenschaft, Autumn 1984.

Deutsches Studentenwerk e.V. Bonn: DSW, August 1984.

Gellert, Claudius. "Politics and Higher Education in the Federal Repubic of Germany." *European Journal of Education*, vol. 19, no. 2, 1984, pp. 217–32.

Peisert, Hansgert, and Framheim, Gerhild. *Systems of Higher Education: Federal Republic of Germany*. New York: International Council for Educational Development, 1978.

Studentenwerke: Social Welfare Organizations at the Universities in the Federal Republic of Germany. Bonn: DSW, September 1984.

Teichler, U., and Sanyal, B. C. "Higher Education and the Labour Market." *Higher*

Education and Employment in the USSR and in the Federal Republic of Germany, edited by R. Arakov, B.C. Sanyal, M. Buttergeit, and U. Teichler. Paris: International Institute for Educational Planning (UNESCO), 1984.

von Dohnanyi, Klaus. *Education and Youth Employment in the Federal Republic of Germany*. Berkeley: The Carnegie Foundation for the Advancement of Teaching, 1978.

France

Bienaymé, Alain. "Efficiency and Quality of Higher Education." English translation of "Efficience et qualité de l'enseignement supérieur." *Chroniques d'Actualités de la SEDEIS*, 15 June 1984.

———. "The New Reform in French Higher Education." *European Journal of Education*, vol. 19, no. 2, 1984, pp. 151–64.

———. *Systems of Higher Education: France*. New York: International Council for Educational Development, 1978.

Infos-Etudiants: 1984. Paris: CROUS de Paris, 1984.

Levy-Garboua, Louis, and Orviel, François. "Inefficiency in the French System of Higher Education." *European Journal of Education*, vol. 17, no. 2, 1982, pp. 153–60.

Millot, Benoit, and Orivel, François. *L'Economie de l'Enseignement Supérieur*. Paris: Cujas, 1980.

Orviel, F.; Guerrin, S.; and Perrot, J. "Les coûts et les dépenses de l'enseignement: le cas de la France." Paris: OECD, 1984. (Mimeograph; authors are at University of Dijon Institute for Research on the Economics of Education.)

Sweden

Centrala Studiestödsnämden. *Studiestöd 1983/84*. Stockholm: Statistics Sweden, 1985.

Centrala Studiestödsnämden. *A Survey of National Benefits for Students*. Sundsvall: CSN, 1981.

Kim, Lillemor. "Admission to Higher Education in Sweden and its Implications for Integrated Higher Education." *The Compleat University: Break from Tradition in Germany, Sweden, and the U.S.A.*, edited by Harry Hermanns, Ulrich Teichler, and Henry Wasser. Cambridge, Mass.: Schenkman Publishing Company, Inc., 1983, pp. 101–28.

Kim, Lillemor. *Widened Admission to Higher Education in Sweden*. Stockholm: National Board of Universities and Colleges, 1982.

Marklund, Sixten, and Bergendal, Gunnar. *Trends in Swedish Educational Policy*. Uddevalla: The Swedish Institute, 1979.

National Board of Universities and Colleges (UHÄ). *Brief Survey of Higher Education in Sweden* (various issues).

Premfors, Rune, and Ostergren, Bertil. *Systems of Higher Education: Sweden*. New York: International Council for Educational Development, 1978.

The Swedish Institute. *Fact Sheets on Sweden* (various issues).

The United States

Barks, Jeffrey A. "Parental Contributions for Higher Education: An Analysis of Expected and Reported Contributions." *Journal of Educational Finance*, vol. 5, Summer 1979, pp. 87–101.

Beck, Norman E. "Financial Aid Today: An Economic Perspective." *The College Board Review*, no. 137, Fall 1985, pp. 2–5.

Christoffel, Pamela. *Working Your Way Through College: A New Look at an Old Idea*. New York: College Entrance Examination Board, October 1985.

The College Board. *Trends in Student Aid: 1980–1984, Update*. Washington, D.C.. The Washington Office of the College Board, 1984.

College Scholarship Service. *CSS Need Analysis: Theory and Computation Procedures for the 1985–86 FAF.* New York: College Entrance Examination Board, 1984.

College Scholarship Service. *Proceedings: College Scholarship Service Colloquium on Student Loan Counseling and Debt Management.* New York: College Entrance Examination Board, 1986. (Colloquium held 2–4 December 1985 in Denver, Colorado.)

Gillespie, Donald, and Carlson, Nancy. *Trends in Student Aid: 1963 to 1983.* Washington, D.C.: The Washington Office of the College Board, December 1983.

Gladieux, Lawrence E. "The Future of Student Financial Aid." *The College Board Review,* no. 126, Winter 1982–83, pp. 12–22.

Gladieux, Lawrence E. "The Issue of Equity in College Finances." In *The Crisis in Higher Education,* edited by Joseph Froomkin. New York: The Academy of Political Science, 1983.

Hansen, Janet S., and Wolfe, Mark L. *Student Loan Guarantee Agencies and Their Financing.* New York: College Entrance Examination Board, September 1985.

Hearn, James C., and Longnecker, David. "Enrollment Effects of Alternative Postsecondary Pricing Policies." *The Journal of Higher Education,* vol. 56, no. 5, Sept./Oct. 1985, pp. 485–508.

Henderson, Cathy. "Forecasting College Costs Through 1988–89." *American Council on Education Policy Briefs,* January 1986.

Johnstone, D. Bruce. "The Future of Financial Aid: Principles, Problems, and Probable Outcomes. *The College Board Review,* No. 141, Fall 1986.

King, Reatha Clark. "The Changing Student." *National Forum,* vol. 65, no. 3, Summer 1985, pp. 22–27.

Kramer, Martin A. "The Costs of Education: Who Pays and Who Should Pay?" *An Agenda for the Year 2000* (Thirtieth Anniversary Colloquia Proceedings of the College Scholarship Service). New York: College Entrance Examination Board, 1985, pp. 55–94.

Kramer, Martin A., and Van Dusen, William D. "Living on Credit." *Change,* May/June 1986, pp. 10–19.

Miller, Scott E. "College Costs: How Do Families Pay?" *Educational Record,* vol. 66, no. 3, Summer 1985, pp. 40–43.

Miller, Scott E., and Hexter, Holly. *How Low Income Families Pay for College.* Washington, D.C.: American Council on Education, July 1985.

———. *How Middle Income Families Pay for College.* Washington, D.C.: American Council on Education, July 1985.

National Association of Student Financial Aid Administrators. "Student Financial Aid . . . Making a Lifetime of Difference." Washington, D.C.: NASFAA, 1985.

Stampen, Jacob O. *Student Aid and Public Higher Education: Recent Changes.* Washington, D.C.: The American Council on Education, the American Association of State Colleges and Universities, the American Association of Community and Junior Colleges, the National Association of State Universities and Land Grant Colleges, March 1985.

The State Education Department [New York]. *A Report by the Board of Regents to the Governor and Legislature on State Student Financial Aid Programs.* Albany: The State Education Department, December 1984.

U.S. Department of Education. *The Student Guide: Five Federal Aid Programs, 1984–85.* Washington, D.C.: U.S. Department of Education, 1984.

Van Dusen, William D., and Hill, Donald E. "A Review of Current Practices Regarding Contributions Expected from Students Toward Post-Secondary Education Expenses." *Journal of Student Financial Aid,* vol. 13, no. 3, Autumn 1983, pp. 18–26.

Wagner, Alan P. "Student Financial Aid in the 1980's." American Education Finance Association, 1986 *Yearbook* (forthcoming).